Commodities and Globalization

Society for Economic Anthropology Monographs

Deborah Winslow, University of New Hampshire
General Editor for the Society for Economic Anthropology

Monographs of the Society for Economic Anthropology contain a peer-reviewed selection of papers from the annual meetings of the Society. Each year's meeting focuses on a different theme in economic anthropology.

Commodities and Globalization

Anthropological Perspectives

Edited by Angelique Haugerud,
M. Priscilla Stone, and Peter D. Little

Published in cooperation with the Society for Economic Anthropology

SOCIETY for ECONOMIC ANTHROPOLOGY

ROWMAN & LITTLEFIELD PUBLISHERS, INC.
Lanham • Boulder • New York • Oxford

ROWMAN & LITTLEFIELD PUBLISHERS, INC.

Published in the United States of America
by Rowman & Littlefield Publishers, Inc.
4720 Boston Way, Lanham, Maryland 20706
http://www.rowmanlittlefield.com

12 Hid's Copse Road, Cumnor Hill, Oxford OX2 9JJ, England

Copyright © 2000 by Society for Economic Anthropology

British Library Cataloguing in Publication Information Available

Library of Congress Cataloging-in-Publication Data

Commodities and globalization : anthropological perspectives / edited by Angelique Haugerud, M. Priscilla Stone, and Peter D. Little.
    p.   cm.
Includes bibliographical references and index.
ISBN 0-8476-9942-0 (cloth : acid-free paper) — ISBN 0-8476-9943-9 (paper : acid-free paper)
    1. Commercial products.   2. International trade.   3. International economic integration.   4. Economic anthropology.   I. Haugerud, Angelique
II. Stone, Margaret Priscilla.   III. Little, Peter D.

HM1040.7 .C65   2000
306.3—dc21   00-026957

Printed in the United States of America

♾™ The paper used in this publication meets the minimum requirements of American National Standard for Information Sciences—Permanence of Paper for Printed Library Materials, ANSI/NISO Z39.48-1992.

Contents

1

Commodities and Globalization: Anthropological Perspectives

M. Priscilla Stone, Angelique Haugerud, and Peter D. Little

World Bank president James Wolfensohn recently spoke of becoming an honorary chief in a Côte d'Ivoire village, where he talked with two Ivoirians connected by computer to the Chicago Board of Trade, as well as to London and Paris.[1] These two West Africans were obtaining on-line commodity price information to pass on by cellular phone to local coffee and cocoa farmers and traders. Wolfensohn's anecdote, and others like it, challenge notions of the integrity of "local systems." Today translocal connections and global flows capture the imaginations of scholars and policymakers. For example, in 1997–1998, it took just nine months for the collapse of the Thai currency (the *baht*) to affect a new American Internet bank established by a Bethesda neighbor of journalist Thomas L. Friedman, and in 1998 it took just one week for a Brazilian economic crisis to affect the Internet corporation Amazon.com (Friedman 1999, ix–xiiii). In a world where globalized information circuits and new technologies connect agricultural commodity producers in Africa, Asia, and Latin America to financial and trading centers in Chicago, London, Paris, and New York, updated analytical models need to account for the new velocity, volume, and intricacy of flows of information and goods. These networks transmit more than economic data and commodities; they also embody cultural categories and political and social relationships that define a world that is globalized in new ways.

This volume is premised on the notion that studying commodities and their movements can help to advance economic anthropology, in concrete and comparative ways, into a fuller engagement with globalization. A commodity focus offers a window on large-scale processes that are profoundly transforming our era.[2]

One of the challenges of contemporary ethnography is to link its traditional concerns with everyday life in particular times and places to new conceptualizations of

1

the connections across such times and locations. Theorists disagree sharply about the nature of the connections, with some discerning orderly causal chains and others chaos.[3] For some the "global" becomes "an emergent dimension of arguing about the connection among sites in a multi-sited ethnography" (Marcus 1995, 99). For others, understandings of the global rest on master narratives of the history of colonialism and capitalism. Scholars such as Polier and Roseberry (1989, 254) caution against both world-systems theorists' view of the capitalist system as determinant, and postmodernists' rejection of such determinism and systemic relationships altogether. Contributors to this volume vary in their emphases on determinism versus historical contingency, but all recognize important structural or historical connections across time and space.

GLOBAL ECONOMIC INTEGRATION

Global economic integration itself is not new.[4] The period from the 1870s to 1914, for instance, was the first age of globalization[5] —a time of laissez-faire policies well suited to an era of imperialism. These policies were subsequently modified by government economic interventions prompted by the Great Depression of the 1930s. As those "Keynesian" programs came under attack in the 1970s and 1980s, economic neoliberalism became dominant. Today global integration of trade and finance is greater than it has been during much of the postwar era, but only slightly greater than it was early in the twentieth century.[6] Protectionist measures continue to offset forms of economic integration. Labor is less mobile today than it was in the 1800s, when passports were unnecessary.[7] In 1900, 14 percent of the U.S. population was born abroad; today the comparable figure is 8 percent.[8]

Recent transformations in the world economy, however, do define a distinctive era.[9] What distinguishes the contemporary historical moment is change fueled by the 1973 demise of the Bretton Woods financial and trading regime, the removal of national and international controls over capital movements, new computer and telecommunications technologies, and the extension of global free trade with the 1993 Uruguay Round of the General Agreement on Tariffs and Trade (GATT). Especially important in economies of the South have been the increasing instability of currency values and commodity prices, as well as international financial institutions' promotion of "free-market" or neoliberal policies in the indebted nations of Africa, Asia, and Latin America.

Caught in an international finance system over which they have little control, debt-ridden states forgo sovereignty over monetary and trade policies and pursue foreign investment and export commodity production to pay off loans (often sacrificing social welfare concerns in the process).[10] As McMichael (1994, 2–3) demonstrates, the global financial system drives recent changes in commodity markets, with national capitalism tied to a dollar/gold standard giving way to a single international finance system increasingly policed by the International Monetary Fund (IMF) and its backers (the United States, Japan, and Europe). Many of the commodity producers described in this volume now figure in a complex web of financiers, international institutions, and corporate executives.

GLOBAL ECONOMIC INEQUALITY

However dense such global networks may be, globalization is an uneven and contradictory set of processes that takes on very different forms in particular places. An innovative anthropological approach to such global disjunctures is Appadurai's (1996) formulation of ethnoscapes, mediascapes, technoscapes, financescapes, and ideoscapes. He uses the suffix "-scape" to "point to the fluid, irregular shapes of these landscapes, shapes that characterize international capital as deeply as they do international clothing styles" (Appadurai 1996, 33). Ethnoscapes deal with people and their networks of relationships; technoscapes are the rapidly changing technologies that move across national boundaries at startling speed; and financescapes, the most mystified dimension, encompass the apparatus of global capital flows: currency markets, national stock exchanges, commodity speculators, and so on. It is the disjunctures among these latter three "-scapes" that are most central to this volume and that help to make sense of the contradictions associated with the concept of globalization (see also Comaroff and Comaroff 1993; Coombe 1995; Hoogvelt 1997; Scott 1997).

Globalization is as likely to polarize and exclude as it is to connect people and places. Economic inequality is increasing even as larger numbers of people are drawn into globalized markets and telecommunications networks.[11] Côte d'Ivoire commodity traders who can afford cellular telephones, for example, constitute a tiny minority among West Africans. An economic anthropology of commodities must address these uneven global economic forces. Rapid changes in global finances, technologies, and the division of labor underpin the transformations in global commodity markets that are explored in this volume. In the context of agro-food commodities this has meant profound changes in the organization of production and exchange relations. International capital, often with the encouragement of World Bank or IMF adjustment programs concerned with debt refinancing, increasingly engages rural communities through the guise of agribusiness and such institutions as contract farming (Bonanno et al. 1994; Little and Watts 1994; McMichael 1995). The Gambian woman or the Mexican peasant who grows vegetables under contract for a transnational firm is an integral part of this new landscape of increasingly global networks of finance and technology. Thus the global commodity chains analyzed by some contributors to this volume (Little and Dolan; Collins; Stanford) reflect broader processes of global restructuring, particularly in the domains of finance, technology, and labor.[12] One of the most visible faces of economic neoliberalism in the world's poorer nations of course is the so-called structural adjustment reforms mandated by the World Bank and IMF.[13] Uniform neoliberal policy prescriptions overlook the ways changing global economic conditions affect the success of particular development strategies and the very different positions individual nations occupy within a larger set of transnational economic and political forces (see Mitchell 1995; Leys 1996). The World Bank's projections frequently overestimate growth in both export prices and volumes, and the Bank's uniform prescriptions to maximize export production carry the risk of gluts and declining export commodity prices for all (George and Sabelli 1994, 86–88).[14] Europe's demand for Egyptian fresh flowers and winter tomatoes, for example, is unlikely to grow by even a fraction of the amount that would be required to meet the export growth targets implied by the World Bank and the U.S. Agency for International Development.[15]

Drawing on careful field studies, this volume explores how a variety of producers fare in the new global marketplace.[16] By addressing questions such as how changing consumer demand affects the organization of production (e.g., feminization of labor, as discussed in Collins's chapter), we bring production, as well as consumption, circulation, and exchange into one analytical framework. Many of the essays assembled here address the political and social relations that structure economic exchange and help to define the value of commodities.[17] Contributors examine globalization from the perspectives of Sardinian pastoralists, Congolese musicians, St. Louis artists, New Guinean vegetable growers, Gambian export crop producers, Mexican melon farmers, and Brazilian grape growers, among others. These economic-anthropological studies help to make globalization processes more concrete, particular, and comparative than much scholarly literature portrays them to be. Or, as Coombe (1995, 809) puts it, "The macrostructural approach to global capitalism, although necessary as a point of departure, is but an empty scaffold, incapable of doing justification to the complexities of the lives of those whose energies construct it." Globalization processes are always experienced and mediated locally (see Watts 1992, 18; Featherstone, Lash, and Robertson 1995). Hence we must look beyond the numerical schematics of global flows captured on computer screens to consider the farmers, herders, popular musicians, artists, and others whose activities power the global flows.

THE ECONOMIC ANTHROPOLOGY OF COMMODITIES

This collection considers how conceptions and roles of commodities may change in response to widening spheres of economic interaction and exchange. The chapters all focus on the production process as it responds to, is distorted by, and is increasingly controlled by the determination of the value of those commodities outside a "locality." This alienation of the commodities from the producers of the goods has been seen by Mauss (1990), Marx (1954), and others as *the* capitalist transition (see below). Commodities offer a particularly useful window on globalization processes partly because they, unlike electronically conveyed capital, transport cultural messages. A painting or a musical work carries more than a price tag; the circulation of the object conveys images, ideas, information, and meanings as well. As we discuss below, these ideological or symbolic transfers, while not automatic, are of particular interest to economic anthropology.

We begin with the definitional problem: What is a commodity and how is it distinguished from a good or a gift? We then briefly review the history of anthropological thought on commodities and examine how contemporary understandings of globalization affect current conceptions of commodities. These issues suggest a large and ambitious project, and we can only be grateful that important aspects of it have already been covered well in previous collections in this series, notably in *The Social Economy of Consumption* (Rutz and Orlove 1989), *Markets and Marketing* (Plattner 1985), and *Marxist Approaches in Economic Anthropology* (Littlefield and Gates 1991), as well as in many of the other volumes. The issue of commodities touches on central debates and concepts within our field and as such is both highly suggestive and complex.

DEFINITIONAL ISSUES

What begins as a seemingly simple definitional problem—What, for an anthropologist, is a commodity?—ends in a prolonged discussion about the very nature of social systems and how they operate through time and space. One would think a definition such as "a commodity is a socially desirable thing with a use-value and an exchange-value" (Gregory 1982, 10) would be relatively straightforward, yet, as this volume illustrates, it clearly is not. For the economist it may well be so: "certain things and rights to things are produced, exist, and can be seen to circulate through the economic system as they are being exchanged for other things, usually in exchange for money" (Kopytoff 1986, 64). But, as Kopytoff goes on to ask, why out of the total range of things available in a society are only some considered appropriate for marking as commodities, and why is the same thing treated as a commodity at one time and not another? Furthermore, whether money is required to mark a thing as a commodity is, as discussed further in this introduction and in Rothman's chapter, the subject of some debate.

USE-VALUE AND EXCHANGE-VALUE

A helpful starting point is the terms "use-value" and "exchange-value." The use-value, following Aristotle's example of a shoe, refers to the value the shoe has for the person who wears it—whether that be comfort, fashion, ease of walking, and so on. Although the use-value is thought to be something intrinsic to the thing, it is still culturally defined and mediated. The same thing—let us say a carnation grown by a Kenyan farmer—may have almost no use-value to the producer but only to the Dutch consumer who buys it the next day. Alternatively, there are goods with substantial use-values (such as land) that may have, at different historical periods, no exchange-value at all to anyone.

The exchange-value of a commodity has been taken to be quite separate from its use-value and refers to the value of the thing for obtaining other things or for generating currency. The exchange-value may well be the defining characteristic of a commodity, and it is again a product of historically and culturally specific criteria. A painting by a St. Louis artist may be worth $50 or $5,000, depending on very complicated cultural reckonings (see Plattner's chapter). Much of the determination of exchange-value may be out of the hands of producers, and the resulting vulnerability of producers to unexpected changes in the market for their commodities has left many farmers, whether in Mexico, Iowa, or elsewhere, in highly precarious economic positions. Indeed, many of the authors in this collection examine just this process—the growing alienation of the producer from not only the product of her or his labor but from the value of that product. Producers are increasingly subject to the whims of the larger marketplace. Some globalized commodities, on the other hand, retain (crucially) visible signs of producer identity. In the case of "world music," as discussed in White's chapter, African identities are reinserted into products intended for sale in global markets.

Even the expansiveness of this definition does not mean that all things that could be commodities are. In every society, Kopytoff (1986) argues, there are things that are publicly precluded from being commoditized, such as public lands or people. There is considerable debate about whether people can be considered commodities—whether as slaves, brides, or exploited labor. Levi-Strauss (1969), for example, thought of marriage as a system of gift exchange of women.[18] Labor, in Marx's (1954) model, becomes a commodity in a capitalist society. Debates about bride wealth in Africa and changes in the balance of cash, other goods, and labor (Hutchinson 1996; Feierman 1993) also often involve a discussion of whether women as wives are becoming more commodified through time. Even Berry's (1989) formulation of investments in social relations in a sense commodifies people's networks of support, if not the people themselves. But as Miers and Kopytoff (1977) point out in discussing African slavery, there is not a clear division between slave (thing-like commodity) and nonslave (person). Rather, there is a continuum of rights in people and things that encompasses all people of whatever status (cf. Feierman 1993, 187–196; Cooper 1997). In the end, Kopytoff (1986, 73) argues, "excessive commoditization is anti-cultural,"[19] a statement that alerts us to the limits of calling everything at all times a commodity (as is emphasized when we too easily label people as potential commodities).

It is also clear, however, that restrictions on exchange can change and relax quite dramatically and quickly. A sacred African mask may be found in an art store in London; a slave may be a free man not by buying himself out of servitude but by changes in legal rules; a communal pasture may be sold and fenced piece by piece. Things move in and out of commodity status in culturally and historically specific ways (Appadurai 1986; Kopytoff 1986; Mintz 1985). Objects have "a life history

... as in the case of an heirloom which family members will not sell until a particular point in the family's life cycle when it becomes available for sale" (Feierman 1993, 180). We wish to understand trends in these sorts of conversions.

CURRENCIES AND COMMODITIES

Many authors have discussed a global trend of monetization of economies that were until recently precapitalist.[20] Once general-purpose currencies are introduced, it is argued, then every good has the potential to become commoditized. Goods may be consumed and exchanged as gifts, but if they are to be considered commodities there must be prices and money and profits. Taussig (1980, 25), for instance, argues that "known as 'commodities,' goods and services under capitalism thus differ enormously from their counterparts in pre-capitalist systems of livelihood. Although they may in fact be the same articles, socially and conceptually they are very different." He further suggests that all social relations become dominated by the exchange ratio of commodities. Earlier Polanyi (1968, 133) defined commodities as "goods produced for sale" in "price-making markets." Gregory (1982) also endeavors to distinguish commodities that involve the exchange of alienable objects between independent actors from gifts that involve exchange of inalienable objects between interdependent transactors.[21] Money, which is meant to allow exchange between strangers, greatly facilitates the process of commoditization in this view.

In a similar way, Bohannan (1959) described transitions in the Tiv economy from multicentric spheres of exchange to general-purpose currency. He argued that the three moral spheres of exchange in the Tiv economy (subsistence, prestige items, and rights in people) were destroyed by the penetration of colonial currency. General-purpose money, in Bohannan's (1959, 503) terms, "creates its own revolution."

Others have taken issue with these strict divisions between goods or gifts and commodities, precapitalist and capitalist systems, restricted currencies and general-purpose money.[22] They choose to use the more inclusive definition of commodities—any object intended for exchange (Appadurai 1986, 9)—and argue that a great deal of exchange occurs without money and is regulated by cultural factors other than "the market" (see also Miller 1994).

THE *KULA* RING, GIFTS, AND COMMODITIES

Perhaps the most famous case of nonmonetary exchange is drawn from Malinowski's (1922) description of the *kula* ring, upon which Mauss and others built theories of gifts and reciprocal exchanges.[23] In the gift economies described by Mauss (1990), the material qualities of an object of exchange and the personal qualities of the exchanger are inseparably bound with each other: exchange is a "total social fact." The *kula* ring, which was a regional system for the circulation of particular kinds of valuables in the Massim group of islands off New Guinea, operated in the absence of money. These exchanges of decorated necklaces and arm shells allowed men of substance to solidify and enhance their wealth, power, and reputation without any actual profit from the exchange itself. Are these commodities? For classical political economy, probably not since this exchange does not operate independently of the exchangers, who are bound by more than their economic relationship (Marx 1954; Gregory 1982). But given the emerging consensus that the marketplace is a culturally defined institution that not only varies through time and space (Appadurai 1986; Taussig 1980) but in which cultural as well as economic information and exchanges occur, this division does not seem useful. Just as Mauss debunked the prevailing beliefs among economists that there were natural economies that produced for subsistence rather than exchange and concluded that there never has been such a thing, so too does it seem that a division between gift and commodity exchanges is one of degree rather than kind.[24]

Such divisions cannot be directly equated with simple historical or evolutionary sequences of change from personal to impersonal exchange in particular societies (usually transposed as an opposition between the modern West and primitive non-West). Carrier (1995, 192) makes this argument as he treats gift and commodity as ideal types, or "analytical tools rather than empirical descriptions." Contemporary commerce in the "West" is not uniformly impersonal, nor were impersonal economic relationships absent before 1800 (Carrier 1994, 362). Possessions that carry personal identities and commodities that do not constitute two poles Carrier (1994, 1995) believes to define a continuum of forms of circulation.[25] Similarly, Appadurai (1986, 12–13) argues the importance of recognizing forms of solidarity and cultural dimensions of exchange in societies assumed to be dominated by "market exchange," as well as the calculative dimensions of exchange in societies taken to be defined by solidarity and reciprocity. Thus we need to address the "calculative dimension in all . . . forms of exchange, even if they vary in the form and intensity of sociality associated with them" (Appadurai 1986, 13).[26]

To clarify the nature of historical transitions in which commodities figure, Carrier (1994) urges attention to the "social relations of circulation" in the West.[27] He highlights the importance of understanding not just how objects are produced but how individuals relate to them and transact them with one another. Such transactions "shape people's perceptions of objects and endow them with a personal specificity that weakens their impersonal symbolic meanings, their sign values" (Carrier 1994, 361). Thus changes in circulation, as well as those in production and mass media, shaped modern consumer culture and the emergence of impersonal markets.

THE ENVELOPE PLEASE . . .

If we are to accept the more expansive definition of commodities, then the presence of money is not necessarily an indication that commodified relationships exist (Parry and Bloch 1989; Guyer 1995). Some of the chapters in this collection (Creamer; Rothman) debate this issue in the archaeological record, and the answers often hinge on how restrictive a definition of commodity is used. Although the chapters that follow may not all use precisely the same definition of commodity, in this introductory chapter we opt to use a broad one:

> A commodity is any good that can be exchanged for other goods. Commodities existed in precapitalist economies, are culturally defined and molded, and are embedded in political and social systems which they both reflect and help to shape.

A commodity, for example, by its value in a global marketplace, may reflect increasing inequalities in global economic and political systems, a point highlighted by Stanford. The same commodity also contributes to the way that the marketplace operates, not only by its physical participation in a commodity chain but through the cultural and political meanings attached to it. The question then becomes how do these ideologies and culturally defined variations in practices and meanings of commodities and exchange operate in ever-widening "global" markets? This is not necessarily a new question—we know of long-distance trade prehistorically in many parts of the world—but it has become an increasingly urgent one as "local" systems of value and exchange become incorporated in new ways into wider global market networks.

Other questions explored here originate in the global arena itself and focus on how the ethnography of economic anthropology can study these globalizing financial and political processes in particular times and places. While a grape or melon grower may be a link in a "global commodity chain," how he or she experiences those connections may be anything but global and merits close ethnographic attention.

GLOBALIZATION AND COMMODITIES

This volume, and the conference on which it is based, were inspired by the relatively new interest in global commodities and commodity chains that link local economic systems to what many believe are newly globalized (or recently reglobalized) ones. Many of the volume's contributors do document startlingly close connections between peasants—whether Gambian farmers or Mexican melon growers—and markets in the North. Such connections also are striking among the Congolese popular musicians White analyzes, many of whom leave their home country to perform (produce) for foreigners abroad. These webs of economic, social, and political relationships represent new puzzles to the anthropologists whose field techniques of ethnography and participant observation are by nature localized in time and place (cf. Gupta and Ferguson 1997; Marcus 1995).

Globalization would seem, at first glance, to change also the ground rules of many of the definitional debates (Featherstone 1990; Friedman 1994; Hall 1991). How can one conceive of a "socially desirable thing" in a marketplace in which the producer and the consumer are not only very far from one another geographically, but may live in completely different cultural, political, and social worlds? Does the "thing" take on multiple meanings? Do these meanings operate independently or do they overlap? Even with the facilitating effects of exchangeable currencies, anthropologists have found that exchange still contains and relies importantly on social relations, and inequities of power are still significant (Carrier 1995; Guyer 1995; Shipton 1989). Similarly, the identification of use- and exchange-values seems highly variable, unstable, and subject to many noneconomic influences in this globalized arena.

Some early thinking on globalization assumed that these differences would disappear eventually, and that a unified and homogenous capitalist global economy would emerge. This prospect caused considerable dismay among anthropologists and cultural theorists who viewed the process of cultural homogenization and economic conformity as antithetical to everything they studied and cherished (Edwards 1994). More recent studies of globalization, however, have documented the persistence of cultural distinctiveness and the localized and diverse responses to these global systems. Whether the rise of ethnic politics, the increased importance of religion in many nations' politics, or the emergence of modern, yet non-Western, forms of family and domestic organization, the globalization process seems as fragmentizing as it does unifying (Bayart 1993; Geschière and Raatgever 1985; Geschière 1992; Harvey 1989; Parry and Bloch 1989; Pred and Watts 1992).

Similarly, capitalism, far from being an "impersonal machine," turns out to be highly cultural, with a specific history (Appadurai 1986, 48; Carrier 1995). The penetration of all-purpose currencies, as noted, has not followed the expected route (Shipton 1989; Guyer 1995; Hutchinson 1996; Ferguson 1990). As Ekejiuba describes for Nigeria (1995, 148), "in the face of the multiplicity of currencies, periodic loss of stores of wealth, and fluctuations in the value and quantity of money in circulation, it is hardly surprising that commodity production, social life and social payments were only partially monetized despite the impressively long history of currency use in Eastern Nigeria."

Global capital, however, is more than currency; it is also about politics, and has been for an impressively long history. Mintz's (1985) study of the growth of sugar as a commodity documents how the combined effects of industrialization and urbanization in England, together with the establishment of colonies and plantation economies fueled by slave labor, help to explain the growing presence of sugar in the English diet from the seventeenth to the nineteenth centuries. Part of the political dimension of global commodities resides in what has come to be called cultural politics. As Harvey (1989, 300) notes, we now have access to cultural forms from all over the world, whether it be food, music, television, or cinema:

> it is now possible to experience the world's geography vicariously, as a simulacrum. The interweaving of simulacra in daily life brings together different worlds (of commodities) in the same space and time. But it does so in such a way as to conceal almost per-

fectly any trace of origin, of the labour processes that produced them, or of the social relations implicated in their production.

The contemporary Northern consumer of Brazilian grapes, Gambian beans, or Italian cheese, perhaps not so differently from the nineteenth-century British consumer of sugar, can sample from the goods of many different parts of the world without having to acknowledge the political inequities that keep the prices low or the supplies abundant. Several chapters in this collection discuss the implications of incomplete information about the market both for the producers (Stanford; Collins; Plattner; Vargas-Cetina) and the consumers (Ziegenhorn; Plattner), exploring both disadvantages and advantages associated with this unevenness for different actors.

But to return for a moment to the aspects of culture that Harvey (1989) listed as being accessible to us from all over the world—food, music, television, or cinema— it might seem at first glance that only the first—food—enters the global arena in any significant numbers from Southern countries, while what we often think of as global cultural commodities—music, television, cinema—might appear to have originated mainly from the North.[28] The first cultural theorists who studied globalization borrowed from world systems theory and indeed have been criticized for presuming that what is "global" emerged principally from the North ("core") and was imposed on the recipient South ("periphery"). As Tsing (1993) notes, these scholars of globalization perpetuated a division between a complex and transcontinental core and a static and recipient periphery (see also Feierman 1993). Some places seem to generate the global, in her critique, while others (the rural, the tribal, the third world) are stuck in the local.

Political economists worked with many of these assumptions as well. Moore (1994, 373) noted about the political economy approach that "the center of analytic attention [is on] the penetration of the world economy into the fieldwork site. . . . In most instances the logic cannot go in the reverse direction." The small-scale producer, a familiar subject of anthropological study, is often portrayed as the victim of imposed foreign models and global forces (whether cultural, political, or economic) that progressively undermine "traditional" ways of life. This bias, however, tended to obscure not only the active resistance to and reconfiguring of capitalist structures undertaken by "third world peasants,"[29] as suggested above, but in a more general way diverted attention away from the producers as global actors.

Although many of the chapters in this volume do see the increasingly powerful reach of global economic forces into the lives of more and more people throughout the world (for example, Collins; Little and Dolan; Stanford; White), analytic attention is beginning to move to the producers themselves. This shift entails a focus on local producers, but in a global frame, whether studying peasant resistance to global markets (Stanford), or small farmers' or Congolese musicians' responses to global consumer demand (Collins; Little and Dolan; White). Related literature in the environmental field also exhibits a gradual shift in attention away from overwhelming concern with the imposition of unfair economic and environmental burdens from the North on peasants in the South, to the green movements that originate from the periphery and constitute a new form of global political movement.[30] So too may the next generation of studies of commodities analyze the cultural, political, and economic contributions of the "periphery" to the global marketplace.

This approach, which we believe is already well begun in this collection, may help us resolve remaining puzzles about global commodities and their circulation. Collins and Stanford, for example, offer the valuable insight that the small producer in the periphery now sees the production process itself more than profits from the sale of his or her commodity as a decisive criterion of what makes economic sense. Thus Stanford notes that the sale of labor or inputs is a more reliable source of income than the sale of a perishable product such as melons, and Collins observes that it is the marketing advantage of large grape farmers (especially their better access to postharvest cold storage and refrigerated transport services) rather than the efficiencies of their production that gives them the upper hand. (Indeed Collins remarks that production costs are lower and quality higher among small-scale producers.) Similarly, White suggests that many Congolese musicians view live performances—rather than commercial sale of their product—as their source of livelihood. Global capitalism unfolds in unexpected ways in the cities and on the farms of The Gambia, Kenya, Iowa, Mexico, Congo, and Brazil. The economic anthropologist whose frame is a global one may be well positioned to unravel some of that startling difference.

As our discussants all noted at the conference (Catherine Besteman, Sutti Ortiz, and Mahir Saul), what commodities are and how they are validated as commodities are surely variable phenomena, but they are always deeply social, cultural, and political as well as economic.

ORGANIZATION OF THIS VOLUME

The essays in this volume are ordered under two themes. Those included in the first section, "Commodities in a Globalizing Marketplace," address historically and culturally defined variations in meanings and practices associated with commodities in globalizing markets. These chapters illustrate the relevance of economic ethnography to globalization processes set in motion by reconfigurations of financial and currency exchange markets, new telecommunications technologies, economic liberalization processes, structural adjustment reforms, possible erosion of nation-state autonomy over fiscal policies, and neoliberal reforms as they affect the ideologies and practices of rural producers.

Bob White's chapter, "*Soukous* or Sell-Out?: Congolese Popular Dance Music as Cultural Commodity," concerns a quintessentially global commodity—emergent "world music"—that has benefited from the post-1980 global economy. Popular music raises important questions about deregulation and property rights, and about how "cultural" commodities may differ from other types of commodities.[31] White explores the particular process by which the Congolese popular dance music known as *soukouss* has been commodified, what meanings and identities are associated with it, how it is valued, and how it has become enmeshed in increasingly global commercial networks of social and political relationships. Contrary to the assumption that cultural exports from the West inevitably displace local goods and producers, the Congo-Kinshasa exports more music than it imports, and its own music has enjoyed increasing commercial success and popularity.

Congolese musicians use notions of African authenticity to promote their music abroad and, White suggests, the commercialization of such music helps to constitute national identity without necessarily compromising or "selling out" African culture. *Soukouss* world music is an example of commodity exchange that may be unusual in that it does not progressively alienate the producer from her or his product. Such global music commodification, however, may involve cooptation, romanticization, essentialization, or invention of identities with particular symbolic value. The relationship between commodities and identity is complex. *Soukouss*, White notes, "has been consciously adapted for foreign audiences and distribution channels." Most people in Kinshasa view *soukouss* as inauthentic (because of its fast tempo and shortened lyrics). A music star can be trapped or alienated by an image associated with his or her success, and new meanings are just as easily romanticized or essentialized as older ones, White observes.

Peter Little and Catherine Dolan's chapter, "What It Means to Be Restructured: Nontraditional Commodities and Structural Adjustment in Sub-Saharan Africa," examines a new category of agricultural export called "nontraditional" commodities, which have been encouraged by institutions such as the World Bank and the IMF. These high-value commodities are intended to increase and diversify export earnings for countries undergoing structural adjustment. The labor and land demands of these commodities have significant consequences for local labor and gender relations. Little and Dolan explore these effects in the Gambian economy of the 1980s and 1990s, when new investments in horticulture and contract farming were undertaken. The authors examine the promotion in The Gambia of so-called nontraditional export commodities such as French beans and chili peppers, and show how the reclassification of certain commodities as nontraditional is associated with a wider set of economic, social, and political processes and inequalities. How powerful institutions categorize commodities has profound social and economic consequences. Under the auspices of nontraditional commodity programs and structural adjustment policies, there have emerged a variety of new opportunities for private capital to reconfigure African agriculture and to force out small-scale commodity growers. Little and Dolan's chapter raises important issues about the economic and ideological significance of ostensibly neutral crop categories used by international agencies, the direct impact of new foreign investment, economic and social differentiation processes that accompany recent neoliberal economic reforms, and the impact on Gambian farmers of practices originating in trade agreements within European Community states.

Horticultural commodities in global markets are also at the center of Lois Stanford's chapter, "The Globalization of Agricultural Commodity Systems: Examining Peasant Resistance to International Agribusiness." Stanford considers how agribusiness and the new NAFTA (North American Free Trade Agreement) affect small-scale vegetable growers in Mexico. She analyzes the experiences of peasant farmers in Michoacán who participated in the development of Mexico's fresh fruit and vegetable export industry beginning in 1950. With the passage of NAFTA, these growers found themselves increasingly disadvantaged relative to international agribusiness. Indeed one farmer told Stanford that peasants were losing everything under globalization or economic opening. The chapter documents several instances where Michoacán peasants attempted to resist unfavorable market conditions but were defeated by state-sponsored programs of privatization and investment, all carried out under the "free" trade mandate of NAFTA. Stanford uses a commodity systems approach to explore negotiation and conflict at different levels of Mexico's horticulture industry and to show how peasants attempted to defend their interests in the face of strong national and global market pressures. In spite of the rhetoric of free trade and privatization, the state played a key role in supporting the interests of agribusiness capital over those of peasants.

Stanford innovatively connects Scott's (1990, 1985) framework of "public" and "hidden" transcripts to the ideology of late capitalism in a rural region of the new global marketplace. She suggests that peasants defend their interests under capitalism rather than reject the latter in the manner Scott (1976) emphasizes. Connecting forms of resistance to levels of repression and changes in national and international economic policies, Stanford shows how small farmers shifted from public confrontation with local elites and foreign agribusinesses in the 1960s and 1970s to private, hidden acts of sabotage that eroded agribusiness profits in an increasingly corrupt commodity system in the 1980s and 1990s. Peasants were further marginalized from the privatized economy by their less open resistance against an "export commodity system dominated by an alliance between the state and foreign agribusinesses." Stanford suggests that Michoacán farmers and entrepreneurs "now recognize the need for new forms of association to defend their common regional interests in an open, market economy." Such organization against neoliberal economic policies is a promising new area of inquiry, as evidenced in Edelman's (1990, 1996, 2000) work on Costa Rican peasants and a transnational peasant movement in Central America.

Jane Collins's chapter, "Tracing Social Relations in Commodity Chains: The Case of Grapes in Brazil," also discusses the fate of Southern Hemisphere producers of fruits. Here the issue is not (as in Stanford's chapter) the politics of production and marketing, but rather the gender-specific effects on production relations of globalizing markets in "luxury" edibles.[32] Using the concept of commodity chains, Collins examines the production of grapes in the São Francisco valley of northeastern Brazil and compares the very different labor processes involved in production of grapes for export and for the national market. In particular, she examines the labor implications of changing quality standards, competition with other Latin American producers, and "nontraditional" marketing strategies. The grape commodity chain is an example of the feminization of labor to meet quality requirements. Commodity chain analysis offers, Collins says, a means of moving beyond models of local communities connected to abstract global forces; her approach offers instead understanding of specific social relationships that constitute the growing distance between points of production and consumption.

Contemporary consumers in the North often have little knowledge of how or where their food is produced. Collins's and Stanford's chapters suggest the potential influence of ethnographic research on the cultural politics of consumer demand, or on an international consumer conscience that addresses the conditions of production of global commodities.[33] As Appadurai (1986, 33) reminds us, "demand can be manipulated by direct political appeals" such as lettuce or grape boycotts or unofficial and official forms of protectionism. Commodities, he notes, vary in their susceptibility to instrumental transmission of social or political messages. Whatever the possibilities of shaping the politics of consumer demand in the North, new forms of transnational organization in the South, among some of those most negatively affected by neoliberal economic reforms, are emerging in places such as Central America (see Edelman 1996). Such organizations must confront the challenges faced by so many of the marginalized peoples described in this volume—namely, how to "defend themselves in the increasingly distant spheres where decisions are taken that affect their livelihood" (Edelman 1996, 42). Economic globalization demands new types of political organization, new strategies of resistance and negotiation, and new forms of professionalization among popular movement members and leaders.[34]

In part two, "The Circulation and Revaluation of Commodities," contributors analyze how commodity producers' experiences are informed by colonial and postcolonial history, state directives in the marketplace, and locations in dependent or marginalized regions. Some of the chapters in part two include attention to the intricacies of local exchange and politics in time periods that precede the globalization processes that have defined so powerfully the past two decades. Here we see crucial antecedent processes of monetization, revaluation of commodities, and changing social relations of exchange and production (Creamer; Polier; Roberts; Rothman; Vargas-Cetina; Ziegenhorn). Other themes include contemporary puzzles in the valuation of commodities such as avant-garde art (Plattner), the hidden knowledge about composition embodied in corporate brands of hybrid corn (Ziegenhorn), and the contradictory effects of cash and commoditization on social relations (Polier). Many of these contributions offer the kind of historical perspective on contemporary economic processes that scholars such as Mintz (1998, 120, 131) have suggested is often missing in anthropological studies of globalization.

Stuart Plattner's chapter, "Profit Markets and Art Markets," explores economic paradoxes of avant-garde art as commodity. Avant-garde artists, for example, often ignore the preferences of potential customers while art dealers adopt monopolistic practices that would leave them without customers in a classical market situation.

And lower prices of art do not necessarily increase demand. To explain these anoma-lies, Plattner considers the twentieth-century growth of wealth in the United States, the postmodern state of aesthetic theory, the goals of producers of art, and the in-formation constraints of consumers. Drawing on ethnographic examples from re-search among artists in St. Louis, he analyzes why aesthetic excellence does not nec-essarily enhance the marketability of art, how art commodity markets are shaped by the hegemony of elite taste, and how the identity (e.g., exhibition pedigrees) of the producers of art affects the value of the product. Some of the artists he studied produce and consume art mostly in St. Louis and mostly in private, rather than for investors in New York or "global cities."[35] It is a small number of elite dealers, crit-ics, and collectors in New York, however, who crucially shape the values of art as commodity. Thus some St. Louis dealers and collectors consult authorities in New York before making purchase decisions. For them, "legitimacy means status in a nonlocal market." Plattner shows how conventional economic theory can explain the unconventional behavior of many artists, dealers, and collectors.

Like Plattner's, Randy Ziegenhorn's contribution, "The Commodification of Hybrid Corn: What Farmers Know," is about a commodity that may appear to defy neoclassical economic logic. Invoking Appaduari's (1986, 56) turnstile of knowledge and ignorance, which allows the flow of some things and hinders the movement of others, Ziegenhorn analyzes a commodity whose composition is intentionally dis-guised in marketing. The Iowa farmers Ziegenhorn describes are no strangers to capitalized agriculture and yet the development and marketing of hybrid corn since the 1920s gradually decreased farmers' control over their productive enterprise (sepa-rating farmers from the reproduction of the seed). He outlines the history of the development of the U.S. hybrid seed corn industry, which progressively deskilled farmers in the breeding and improvement of their own seeds, and made them in-creasingly dependent on the seed industry. The creation of barriers to knowledge, done by disguising the origin and composition of corn hybrids, boosted the success of hybrid corn by confusing farmers and limiting competition, but also provided the necessary conditions of capital accumulation in the seed industry. Through co-operation with U.S. land grant universities, the hybrid seed corn industry created a system of nomenclature and trade secrecy that prevents farmers from making in-formed choices and insulates individual companies from competition. The closed pedigree system for hybrid corn also threatens the genetic diversity of the U.S. corn crop. The chapter illustrates how U.S. capitalism, advertising, and state regulators shape a commodity's social and economic characteristics and its market success.

Ziegenhorn's work is part of a much larger tale of how crop seed historically has been "transformed from a public good produced and reproduced by farmers into a commodity that is a mechanism for the accumulation and reproduction of capital" (Kloppenburg 1988, xii). The development of hybrid corn is a striking example of the use of science to speed commodification (Kloppenburg 1988, xiii). Corporations operating globally now have a significant capacity to mask and confuse the identi-ties of key commodities such as the seeds of the food crops on which we all depend.

Today, Ziegenhorn notes, biotechnology contributes to the mysterious nature of seeds, creating new forms of knowledge over them that are even more remote from farmers in the United States and elsewhere (cf. Kloppenburg 1988). The development of hybrid corn, then, points to much broader issues concerning property rights in plant genetic material and threats to crop genetic diversity in the United States and abroad.

The chapters by Creamer and Rothman examine commoditization in much earlier times. Winifred Creamer's chapter, "The Impact of Colonial Contact on the Production and Distribution of Glaze-Paint Decorated Ceramics," explores a series of changes in ceramic forms and design elements with the colonization of northern New Mexico in the late sixteenth century. The new forms and designs were borrowed from European ceramics and presumably were made for the colonists, while changes in execution of decoration, and even glaze color, were likely to be responses to increasing exchange of ceramics with European settlers and decreasing exchange among Pueblo people. Although the Europeans profoundly changed the market for ceramics, an indigenous process of commoditization of pottery had been under way at least since A.D. 1400.

Mitchell Rothman, in "The Commoditization of Goods and the Rise of the State in Ancient Mesopotamia," explores how commodities emerged in the context of early state formation in Mesopotamia. Control of trade and of commodities such as pottery and metals bolstered early state authority and the administrative and economic structures that underlie a complex state. Commoditization and state formation, he argues, coevolved even in the absence of a modern economic system—a historical pattern that prompts Rothman to argue for a somewhat more narrow definition of commodities than the one we propose above. In the absence of modern markets, he suggests, the value of commodities was shaped politically by the state. Rothman shows that by the middle of the fifth millennium B.C. the state had refined ruling structures and techniques (including force and repression) to monitor and control high-value commodities.

Bruce Roberts, in "Always Cheaply Pleasant: Beer as a Commodity in a Rural Kenyan Society," examines the place of beer in a rural Kenyan locale. He suggests that beer among Keiyo peoples of the Rift Valley is equivalent to the luxury foods enjoyed by the English poor of the 1930s. Roberts's chapter explores the social contexts in which beer is consumed, and its income-generating role in rural households that produce it. That is, beer is a commodity imbued with a rich set of meanings associated with a long history of consumption in socially significant contexts (communal labor, sacrifices to ancestors, weddings, naming ceremonies, bride wealth). Roberts examines variations across ecological zones in the use of beer in communal labor and household production of beer for sale, the latter being highest in areas where salaried employment and small business opportunities are least available. He also considers how the colonial and postcolonial states have influenced social and exchange relations centered on beer.

Parallel historical themes on a different continent emerge in Nicole Polier's chapter, "Commoditization, Cash, and Kinship in Postcolonial Papua New Guinea." Polier reconsiders Sahlins's (1972) model of reciprocity and social distance as she explores local dimensions of commoditization among villagers in the Western Province of Papua New Guinea. Since the early 1980s, people in this region have been incorporated within global commodity circuits associated with a multinational mining company. The mine created a local market for labor and crops. Polier analyzes consequent changes in the moral foundations of exchange as cash flows into previously nonmonetized social networks of kin, clan, and community relationships. Among the results are attenuation of laborers' extended kin ties, new forms of mistrust and tension in core kin relations, a blurring of the boundary between kindred and "others," and emergence of new lines of social differentiation. Global commodity production and newly concealable and privatized forms of wealth and accumulation have reconstituted social and kinship relations (including those of food sharing and trade between regional partners). While commoditization contributes to revaluation of both goods and close kin, the causes of such changes are complex and need not be reduced to the penetration of money per se (cf. Parry and Bloch 1989, 21–23). As Polier's analysis suggests, cash can sustain as well as subvert social relations. When is a man who visits an employed kinsman a wolf at the door from whom cash must be concealed, as opposed to a valued family member with whom cash is shared willingly? Both images are culturally recognized among the villagers Polier studies; both are crucial to processes of postcolonial change and are situationally defined and constantly renegotiated.

Gabriela Vargas-Cetina's chapter, "From Handicraft to Monocrop: The Production of Pecorino Cheese in Highland Sardinia," analyzes local social effects of growth in the international market for Pecorino cheese. While Pecorino cheese has existed since the Middle Ages, its export commodity status is relatively recent. Sardinian agro-pastoralists have been producing cheese for international markets at least since the mid-nineteenth century. The terms of trade for their cheese, however, have changed significantly during the past 150 years, and recent measures introduced by the new European Community have contributed to further changes. Vargas-Cetina explores the responses of the pastoralist families to expansion of the international market for Pecorino cheese and shows how growth in such cheese exports has altered local exchange patterns and relations of gender, family, friendship, and patronage. Through household organization of production and trade of cheese, Sardinian pastoralists retained some flexibility in responding to the market, a capacity that has helped them to deal with new European commodity regulations and global market pressures. To highlight the historical processes associated with the transformation to export production, Vargas-Cetina suggests a five-phase model that traces the transition from an initial stage of market expansion to market saturation and then underdevelopment. Rather than being "backward," as the Italian politicians have depicted them, Sardinian pastoralists' current economic vulnerability derives precisely from their long-term participation, as export commodity producers, in international and global "modern" markets.

Today Sardinian pastoralists, like African or Latin American farmers, must search for alternative means of survival (such as migration or diversification into other agricultural or nonagricultural activities). In addition, Sardinian pastoralists manipulate the symbolic content of their primary export commodity. During the early 1990s, as they faced increasing world market competition for their product, associations of Sardinian shepherds demanded that their cheese be marketed under its own trademark *(pecorino di Sardegna)* to distinguish it from similar products of countries such as Argentina. Thus changes in global markets have prompted Sardinian shepherds to commoditize their identity. Once again, the local is globalized.[36]

CONCLUSION: FOLLOW THE COMMODITY

Globalization, as noted, is not entirely new and does not necessarily demand a reinvention of anthropology (Mintz 1998). Today's growing fascination with flows of people, commodities, technology, capital, images, and ideas across national and other boundaries, however, does pose theoretical and methodological challenges. One response has been the current popularity of multisited ethnographic research. In a recent overview, Marcus (1995, 106–107) mentions several "tracking" strategies in multisited research, one of which is to "follow the thing" or commodity: "tracing the circulation through different contexts of a manifestly material object of study (at least as initially conceived), such as commodities, gifts, money, works of art, and intellectual property." Thus commodity analysis is one means of taking up the challenge to contemporary anthropologists to understand better the connections, discontinuities, and contrasts among multiple research sites.[37]

A focus on particular commodities such as grapes (Collins), or Congolese popular music (White), or avant-garde art (Plattner) reveals some of the scarcely visible social, political, and economic relations that define this globalizing era. Collins's chapter, for example, illustrates how Northern consumers' year-round demand for fresh grapes helps to reshape the conditions of work for women in the South. Studies of sugar, coffee, tea, and chocolate—commodities Mintz (1979) termed "proletarian hunger killers"—link class dynamics in consuming countries to relations of production among peasants, slaves, and others who grow or harvest the products (Roseberry 1996, 770).[38] Case studies of such processes in particular times and places, like those assembled in this volume, illuminate the human dimensions of globalization processes that too often become remote abstractions.

One of the analytical difficulties of such a task is to capture the relationship of part to whole, of locale to wider system, of cases to more general processes. Thus Marcus (1995, 102) notes the need to "posit logics of relationship, translation, and association among these sites" (cf. Wolf 1982). Comprehending these relationships is not easy or straightforward. In this time of displacement of earlier models of macroprocesses, some argue that it is not enough to adopt a postmodernist juxta-position of sites or construction of ethnographic "collages" (Polier and Roseberry 1989).[39] Among the analytical challenges is how to capture both determinism and historical contingency. As Polier and Roseberry (1989, 256) suggest, we should not be too quick to dismiss the notion of totalities or to "invalidate an attempt to see things whole, to see structural connections among particular customs or institutions, to see historical connections between social groups or states, to see *relationships* of exchange, domination or resistance" (emphasis in original; see also Pred and Watts 1992; Cooper et al. 1993). Polier and Roseberry (1989, 257) note that the connec-tions and relationships we posit may be contradictory and their development un-even; "we may see totalities as differentiated, understanding that differentiation in terms of a series of connections and relationships that have histories." A focus on commodities, then, offers one means of tracing historical connections and structural relationships in this era of both "globalization" and apparent disconnection and frag-mentation.

Such an approach poses methodological challenges. The fieldwork is not com-plete once the anthropologist leaves the rural area, but extends to following a com-modity chain and communications network into the global arena. To understand the commodification history of hybrid seed corn (Ziegenhorn), for example, one needs to combine attention to several sites: multinational corporations that sell seed, national and regional seed companies, U.S. land grant universities, legislation gov-erning marketing, and farmers in Iowa and elsewhere. Furthermore, multisited eth-nography must deal with fieldwork "knowledge bases of varying intensity," bring-ing into a single frame of study knowledge of varying depth and quality gained at different sites (Marcus 1995, 100–101). Thus a single study might combine atten-tion to the production of international discourses of development, or particular policies such as those favoring "nontraditional" commodity exports, as well as ev-eryday economic life in communities affected by such policies.

Also important is the wider "system-awareness" that is evident in commodification as seen from the margins: the "everyday consciousness and actions" of subjects within a single site (Marcus 1995, 111)[40]—as illustrated in the telling remark by one of the Gambian farmers in Little and Dolan's study:

> The supermarket chains in Europe know nothing about farming or the needs of farmers. . . . They think our farms are like factories where we can turn out a bean of 10 centimeters every time. Farming is not like factory work.

Gambian farmers and exporters are aware of their relationships to nonlocal sites and agents, and they recognize that they themselves lack the power to shape those rela-tionships as they wish (see also Stanford's chapter).

Many of the commodities analyzed in this volume—grapes, melons, Congolese popular music, chili peppers, Gambian French beans—are produced by poor or marginalized peoples of the South and exported to wealthier consumers in the North who are unlikely to have direct knowledge of the conditions of their production. Yet both Northern consumers and Southern producers are entwined (in very different ways) in the same global networks of capital and commodities. Non-Southern producers of other commodities considered here—Pecorino cheese, avant-garde art, hybrid corn—also are disadvantaged by incomplete information about and peripheral positions in relation to markets for the goods they produce. Since commodities such as grapes or coffee not only embody economic value but also transmit social and political messages, they offer a useful window on the volatile and diverse historical processes we call globalization.

Growing economic disparities accompany globalization in both North and South and these have become troubling even to globalization cheerleaders (see, for example, Friedman 1999). Such inequalities help to fuel new modes of local and transnational political mobilization against economic neoliberalism (see Edelman 1996, 2000). Although the market economy is often construed as a "natural" rather than a socially constructed and state-mediated entity, globalization is a political process, not a "natural" one, and it can stimulate political countermovements.[41]

In short, the topic explored in this volume is a lively area of research and one that is likely to bedevil economic anthropologists for years. As our theories of globalization improve, and as our methods for studying these complex and by definition far-flung processes catch up, we are confident our understanding of the ways contemporary commodities behave will gain increasing conceptual clarity. Future collaboration with our colleagues in history, economics, cultural studies, and political science will also, we believe, better allow us to grasp what often seems to be an unmanageable and unbounded set of data and theories. A "commodity chain" may sound like a logical and ordered system we can follow link by link, but that is not an easy task. The chapters in this collection, nonetheless, take an important step in organizing and pointing the way through these complex networks and the rethinking of commodities this requires.

NOTES

The editors wish to thank two anonymous reviewers for extremely helpful comments and suggestions. In addition, we are grateful to Deborah Winslow, publications coordinator of the Society for Economic Anthropology, who provided very useful suggestions and support, and to Bob White, who offered helpful comments on an earlier draft of this introduction. Generous funds to assist in the preparation of this volume were given by the Society for Economic Anthropology and the University of Kentucky. We also thank Washington University (St. Louis) for administrative support. We are grateful to graduate students Brian George, Elisabeth Hildebrand, Nicholas A. Jackson, and Michele Pietrowski for superb research and editorial assistance.

Earlier forms of the chapters included here were presented at the 1995 annual meeting of the Society for Economic Anthropology in Santa Fe, New Mexico. The three co-editors were program chairs of that conference, whose theme was "Rethinking Commodities."

1. The World Bank Group, transcript of a press conference with James D. Wolfensohn, Washington, D.C. [http://www.worldbank.org/html/extdr/spring99/jdwts042299.htm]. 1 October 1998.

2. Fine examples of how a single-commodity focus can illuminate large historical changes include Mintz's (1985) work on sugar and Roseberry's (1996) on yuppie coffees.

3. See, for example, Mintz (1985), Wolf (1982), Taussig's (1989) critique of Mintz and Wolf, and Mintz's (1989) response. See also Featherstone and Lash's (1995, 3–4) discussion of global homogenizers (who subscribe to some notion of world system) versus heterogenizers (who dispute the existence of such a system).

4. See, for example, Wallerstein (1974, 1980, 1989), Wolf (1982), and Mintz (1998).

5. Fareed Zakaria, review of John Gray, *The Delusions of Global Capitalism* (New York: Free Press, 1999). *New York Times*, Sunday Book Review, 25 April 1999, pp. 16, 18. See also Friedman (1999, xiv–xvi).

6. DeMartino (2000). See also Leys (1996, 20), Hart (1992), and Zevin (1992).

7. Mintz (1998) examines the history of migration during the nineteenth century and argues that the contemporary view of transnationalism as qualitatively different from earlier times is exaggerated, as is the notion that the contemporary mobility of people requires a new anthropology.

8. Capital mobility (capital movements as a proportion of economic output) may also be lower today than in the 1880s, according to a 1997 IMF report. On the other hand, with new electronic technologies, capital today moves around the globe much more quickly and with greater geographic reach than it did in the past. The figures on proportions of the U.S. population born abroad and that on capital mobility are from Nicholas D. Kristoff, "At This Rate, We'll Be Global in Another Hundred Years," *New York Times* 23 May 1999, p. WK5.

9. On recent globalization processes, see, for example, Coombe (1995), Featherstone, Lash, and Robertson (1995), Friedman (1999), Hoogvelt (1997), Leys (1996), McMichael (1996), and Schaeffer (1997).

10. Scholars disagree on the implications of globalization for national sovereignty. For example, Panitch (1994, 63) argues that globalization has not necessarily diminished the role of the state, and suggests that "today's globalization both is authored by states and is primarily about reorganizing, rather than bypassing, states." Keller and Pauly (1997, 370) similarly suggest that "markets . . . are not replacing states as the world's effective government." McMichael (1996, 28), on the other hand, observes that "precisely because of the non-territorial character of financialization, all states are constrained to manage their finances according to global criteria."

11. According to the United Nations Development Program's 1992 *Human Development Report*, the world's wealthiest countries constitute 20 percent of the planet's population and receive 82.7 percent of its income, while the poorest 20 percent receive a scant 1.4 percent of the world's income. Furthermore, if we consider individual statistics rather than these national averages, we find that "the incomes of the richest 20 percent of the world's people are approximately 140 times those of the poorest 20 percent" (Korten 1996, 16). That gap

has more than tripled since 1960, when the wealthiest 20 percent received just thirty times the income of the poorest 20 percent (Korten 1996, 16).

12. Again, in Appadurai's (1996) terms, these domains would correspond to financescapes, technoscapes, and ethnoscapes.

13. These loan agreements carry conditionalities requiring liberalization of currency markets, budget reforms, and expansion of agricultural exports.

14. Examining 1993 commodity prices, George and Sabelli (1994, 86) found that the actual prices were "catastrophically (for producers) lower than the [World] Bank had said they would be only two years previously. The Bank's 1991 projections were off by 47 per cent on coffee, 56 per cent on cocoa, 74 per cent on sugar, 30 per cent on aluminum, 52 per cent on lead and 37 per cent on zinc. They got petroleum, copper and silver about right; palm oil, alone among the commodities we were able to check, did better than the Bank said it would, by 15 per cent."

15. Mitchell (1995, 147–148).

16. Consumers of commodities and the effects of globalization on consumer society have received much recent attention (see, for example, Howes 1996; MacKay 1997). We now have a good understanding of the marketing of culture and of "tradition," resistance by Southern consumers to Western ideologies, as well as the indigenous appropriation of communications technologies and networks. All of these topics, while of great importance, are distinct from the main purpose of this volume.

17. See Appadurai's (1986, 3–63) discussion of what is meant by economic value, how it is created in culturally and historically specific ways and mediated politically, and why "commodities, like persons, have social lives." To understand the circulation of commodities in actual times and places we must "follow the things themselves, for their meanings are inscribed in their forms, their uses, their trajectories. It is only through the analysis of these trajectories that we can interpret the human transactions and calculations that enliven things" (Appadurai 1986, 5).

18. See also Bourdieu's (1997) analysis of Kabyle marriage practices.

19. All economies of course are culturally constituted.

20. But see Parry and Bloch's (1989) discussion of why it can be misleading to transpose the nonmonetary/monetary and traditional/modern dichotomies into congruent historical sequences of societal change, and how some Western cultural discourses condemning money have been overgeneralized.

21. This phrasing is close to that of Parry and Bloch (1989, 8).

22. See, for example, Carrier (1995), Parry and Bloch (1989), and Roseberry (1989). Carrier (1995, 201–202) observes that Mauss underplayed the presence in the Melanesian societies he described of "impersonal transactions between autonomous transactors, most notably in local markets where people from different villages traded for each other's produce . . . [though] such impersonal markets may well have been less significant in these societies than impersonal markets were in France in the 1920s when Mauss wrote." Carrier's (1995, 202) point is that Mauss exaggerates by "convert[ing] a difference of degree into a difference of kind: the West has impersonal markets and autonomous actors, the societies of Melanesia do not." He argues the need to avoid this "twinned orientalism and occidentalism" (Carrier 1995, 202).

23. See the edited collection on this topic by Leach and Leach (1983).

24. See also Appadurai (1986, 9–13), Carrier (1994, 1995), and Alexander and Alexander (1991).

25. Possessions, Carrier (1994, 361) writes, "inalienably bear the personal identities of the people who have them, of those from whom those people received them, and of the personal relationship between givers and receivers. . . . At the other pole . . . commodities [are] objects that carry no personal identities, being alienated from those who have them, from those from whom they received them, and from the relationship between givers and receivers."

26. See also Hart's (1992, 224–225) discussion of models of market relations; he notes that market exchange usually requires economic actors to "engage with social organization as a means of reducing the uncertainties involved."

27. Carrier extends Mauss's model of forms of circulation to an analysis of changes in retail trade relations in England since about 1800, when anonymous transactions between shopkeepers and buyers developed. He describes a sixteenth- and seventeenth-century English moral order in which traded objects were to "pass through as few hands as possible," sellers and buyers usually were previously known to one another, and producers and consumers traded directly with one another (Carrier 1994, 364–365). As factory production increased after about 1750, "it became easier for seller and buyer alike to impose new, symbolic meanings on commodities" (Carrier 1994, 370), and it became easier for sellers to hide information about quality or composition from buyers (Alexander 1992).

28. This view is misleading, as Bob White (personal communication) observes. For example, mainstream American popular music takes many of its cues from African traditions long found in much of the Atlantic (Gilroy 1993), and forms such as Afro-Cuban rumba became enormous commercial successes in post–World War I Europe and North America.

29. See, for example, Cooper et al. 1993 for essays that critically assess earlier historical paradigms in relation to such contemporary theoretical and empirical concerns.

30. See, for example, Peet and Watts (1994, 1996), and Princen and Finger (1994).

31. All commodities of course are cultural (Wade 1998); see endnote 7 in White's chapter for his definition of "cultural" commodities.

32. Cf. Appadurai (1986, 38–39) on the definition of "luxury" goods: he defines luxury as a "special 'register' of consumption . . . [rather than] as a special class of thing."

33. This point was raised by Catherine Besteman in her commentary on Collins's and Stanford's papers at the 1995 meeting of the Society for Economic Anthropology.

34. Again, see Edelman's (1996) thoughtful discussion of these points in relation to a recent transnational peasant movement in Central America.

35. See Sassen (1991) on "global cities" that are, as Coombe (1995, 800) puts it, "strategically positioned to coordinate and dominate global flows of information, people, capital, and things . . . [and] have become centers for a vast international web of communications that manages a global network of factories, service outlets, and financial markets." Art markets could be added to this list.

36. Such a product labeling strategy accords with patterns of innovation associated with the flexible regimes of accumulation that succeeded Fordism, as discussed by Harvey (1989).

37. Cf. Marcus (1995), as well as Wolf's (1982) earlier discussion of "connections" and Polier and Roseberry's (1989) critique of postmodernist tendencies to dismiss systemic relations altogether.

38. Of course, as Roseberry (1996, 773–774) observes, the specialty coffees that emerged later are not "proletarian hunger killers" but rather were initially targeted toward more privileged market segments (professionals, yuppies, college students). More recently, he notes, the gourmet coffees themselves have become more standardized and widely marketed, though there are limits to their mass marketability.

39. Polier and Roseberry (1989, 254) criticize postmodernists' celebrations of ethnography as pastiche or collage—that is, their attention to "fragments . . . brought together in ways that emphasize their lack of [historical] connection."

40. Cf. Scott (1985), contributions to Cooper et al. (1993), and Ortner (1995).

41. Many believe that globalization has shrunk the political arena. Leys (1996, vi) argues that development theory has been demobilized by a "retreat from politics in the face of the seemingly irresistible success of capital in subordinating everything to the arbitration of 'global market forces.' But a broader, more historical view of development shows that no such victory is ever really irresistible."

REFERENCES

Alexander, Jennifer, and Paul Alexander. 1991. What's in a Fair Price? Price-setting and Trading Partnerships in Javanese Markets. *Man* 26(3): 493–512.

Alexander, Paul. 1992. What's in a Price? Trading Practices in Peasant (and Other) Markets. In Roy Dilley, ed., *Contesting Markets: Analyses of Ideology, Discourse, and Practice.* Edinburgh: Edinburgh University Press.

Appadurai, Arjun. 1986. Introduction: Commodities and the Politics of Value. In Arjun Appadurai, ed., *The Social Life of Things: Commodities in Cultural Perspective.* Cambridge: Cambridge University Press.

———. 1996. *Modernity at Large: Cultural Dimensions of Globalization.* Minneapolis: University of Minnesota Press.

Bayart, Jean-François. 1993. *The State in Africa: The Politics of the Belly.* New York: Longman.

Berry, Sara. 1989. Social Institutions and Access to Resources. *Africa* 59: 41–55.

Bohannan, Paul. 1959. The Impact of Money on an African Subsistence Economy. *The Journal of Economic History* 19: 491–503.

Bonanno, Alessandro, Lawrence Busch, William Friedland, Lourdes Gouveia, and Enzo Mingione, eds. 1994. *From Columbus to ConAgra: The Globalization of Agriculture and Food.* Lawrence: University Press of Kansas.

Bourdieu, Pierre. 1977. *Outline of a Theory of Practice.* Cambridge: Cambridge University Press.

Carrier, James. 1994. Alienating Objects: The Emergence of Alienation in Retail Trade. *Man* 29(2): 359–380.

———. 1995. *Gifts and Commodities: Exchange and Western Capitalism Since 1700.* London and New York: Routledge.

Comaroff, Jean, and John Comaroff, eds. 1993. *Modernity and Its Malcontents: Ritual and Power in Postcolonial Africa.* Chicago: University of Chicago Press.

Coombe, Rosemary. 1995. The Cultural Life of Things: Anthropological Approaches to Law and Society in Conditions of Globalization. *The American University Journal of International Law and Policy* 10(2): 791–835.

Cooper, Frederick. 1977. *Plantation Slavery on the East Coast of Africa.* New Haven, Conn.: Yale University Press.

Cooper, Frederick, Florencia E. Mallon, Steve J. Stern, Allen F. Isaacman, and William Roseberry. 1993. *Confronting Historical Paradigms: Peasants, Labor, and the Capitalist World System in Africa and Latin America.* Madison: University of Wisconsin Press.

DeMartino, George. 2000. *Global Economy, Global Justice: Theoretical Objections and Policy Alternatives to Neoliberalism.* New York: Routledge.

Dilley, Roy, ed. 1992. *Contesting Markets: Analyses of Ideology, Discourse and Practice.* Edinburgh: Edinburgh University Press.

Edelman, Marc. 1990. When They Took the "Muni": Political Culture and Anti-Austerity Protest in Rural Northwestern Costa Rica. *American Ethnologist* 17(4): 736–757.

———. 1996. Reconceptualizing and Reconstituting Peasant Struggles: A New Social Movement in Central America. *Radical History Review* 65: 26–47.

———. 2000. *Peasants Against Globalization: Rural Social Movements in Costa Rica.* Stanford: Stanford University Press.

Edwards, David. 1994. Afghanistan, Ethnography and the New World Order. *Cultural Anthropology* 9(3): 345–360.

Ekejiuba, Felicia. 1995. Currency Instability and Social Payments among the Igbo of Eastern Nigeria, 1890–1990. In Jane Guyer, ed., *Money Matters.* Portsmouth, N.H.: Heinemann.

Featherstone, Mike, ed. 1990. *Global Culture: Nationalism, Globalization and Modernity.* London: Sage.

Featherstone, Mike, and Scott Lash. 1995. Globalization, Modernity and the Spatialization of Social Theory: An Introduction. In Mike Featherstone, Scott Lash, and Roland Robertson, eds., *Global Modernities.* London: Sage.

Featherstone, Mike, Scott Lash, and Roland Robertson, eds. 1995. *Global Modernities.* London: Sage.

Feierman, Steven. 1993. African Histories and the Dissolution of World History. In Robert H. Bates, V. Y. Mudimbe, and Jean O'Barr, eds., *Africa and the Disciplines: The Contributions of Research in Africa to the Social Sciences and Humanities.* Chicago: University of Chicago Press.

Ferguson, James. 1990. *The Anti-Politics Machine: "Development," Depoliticization and Bureaucratic Power in Lesotho.* Cambridge: Cambridge University Press.

Friedman, Jonathan. 1994. *Cultural Identity and Global Process.* New York: Sage.

Friedman, Thomas L. 1999. *The Lexus and the Olive Tree.* New York: Farrar, Strauss and Giroux.

George, Susan, and Fabrizio Sabelli. 1994. *Faith and Credit: The World Bank's Secular Empire.* Boulder, Colo.: Westview Press.

Geschière, Peter. 1992. Kinship, Witchcraft and "the Market." In Roy Dilley, ed., *Contesting Markets: Analyses of Ideology, Discourse and Practice.* Edinburgh: Edinburgh University Press.

Geschière, Peter, and Reini Raatgever. 1985. Introduction: Emerging Insights and Issues in French Marxist Anthropology. In Wim van Binsbergen and Peter Geschière, eds., *Old Modes of Production and Capitalist Encroachment: Anthropological Explorations in Africa.* London: Routledge and Kegan Paul.

Gilroy, Paul. 1993. *The Black Atlantic: Modernity and Double Consciousness.* Cambridge, Mass.: Harvard University Press.

Gregory, C. A. 1982. *Gifts and Commodities.* London: Academic Press.

Gupta, Akhil, and James Ferguson, eds. 1997. *Anthropological Locations: Boundaries and Grounds of a Field Science.* Berkeley: University of California Press.

Guyer, Jane, ed. 1995. *Money Matters.* Portsmouth, N.H.: Heinemann.

Hall, Stuart. 1991. The Local and the Global: Globalization and Ethnicity. In Anthony King, ed., *Culture, Globalization and the World System: Contemporary Conditions for the Representation of Identity*. Binghamton, N.Y.: SUNY Press.

Hart, Keith. 1992. Market and State after the Cold War: The Informal Economy Reconsidered. In Roy Dilley, ed., *Contesting Markets: Analyses of Ideology, Discourse and Practice*. Edinburgh: Edinburgh University Press.

Harvey, David. 1989. *The Condition of Postmodernity*. Oxford: Basil Blackwell.

Hoogvelt, Ankie. 1997. *Globalization and the Postcolonial World: The New Political Economy of Development*. Baltimore, Md.: Johns Hopkins University Press.

Hutchinson, Sharon. 1996. *Nuer Dilemmas: Coping with Money, War and the State*. Berkeley: University of California Press.

Keller, William W., and Louis W. Pauly. 1997. Globalization at Bay. *Current History* 96(613): 370–376.

Kloppenburg, Jack R. 1988. *First the Seed: The Political Economy of Plant Biotechnology, 1492–2000*. Cambridge: Cambridge University Press.

Kopytoff, Igor. 1986. The Cultural Biography of Things. In Arjun Appadurai, ed., *The Social Life of Things: Commodities in Cultural Perspective*. Cambridge: Cambridge University Press.

Korten, David. 1996. The Limits of the Earth. *The Nation* 263(3):14–18.

Leach, J. W., and E. Leach, eds. 1983. *The Kula: New Perspectives on Massim Exchange*. Cambridge: Cambridge University Press.

Levi-Strauss, Claude. 1969 [1949]. *The Elementary Structures of Kinship*. London: Eyre and Spottiswoode.

Leys, Colin. 1996. *The Rise and Fall of Development Theory*. London: James Currey.

Little, Peter D., and Michael Watts, eds. 1994. *Living Under Contract: Contract Farming and Agrarian Transformations in Sub-Saharan Africa*. Madison: University of Wisconsin Press.

Littlefield, Alice, and Hill Gates, eds. 1991. *Marxist Approaches in Economic Anthropology*. Society for Economic Anthropology Monograph, No. 9. Lanham, Md.: University Press of America.

Malinowski, Bronislaw. 1922. *Argonauts of the Western Pacific*. London: Routledge.

Marcus, George E. 1995. Ethnography In/Of the World System: The Emergence of Multi-Sited Ethnography. *Annual Review of Anthropology* 24: 95–117.

Marx, Karl. 1954 [1887]. *Capital*. Edited by Frederick Engels. Trans. Samuel Moore and Edward Aveling. Vol. 1. London: Lawrence and Wishart.

Mauss, Marcel. 1990. *The Gift: The Form and Reason for Exchange in Archaic Societies*. Trans. W. D. Halls. New York: Norton.

McMichael, Philip.1995. *Food and Agrarian Orders in the World Economy*. Westport, Conn.: Greenwood Press.

———. 1996. *Development and Social Change: A Global Perspective*. Thousand Oaks, Calif.: Pine Forge Press.

———, ed. 1994. *The Global Restructuring of Agro-Food Systems*. Ithaca, N.Y.: Cornell University Press.

Miers, Suzanne, and Igor Kopytoff, eds. 1977. *Slavery in Africa*. Madison: University of Wisconsin Press.

Miller, Daniel. 1994. *Modernity: An Ethnographic Approach*. Oxford: Berg.

Mintz, Sidney. 1979. Time, Sugar, and Sweetness. *Marxist Perspectives* 2: 56–73.

———. 1985. *Sweetness and Power: The Place of Sugar in Modern History*. New York: Viking.

————. 1998. The Localization of Anthropological Practice: From Area Studies to Transnationalism. *Critique of Anthropology* 18(2): 117–133.

Mintz, Sidney, and Eric Wolf. 1989. Reply to Michael Taussig. *Critique of Anthropology* 9(1): 25–31.

Mitchell, Tim. 1995. The Object of Development: America's Egypt. In Jonathan Crush, ed., *Power of Development*. London: Routledge.

Moore, Sally Falk. 1994. The Ethnography of the Present and the Analysis of Process. In Robert Borofsky, ed., *Assessing Cultural Anthropology*. New York: McGraw Hill.

Ortner, Sherry. 1995. Resistance and the Problem of Ethnographic Refusal. *Comparative Studies in Society and History* 37(1): 173–193.

Panitch, Leo. 1994. Globalisation and the State. In Ralph Miliband and Leo Panitch, eds., *Between Globalism and Nationalism*. London: Merlin Press.

Parry, Jonathan, and Maurice Bloch. 1989. Introduction: Money and the Morality of Exchange. In Jonathan Parry and Maurice Bloch, eds., *Money and the Morality of Exchange*. Cambridge: Cambridge University Press.

Parry, Jonathan, and Maurice Bloch, eds. 1989. *Money and the Morality of Exchange*. Cambridge: Cambridge University Press.

Peet, Richard, and Michael Watts. 1994. Introduction: Development Theory and Environmentalism in an Age of Market Triumphalism. *Economic Geography* 69: 227–253.

Peet, Richard, and Michael Watts, eds. 1996. *Liberation Ecologies: Environment, Development, Social Movements*. London: Routledge.

Plattner, Stuart, ed. 1985. *Markets and Marketing*. Society for Economic Anthropology Monograph, No. 4. Lanham, Md.: University Press of America.

Polanyi, Karl. 1968. The Economy as an Instituted Process. In Edward LeClair and Harold Schneider, eds., *Economic Anthropology: Readings in Theory and Analysis*. New York: Holt, Reinhart and Winston.

Polier, Nicole, and William Roseberry. 1989. Tristes Tropes: Post-Modern Anthropologists Encounter the Other and Discover Themselves. *Economy and Society* 18(2): 245–262.

Pred, Allan, and Michael Watts. 1992. *Reworking Modernity: Capitalism and Symbolic Discontents*. New Brunswick, N.J.: Rutgers University Press.

Princen, Thomas, and Matthais Finger, eds. 1994. *Environmental NGOs in World Politics: Linking the Local and the Global*. London: Routledge.

Roseberry, William. 1989. *Anthropologies and Histories: Essays in Culture, History and Political Economy*. New Brunswick, N.J.: Rutgers University Press.

————. 1996. The Rise of Yuppie Coffees and the Reimagination of Class in the United States. *American Anthropologist* 98(4): 762–775.

Rutz, Henry J., and Benjamin S. Orlove, eds. 1989. *The Social Economy of Consumption*. Society for Economic Anthropology Monograph, No. 6. Lanham, Md.: University Press of America.

Sahlins, Marshall. 1972. *Stone-Age Economics*. New York: Aldine.

Sassen, Saskia. 1991. *The Global City: New York, London, Tokyo*. Princeton, N.J.: Princeton University Press.

Schaeffer, Robert K. 1997. *Understanding Globalization: The Social Consequences of Political, Economic and Environmental Change*. Lanham, Md.: Rowman & Littlefield Publishers.

Scott, Alan, ed. 1997. *The Limits of Globalization: Cases and Arguments*. London: Routledge.

Scott, James C. 1976. *The Moral Economy of the Peasant*. New Haven, Conn.: Yale University Press.

———. 1985. *Weapons of the Weak: Everyday Forms of Peasant Resistance*. New Haven, Conn.: Yale University Press.

———. 1990. *Domination and the Arts of Resistance: Hidden Transcripts*. New Haven, Conn.: Yale University Press.

Shipton, Parker. 1989. *Bitter Money: Cultural Economy and Some African Meanings of Forbidden Commodities*. American Ethnological Society Monograph, No. 1. Washington, D.C.: American Anthropological Association.

Taussig, Michael. 1980. *The Devil and Commodity Fetishism in South America*. Chapel Hill: University of North Carolina Press.

———. 1989. History as Commodity in Some Recent American (Anthropological) Literature. *Critique of Anthropology* 9(1): 7–23.

Tsing, Anna. 1993. *In the Realm of the Diamond Queen: Marginality in an Out-of-the-Way Place*. Princeton, N.J.: Princeton University Press.

Wade, Peter. 1998. Music, Blackness and National Identity: Three Moments in Colombian History. *Popular Music* 17(3): 1–20.

Wallerstein, Immanuel. 1974. *The Modern World System: Capitalist Agriculture and the Origins of the European World-Economy in the Sixteenth Century*. New York: Academic Press.

———. 1980. *The Modern World System II: Mercantilism and the Consolidation of the European World-Economy, 1600–1750*. New York: Academic Press.

———. 1989. *The Modern World System III: The Second Era of Great Expansion of the Capitalist World-Economy, 1730–1840s*. New York: Academic Press.

Watts, Michael J. 1992. Capitalisms, Crises and Cultures I: Notes Toward a Totality of Fragments. In Allan Pred and Michael J. Watts, eds., *Reworking Modernity: Capitalisms and Symbolic Discontent*. New Brunswick, N.J.: Rutgers University Press.

Wolf, Eric. 1982. *Europe and the People Without History*. Berkeley: University of California Press.

Zevin, R. 1992. Are World Financial Markets More Open? If So, Why and With What Effects? In Tariq Banuri and Juliet Schor, eds., *Financial Openness and National Autonomy: Opportunities and Constraints*. Oxford: Oxford University Press.

Part I

Commodities in a Globalizing Marketplace

2

Soukouss or Sell-Out? Congolese Popular Dance Music as Cultural Commodity

Bob White

You know, if we did like the Americans, we would be even bigger than they are. First you sell your culture and then all the other goods will follow.
— Student from the former Zaire, May 1995

It is often assumed that aggressive promotion of cultural goods contributes to U.S. political and economic strength. Mass entertainment commodities constitute the second largest U.S. export after aircraft, according to the *New York Times*.[1] Given the accompanying assumption that cultural exports displace local goods and producers, how are we to understand a "developing" country in Africa that is culturally self-sufficient, exporting (at least in terms of its music) more than it imports? Such is the case with Congo-Kinshasa, where for many years musical production has become increasingly commercial and visible. This chapter explores changes in Congolese popular music in order to improve our understanding not only of this particular musical style, but also of a commodification process both within and outside Congolese national borders.

The contagious sound of Congolese popular dance music has made it a "musica franca" of sub-Saharan Africa (Ewens 1990, 126). Within the Congo, the music— referred to locally as "*la musique moderne*"—is everywhere. It occupies a special place in the urban landscape, animating households, storefronts, taxis, and bars, and it dominates the local media. It is far and away the music of choice; estimates from the 1980s suggest that more than 50 percent of national programming was made up of live or rebroadcast concerts and musical performances.[2] Outside the region this music has attracted attention in the emerging "world music" scene, due in part to the success of *soukouss*, a particular form of Congolese popular music that targets primarily non-Congolese audiences. But the point is not just to understand why this particular form of music is so popular. I am also interested in addressing Congolese popular music as a locally privileged form of cultural expression, which, having undergone a particular process of commercialization, offers valuable insight into economic culture and history in this part of Central Africa.

TRANSACTION AND MEANING: SOME THEORETICAL CONSIDERATIONS

I should preface this discussion with several disclaimers. First, this chapter blurs the distinction between the Democratic Republic of the Congo (ex-Zaire, formerly the Belgian Congo) and the People's Republic of the Congo (a former French colony), both independent countries since 1960. I refer to the two countries as "Congo-Kinshasa" and "Congo-Brazzaville," respectively.[3] The war that raged across Zaire in the spring of 1997, bringing Laurent Kabila to power after more than thirty years of Mobutu's rule, significantly affected Congolese culture and economy, but these issues are not my immediate focus here (see White 1997). Second, while this chapter is about a culturally specific musical form, these ruminations are not strictly ethnomusicological. Instead, I consider how local cultural goods, such as popular music, become entangled in commercializing—and sometimes globalizing—networks of social and political relations. My primary focus is not the aesthetics of a particular commodity, but the evolution of a commodity that has aesthetic qualities. Third, it is important to distinguish between Congolese popular music in general and *soukouss,* a specific type of Congolese music that has been consciously adapted for foreign audiences and distribution channels. *Soukouss,* a highly commodified form of Congolese popular music, is the principal focus of this chapter.

Considering Congolese music's strong presence throughout most of Africa, and given the limited academic literature on the subject, what analytical approaches or theoretical frameworks are most useful to understand its impact as a commercial cultural form?[4] In recent years interest has grown in research on cultural goods and the cultural aspects of commodity flows, an area of importance for understanding the commercialization of cultural forms such as music. Foundational studies of commodity exchange (Braudel 1979; Polanyi 1957; Wallerstein 1974) and later more anthropological studies (Mintz 1985; Wolf 1982) examine broad economic and political links that bring together local and regional economies in a global "world system." Studies of this sort tend to portray the flow of commodities as homogenizing, unidirectional, and destructive of precapitalist societies.[5] At issue, however, is the very notion of "commodity," which, as Appadurai (1986) and others have argued, should explain not only the production of goods, but also the production of meaning (Gudeman 1986; Taussig 1980). Furthermore, it should explain not only production, but also exchange and consumption (Barber 1987; Gregory 1982; Wilk 1993). That is, the study of commodities must look beyond their basic characteristics as things and take into account their "total trajectories" (Appadurai 1986).

Treatments of popular music in Western societies, particularly those inspired by the Frankfurt school, have emphasized the political and economic aspects of cultural production, especially in the context of state-sponsored or state-controlled mass media. Recent critiques (particularly of Adorno's work) fault this approach for its monolithic view of the culture industry as a repressive tool of the state and for its conception of consumers as passive vessels (Middleton 1990). Middleton has contrasted Adorno's work to that of Benjamin's, who writes of the large-scale production of music as a potentially liberating force. Manuel (1993) argues that rather than attempt to answer the question of whether mass-produced cultural forms are repressive or emancipatory, we must instead seek a theoretical framework that can account for both of these possibilities (and perhaps others) simultaneously.

This chapter addresses two sets of questions. The first concerns specific social and economic mechanisms involved in the process of commercialization: How do popular forms of cultural expression such as music become commodities, and who stands to lose or gain from this transformation? The second set of questions examines meanings associated with commercialized cultural goods: How is the value of these goods negotiated in a cross-cultural setting? What kinds of identities are expressed and contested through commodities of this type? How are "cultural" commodities different from other commodities? This framework, which sets up a potentially false distinction between the "objective" realities of economic transactions and the "poetics" of cultural meanings, is not an attempt to isolate two distinct analytical perspectives, but rather to open a dialogue, however faint, between the two. *Transaction* will be juxtaposed with *meaning* in the hope that their presence in a common analytical space will provide new insight into processes of social and cultural change in a postcolonial African setting.[6]

After briefly describing important developments in musical style since the 1950s, I discuss the commercialization of cultural goods in general, and music in particular. Next I examine how various meanings are produced and managed through the process of commodification, the particular ways in which commodified music obscures political aspects of its production, and the complex relationships between commodities and identity, especially in light of the recent success of "world music" in the global marketplace. Finally, I consider "cultural" commodities as a particular type of commodity, and conclude with thoughts about why "cultural" commodities are important to our understanding of commodity processes and capitalist development in Africa.[7]

THE TRANSACTION OF COMMERCIAL MUSIC: FROM *RUMBA* TO *SOUKOUSS*

What historical developments led to Congolese music's commercialization in local, regional, and global markets? A particular series of transactions—not only economic, but also social and political—made Congolese *rumba* the first commercialized African music to attract continental listenership outside of its own national borders. More specifically, how did innovations in technology, expanding distribution networks, and corporate sponsorship combine to foster the development of this new, expressly African, area of cultural production? Before addressing these issues, let us look briefly at the history of the musical style.

Congolese *rumba* emerged primarily from the urban centers of the Belgian Congo during the interwar period, and drew heavily from Afro-Cuban styles that were spreading to North America and Europe at that time, as well as from West African *highlife* music and various forms of traditional music in the Pool region between Kinshasa (formerly Léopoldville) and Brazzaville.[8] In its earliest form, Congolese *rumba* was a noncommercialized, guitar-based music performed by itinerant solo musicians who wandered the newly formed urban labor settlements of the French and Belgian colonies.[9] Often with nothing more than a guitar, urban *griots* such as Wendo Kolosoy, Adou Elenga, and Paul Kamba animated Léopoldville's popular neighborhoods, playing music in the bars and bistros that came to symbolize the city's charm and nighttime ambiance.[10] Beginning in the 1940s, when expatriate entrepreneurs opened the first recording houses (*maisons d'édition*), it was this group of roving musicians who became the first to play music professionally, signing contracts as individuals (Leon Bukasa, Lucie Eyenga) or sometimes as groups (Beguen Band, Le Trio Bow, San Salvador). Almost all of the music was written and recorded by local musicians in Léopoldville. Seventy-eight rpm records, intended primarily for sale on the local market, were mass-produced to provide relatively inexpensive, high-quality recordings to large numbers of urban consumers. In 1950 three major studios were producing and distributing records. By 1960, the number had increased to nearly twenty (Radio France International 1992, 6). This growth in production, together with the installation of powerful radio transmitters in Léopoldville, permitted large numbers of people outside of the Pool region to listen to this new sound, which came to be known in many parts of Africa as "Congo Jazz."

Advances in technology were not the only reason this music became popular in other parts of sub-Saharan Africa. With the industry's basic infrastructure in place, a new generation of musicians was forming; their talent and star quality would soon surpass that of their elders and their music would begin to "colonize" the rest of the continent. This was the golden age of *rumba*, the era of big-band–style orchestras, led by the undisputed patriarch of the genre, Grand Kallé (Joseph Kabasele), and his group, African Jazz. Under Kallé's supervision, African Jazz would later provide Congolese music with some of its biggest names, among them Tabu Ley (Seigneur Rochereau) and Nicolas Kasanda (Dr. Nico). None, however, could match the bigger-than-life quality of the "Great Master," François Luambo Makiadi (Franco), co-founder and leader of the country's most well-known band, l'Orchestre O.K. Jazz. The rivalry that developed between O.K. Jazz and African Jazz was accentuated by the emergence of two distinct styles or "schools" of music, which corresponded roughly to their aesthetic signatures: one modernist (African Jazz), one traditionalist (O.K. Jazz); one melody, one rhythm; one for listening, one for dancing; one refined, one *sauvage*. This stylistic distinction continues today, although it has been made more complex by intermingling and borrowing between the two schools.

The strength of these two musical "empires" was not challenged until the early 1970s, when a new generation of musicians emerged with a markedly different style.[11] Taking cues from African American soul music and from the music of young Congolese students studying abroad in Belgium, this new wave of music (*la nouvelle vague*) had a huge impact on the local music industry in part because its accelerated tempo and innovative dancemanship appealed widely to urban youth (Nkashama 1979). During this period, especially after the formation of the youth super-group Zaiko Langa-Langa in 1969, a number of important stylistic innovations were introduced into the music, among them choreographed dancing and the distinct two-part song structure. Not until well into this third generation of musicians, however, did the music take on its most commercial form: Zairean dance music made for export, or *soukouss*.[12]

Congolese musicians on tour found that listeners and concertgoers outside of their country often showed a preference for fast-paced dance music. Thus the now well-established two-part song structure, with a slow lyrical introduction followed by a fast-paced dance section, evolved into a song format that focused primarily on the dance section (*seben*). This format, once elaborated and perfected for non-Congolese audiences, eventually became known as *soukouss,* from the French verb *secouer* (to shake).[13] In the mid-1980s (a time of increasing disillusion with the Mobutu regime), a number of *soukouss* musicians established themselves in Europe, using Paris and Brussels as bases from which they recorded and toured regularly. Groups such as Soukouss Stars, Kanda Bongo Man, and Loketo made their living by playing not only for Europeans (particularly those who had traveled or worked in Africa and had acquired a taste for the sound of *la musique Zaïroise*) but also for a rapidly growing African immigrant community.

CULTURAL GOODS AND THE PROCESS OF COMMERCIALIZATION

Even before independence, Congolese musicians toured and played concerts abroad. During the 1960s and 1970s record sales were considerable; with an extensive network of music retailers and distributors throughout the region, artists such as Franco and Tabu Ley were able to sell more than one million copies of individual songs. The commercial integration of musical styles is signaled by widespread sale of the product, its recognition by a diverse consumer audience, and the presence of stylistic aspects that are shaped partly by perceived consumer needs. Below I will consider several specific aspects of this commercialization process, especially technology, distribution networks, and the role of corporate sponsorship.[14]

Recent research on popular music suggests a variety of influences on the commercial spread of popular music forms (Guilbault 1993; Manuel 1993). Among these, access to music-related technology is probably the most obvious. The Belgian Congo was one of the first African colonies to have the necessary infrastructure to support the production and sale of local music. "For musicians, the development of record players, recording companies, and national radio stations guaranteed an increasingly solid and permanent degree of professionalism in Congolese music" (Radio France International 1992, 17). Record-pressing facilities were owned and operated by expatriate businesspeople, who also monopolized the sale and distribution of records throughout the region. After independence, state-run television and radio brought Zairean music into the homes of thousands of families living outside the capital in urban and semirural settings. Changes in instrumentation (introduction of the electric guitar, the saxophone, and later the jazz drum set) made the music more accessible to audiences already familiar with foreign musical styles. The development of elaborate touring circuits (in Africa and later in Europe and North America) gave the music a wider consumer base, paving the way for a long-term process of technical and artistic innovation.

In more recent years, the music's spread has been linked to new forms of recording and audio reproduction technology, particularly cassettes. As with many industries in Zaire, a large share of the music trade takes place outside officially registered economic activity. During periods of economic hardship, the cassette medium makes music one of the most affordable forms of leisure for Congolese consumers.[15] The market for Congolese music in France is considerable, but by far the largest number of cassettes are sold within Africa. Much of the music's production is controlled by non-Congolese living outside the region, primarily in Paris, but also in Brussels and Brazzaville. Distribution, on the other hand, is much more decentralized, with a multitude of *re-producers* (both local and global) making a living from the sale of pirated audio and video cassettes. What we see, then, is not the mass production of a cultural product, but its mass distribution. Re-producers, who range from large, commercial-scale (sometimes international) cassette pirates to homemade cassette copiers and individual itinerant street vendors, are crucial to the music's spread, but they are seen by most people—especially by musicians—as profiteers, since none of the money they earn actually returns to the artist.

Commercial sponsorship of Congolese musicians first appeared in the 1950s. Musicians were offered renewable contracts with recording houses, which hired them full time and paid them as salaried employees. By the 1960s, however, after musicians began to experience local celebrity status, a large number of artists left the recording houses to form music groups of their own. It was not until the mid-1970s, when the music industry was in full commercial bloom, that various local corporate entities recognized the potential for musicians to promote their products and offered musicians long-term sponsorship agreements. By the 1980s, almost all the big acts in Kinshasa were sponsored by one of the city's major breweries.[16] With the hope that beverage sales would increase if audiences saw their favorite musicians drinking the product, advertising specialists loaded concert locations with brewery paraphernalia, including tablecloths, banners, glasses, backdrops, and, most importantly, performers' outfits with logos. In exchange, musicians received small sums of money, beer every month (which they could drink or resell), and the benefit of having concerts scheduled and promoted throughout the country on a regular basis.

After several years of heavy spending on musicians as a form of product promotion (sometimes as much as 35 percent of advertising budgets), the breweries' owners realized that while people were associating their products with famous musicians, they were not necessarily buying more beer. This, together with early signs of recession at the end of the 1980s, forced the breweries' management to rethink their music sponsorship policy. Since 1990, breweries have canceled almost 70 percent of their sponsorship agreements and have reduced their music advertising budgets by as much as 85 percent.[17] Corporate sponsorship of music still exists in Kinshasa, although there is a trend toward sponsoring events rather than groups, and smaller amounts of money are spent by a larger number of sponsors. Thus the musician is increasingly faced with the insecurity of short-term contracts and a multiplicity of sponsors.[18]

Thus far I have discussed the process by which a form of cultural expression, such as African music, becomes a commercial product, effectively moving (or being moved) between various spheres of production and consumption.[19] More research, however, is needed to determine what effect this movement has on social relations within Africa itself and how it favors some musicians over others.[20] Congolese musicians, even those who specialize in *soukouss,* find it very difficult to earn a living from their music. There is intense competition for already scarce contracts, and Paris, once a *soukouss* mecca, is now saturated with musicians and burdened with audiences whose attention is increasingly difficult to capture.[21] A lack of professional producers and managers interested in promoting Congolese music forces many musicians to produce and manage themselves, a situation that detracts from their "evolution as an artist" (J. P. Busé, personal communication).

Most people who promote music do so on a part-time basis and with insufficient financial resources, which only reinforces the negative stereotype that Congolese musicians are disorganized and unpredictable (see below). Nonetheless, Congolese music is obviously profitable. Distributors who live in Europe, for example, can benefit from high markups on inexpensive products that are created in the Congo and packaged or produced in Paris or Brussels. In recent years, large record labels in Paris and New York (such as Sonodisc and Sterns) have reissued "golden oldies" from as early as the 1950s and have sold them in the form of nostalgia collections (*merveilles du passé*) intended primarily for African audiences. Commercial sponsors also benefit from the highly effective but low-cost advertising that appears on most album covers.

THE MEANING OF COMMERCIAL MUSIC:
BROKERS, POLITICS, AND IDENTITY

Discussions of meaning are most useful when grounded in examples of everyday experience and practice (de Certeau 1984; Ortner 1984). In order to understand meanings associated with *soukous,* I examine the strategies of the music's primary brokers (i.e., the musicians), focusing on how they use the notion of authenticity along with other strategies to promote their music abroad. I also discuss how song lyrics that are on the surface simple texts about love and desire actually hide an underlying social organization of production that is profoundly political. Finally, I consider how commercialized cultural goods such as music can contribute to the crystallization of a national identity, even (or especially) in countries far away from the goods' place of origin. Although this discussion is primarily concerned with the practices of Congolese people who live outside their country, I do not discuss issues raised by the emerging literature on diaspora cultures (e.g., Clifford 1994; Gilroy 1993).

Cultural Brokers and the Production of Meaning

Anthropology has given little attention to intermediaries such as the re-producers discussed above. Perhaps an explanation of the circuitous and multifaceted networks that bind the "local" with the "global" seems too daunting a task. For the purposes of this chapter, *cultural brokers* are of primary importance, for it is they who manage the material and symbolic resources that constitute notions of taste (and thus value) in a given society (cf. Bourdieu 1984). Drawing on Steiner's (1994) work, I see a cultural broker as someone who demystifies demand for the producer and communicates some form of authenticity or cultural identity to the consumer. In Appadurai's (1986) terms, the broker in effect *makes* taste through activities such as "enclaving" or "diverting." Jules-Rosette (1984) refines the term further by suggesting that brokers do not simply manufacture taste, but that taste is the result of a series of dialogues among producers, brokers, and consumers. Paine (1971) makes a crucial distinction between "broker" and "go-between," noting that some intermediaries influence consumer taste while others simply *read* it. For the purposes of this discussion, I see cultural brokers as those who engage in the *management of meaning* (see also Kurin 1997).

In the Belgian Congo, the first brokers of the musical style were non-Congolese. Owners of the first recording houses—mostly local Greek merchants—brought together musicians to play in their studios, and in some cases even acted as musical arrangers. Leading up to the nationalization policies of the mid-1970s (see endnote 11), several musicians began to distinguish themselves as cultural brokers in their own right, the most well-known of whom is Kiamwangana Verckys (Vévé). Probably Zaire's closest resemblance to a media mogul, Verckys owned his own record label, operated his own recording studio, and provided musical equipment for many of the new generation of musicians in Kinshasa during the 1970s. Originally a musician himself, Verckys is known for bringing together young, unknown musicians and molding them into national celebrities (Les Frères Soki, Lipwa Lipwa, Shama Shama), as well as for his entrepreneurial influence on other young groups (Zaiko Langa Langa being the best example). His skill at predicting hit songs and his acute business sense earned him much money and a position of privilege in the 1970s and 1980s Kinshasa music scene. Since Verckys, there have been few full-time professionals working in music promotion, and this conspicuous absence of indigenous entrepreneurs has had serious implications for the region's music production.[22]

Cultural brokerage, however, occurs at many levels. *Soukouss* musicians, perhaps the most active brokers of the musical style, have made consistent efforts to adapt their music to foreign audiences. Often targeting Western (or at least non-Congolese) fans of tropical dance music, *soukouss* musicians write songs that are heavy on dance and light on lyrics. The words, which have been so important to generations of listeners in Congo-Kinshasa, are either shortened or completely eliminated in order to leave plenty of time for dancing. According to Aurlus Mabele, the self-proclaimed "King of *Soukouss*": "You don't understand a word of Lingala, but you dance anyway. You dance, even during the singing, because of the rhythm" (quoted in Cheyney 1989, 40).[23] When included, lyrics are usually in simplified Lingala, but the use of other languages is also very common. Singing entirely in French or singing sections of songs in English and various African languages is a strategy to increase record sales in particular regions. At one time, *soukouss* musicians sped up their music in response to the popularity of the West Indian group Kassav, which was playing its trademark *zouk* music to sold-out audiences all over Europe and Africa. Lokassa ya Mbongo, a founding member of Soukouss Stars, described this change as a conscious strategy: "*Soukouss* was being played much faster then. It was when Kassav had their big hit [he sings the song *Zouk-la Sé Sèl Médikaman Nou Ni*]. So we were all following that" (interview with author, 17 January 1998).[24]

Other strategies to increase concert attendance and record sales include place-naming (mainly countries, but also cities), people-naming (commercial as well as private sponsors), and the choreographed eroticism that is usually associated with the "show chaud" (hot show) of most live *soukouss* performances. After a *soukouss* show in Montreal, I wrote the following notes:

> After a signal from one of the musicians, a woman dressed in spandex shorts and a leopard skin halter top shuffles on stage. She is covered in makeup, extensions in her hair, barefoot with a huge smile. Her gestures are nothing if not suggestive and the hard smile she holds as she isolates the movement of particular body parts creates a strange, grotesque eroticism. She continues to smile while her colleagues on stage remain completely deadpan and she drags an unwilling victim onto the stage with a forced participation that in the end is not offensive. In between songs, singers reinforce the idea:

"Thanks for joining us tonight. Is everybody having fun? This is what African music is all about, people getting together, dancing to the rhythm and having fun. Is everybody having fun?" (April 15, 1995)

Underlying the discourse of live *soukouss* performance are complex assumptions about African music and identity; these assumptions are important tools for *soukouss* performers. As members of the mostly non-Congolese audience, however, we are active participants in a spectacle that conveys subtle messages about what this music means and why it is good (cf. Jewsiewicki 1991). We think: "Look at those women dancing, how do they do that? Did you see what she is wearing?" *African music is erotic.* We think: "I like this music. I don't know why, it just makes me feel happy; it's so upbeat." *African music is childlike.* We think: "This dancing is unbelievable. They have such a good sense of rhythm." *African music is rhythm.* This is the "dancing African other" (Meintjes 1994) that enables the spectator to participate in a state of release, an acceptable way of venting surplus energy (Guilbault 1993, 181):

> Tied to a long history of essentializing and racializing other bodies as possessing a "natural" sense of rhythm, the invention of "world beat" reproduces a Western gaze toward the exotic and erotic, often darker-skinned, dancing body. These othered "beats" thus provide the pulse and groove for Western bodies to throw their inhibitions off on the dance floor." (Feld 1994, 266)

Although *soukouss* and its accompanying "feel good" aesthetic is virtually unknown in Kinshasa, *soukouss* musicians capitalize on foreign fascination with the music by trying to make it stand for the whole of Africa. Not *any* Africa, but an authentic, "real" Africa: "Ça c'est *bon* ça," listeners say, "Ça c'est la *vraie* musique Africaine!"[25] Apart from the leopard skin halter top, however, what we see is a performance filled with non-African markers: brightly colored electric guitars mediated through reverb and distortion, the latest Parisian high fashions and expensive jewelry, fluid four-part parallel harmony, a percussion instrument made from an empty insecticide spray can, and flowing lyrics that are mostly about romantic love.

The Politics of Love Songs

> The embeddedness of the political in the sonic means that the political becomes entangled in and communicated through affective experience. (Meintjes 1990, 38)

> La femme Ivoirienne, chérie
> Tu m'as troublé, oh-oh
> Tu m'as troublé, mon amour
> Je suis à toi, oh-oh . . .[26]

Soukouss includes a high proportion of lyrics about love and matters of the heart (jealousy, heartbreak, infidelity). At first glance, this tendency is difficult to reconcile with the everyday reality of postcolonial crisis in the Congo (in local terms: "déstabilisation," "démocratisation," and "dollarisation"). Why then are some styles of music characterized by political engagement while others are not?[27] It could be argued that the degree of commercialization influences the amount of political content, since "feel good–feel bad" lyrics tend to please a larger audience, but there must be other contributing factors as well. Could it be something as idiosyncratic as the particular sensibility of individual artists, or is thematic content a function of a culturally specific consumer demand? From one perspective, the depoliticization of lyrics is a result of people's need to escape a state of political oppression and economic crisis. Political messages are often nested in seemingly apolitical forms through the use of metaphorical language and political subtexts (Fabian 1998; Onyumbe 1994). But as some cultural critics have observed, perhaps the apolitical *is* the message (Hebdige 1979; Mbembe 1992), not only because declarations of love can be considered subversive (Abu-Lughod 1990; Fabian 1978), but also because the silence surrounding politics speaks volumes about the limitations on freedom of expression in authoritarian regimes (cf. Averill 1997; Ndaywel è Nziem 1993).

Most *soukouss* musicians strictly avoid political content in their music.[28] They prefer to sing about matters of the heart partly because lyrics of a political nature would be lost on an audience that is primarily non-Lingala speaking. But musicians are also concerned about retaining fans who (they believe) might avoid music with political lyrics.[29] Whether or not audiences understand song lyrics, *soukouss* musicians in concert often describe their music as "une musique sentimentale" (a romantic music). In many cases, musicians sing about love because "this is what people want to hear," especially female fans, who are highly valued by musicians because they presumably influence men to buy particular records. Although it is probably true that many musicians sing about love out of personal pleasure, avoidance of political themes may be related to musicians' dependence on patrons and fans for supplemental incomes. Musicians also rely on gifts (usually in the form of money and clothes) from wealthy businesspeople and politicians, and they believe that lyrics with political overtones may reduce their ability to attract and maintain patron-based support.[30] Thus, they sing about the one theme that is sure to offend no one: love. It is in this sense that commercial dance music must be seen as profoundly political.

National Identity and "World Music"

> [Popular music] has entered our social and economic lives like perfume or toothpaste. It has impregnated the rhythm of our work and leisure. We can no longer do without it. (Lonoh 1969, 7, my translation)

Congolese music represents an interesting counterexample to commonly held beliefs about African patterns of consumption, namely, that Africans have an insatiable desire for foreign goods (see Geschiere and Rowlands 1996). In the Congo, where most music is "local, home-grown produce" (Ewens 1990, 126), local commodities are highly valued, and, as the case of *soukouss* shows, they are also exported. Given the influence of Western consumer cultural goods in many parts of the "developing" world, why this preference for local music? It may be that certain types of goods that touch or enter the body (music, food, clothes) are in some way closer to the self, and thus less likely to be displaced by foreign consumer goods. Of course this hypothesis cannot account for the success of *soukouss* music in other African countries, or for the popularity of European and Japanese high fashion in Central Africa (see Gandoulou 1989). Or it may be that the colonial and postcolonial state's peculiar combination of cultural promotion and political neglect encourages self-sufficiency in cultural production, unintentionally making popular music a privileged (if not the only) form of personal political expression (Barber 1987).

As Manuel (1993) has shown for India's music industry, the process of commercialization almost always entails the spread of a dominant form, but this form can open up a new space for local goods. Since the late 1980s, the development of many *soukouss*es has occurred throughout Africa. The Comoro Islands, located off Africa's east coast, provide an example from the periphery. In the Comoros, where *la musique Zaïroise* has dominated the local music scene for some time, musicians often emulate "the Zairean sound" (*le son Zaïrois*), but their ability to imitate these cosmopolitan, imported styles gives them added credibility in local markets and thus helps them to promote their own brand of local music making. A recent cassette produced in the Comoros features four *soukouss* imitations, two *zouk* imitations, one American imitation, and three traditional Comorian songs, all in the local variant of Swahili, Shingazidja.[31] In this way, local cultural styles *piggyback* larger dominant ones. What is most interesting about this case is that the dominant cultural form originates not from the West, or even from a form that is heavily mediated through Western technological and promotional inputs (such as *zouk*), but from within Africa itself.[32]

The relationship between music and identity, especially national identity, is not a simple one (Wade 1998). Music in its most commercial form has the potential to contribute to the crystallization of a national identity, or what Waterman (1990) refers to as "pan-ethnic" identity, a term that takes on special meaning in the Congo, where there are more than three hundred distinct ethnic groups. Most Congolese citizens are aware that their music is very popular in other African countries, but it is difficult to say how this awareness contributes to the feeling of being Congolese.[33] For a Congolese person, listening to a "world music" show on a commercial radio station in Montreal and hearing the strangely familiar *soukouss* for the first time might constitute one such moment. Another might be when she finds herself abroad and meets people who question her eagerly about her country: "Oh, you're from Zaire? Do you like *soukouss*? I love *soukouss*." Lokassa ya Mbongo explains the relationship between popular music and national identity within the country:

There are more than 300 ethnic groups [in the Congo]. A big equatorial forest and it's not even exploited [musically]. One group talks and the group next to them doesn't understand a thing. Each one has its own way of playing, but we all come together on a corner where we play music for everyone. And there is one language that reunites us, Lingala. That is our advantage. When you're in Lumbumbashi, you'll hear other musics, but when we play *soukouss* it brings everyone together.[34]

Although most people in Kinshasa perceive *soukouss* as inauthentic (due to its fast tempo and shortened lyrics), this music contributes to non-Congolese perceptions of what it means to be Congolese. Character traits of Congolese musicians become generalized in the form of nationally based stereotypes. Congolese are perceived by other Africans as being "very cool in their ways" (i.e., good dancers) and "really good-timers" (Chernoff 1979, 149), but also as hedonistic, promiscuous, and lazy—traits often used to describe musicians. In short, the ambiance (party atmosphere) and *frime* (cockiness) often associated with Congolese music has come to stand for the country itself. A Congolese music promoter with whom I spoke explained the stereotypes he encountered while traveling in various parts of West Africa: "'You work?' they said, 'We thought you guys didn't work. We thought you just sing and dance all the time.' They must think we eat music."[35]

While *soukouss* enjoyed some success in Europe and North America in the late 1980s, its popularity was less than that of other "world musics" such as reggae or *zouk,* which have benefited from the backing of major international record labels. In spite of concerted efforts on the part of musicians to adapt their music to European and North American audiences, *soukouss* never became fully integrated in the Western world music market. In sub-Saharan Africa, however, it continues to be produced, distributed, and redistributed in the form of a commodity. In countries all over the continent it is copied, pirated, performed, imitated, indigenized, fetishized, imagined, and integrated into local systems of transaction and meaning. If *soukouss* never "took off" in the West, it is not for lack of talent, since some of Congo's most talented musicians (Lokassa ya Mbongo, Daly Kimoko, Rigo Star, Ngouma Lokito, Kanda Bongoman, Nyboma) have been at the forefront of the Paris *soukouss* scene. Nor is it due solely to the conspicuous absence of indigenous entrepreneurs in the arts, although this has certainly been a contributing factor. Instead I suggest that the commodification of *soukouss* in the West has been limited primarily by its failure to capture what Erlmann (1996) has called the "global imagination" for "world music."[36] Although many internationally marketed African musics appear increasingly "traditional" (Meintjes 1994), *soukouss* (and Congolese popular music in general) has presented itself as "modern," both in terms of the music's sound and its performance. From an outsider's point of view, *soukouss* simply does not *look* African, and this makes it less appealing to "world music" promoters and fans since it is the appearance of African "authenticity" or "difference" that sells most music in this category.

In other words, different phases in the evolution of world music—itself not an ahistorical phenomenon—are to be distinguished by the degree to which the meanings of the past, the tradition, overlap with the overwhelming present or, by the extent to which certain social relations and cultural practices are unhinged from concrete spatial conditions and recombined in ever-changing, disembedded time-space relationships. (Erlmann 1996, 476)

Given today's globalizing discourses of development, with their focus on "empowerment" and "sustainability," the flow of *soukous* from Congo to other African countries is certainly intriguing. In the context of the emerging "world music" scene, however, this pattern of *soukous* exports is probably more the exception than the rule. Recent writing on world music emphasizes how African artists are increasingly alienated by involvement in international music markets:

> Even if local musicians take control in remote locales, how progressive can the world of popular music be when the practices of a transnational culture industry steadfastly reproduce the forms and forces of domination that keep outsiders outside, as "influences" and laborers in the production of pop? (Feld 1994, 263)

Feld, who is otherwise optimistic about the potential benefits of Western-sponsored collaborative music projects, acknowledges that such projects "fulfill the economic and social needs of their makers, reproducing their positions of privileged access and their ability to define just what kind of adventure may be had" (Feld 1994, 284; Meintjes 1990).[37] Although I am skeptical of Feld's notion of collaboration (1994, 283), I agree that musicians themselves do not always agree with the literature about their position in globalizing music networks. As Mali's Salif Keita notes: "White people who collaborate with African musicians want the *inspiration*. It is not bad. They get the inspiration and we get the popularity" (quoted in Troupe 1995, 27).

According to Erlmann (1996, 473), "the omnipresence of commodity production is the roof, as it were, under which differentiation and homogenization now comfortably reside as members of the same family." The multinational machinery that supports a growing market for world music perpetuates a myth of global diversity (i.e., equality) through the Benettonesque celebration of difference. This "production of difference" fuels the global consumer imagination, but does little or nothing to actually challenge structures of inequality fixed in place by the extension of global capitalism. Locality is fetishized, "difference is drawn back into the system," and in the end nothing really changes (Erlmann 1996, 472; cf. Wade 1998).

In commercialized popular music we see not only how the local is globalized (as in the consumption of exotic forms of "world music" or "world beat"), but also how the global is localized (as in the indigenization of foreign styles such as reggae, and more recently hip hop). In this context it could be argued that African musicians are in an unparalleled position to benefit from international commodity markets, since their product is sold on its ability to be both "traditional" and "modern," or what Gilroy (drawing from W. E. B. DuBois) has discussed as the African diaspora's unique "double consciousness" (Gilroy 1993, 73). Guilbault (1993), however, sees this doubleness as a handicap, since practitioners of world music are forced to innovate in important ways, while at the same time gesturing toward an imagined "traditional" past. Waterman's analysis of *juju* music in Nigeria shows that musicians themselves view their special position as an asset: "You know, our Yoruba tradition is a very modern tradition" (1990, 2). For Cameroun's Manu Dibango, this consciousness is not double, but triple. Dibango points out that in his first international hit song ("Soul Makossa"), "Americans said I was doing African music and Africans said I was doing Western music and Europeans said I was doing American music" (Santoro 1994).

COMMODITIES IN MOTION AND VIEWS FROM THE MARGINS

> Capitalism's specificity is due to its ability to draw in goods from far away without making reference to the social matrix in which they were produced. (Wolf 1982, 310)

The question of identity is essential to understanding the distinctiveness of "cultural" commodities. It is especially interesting to look at "cultural" commodities such as music because of what these goods tell us about the people who produce and consume them. "Cultural" commodities are different from other commodities (a bale of cotton or a sack of rice, for example) because at some level they embody the cultural identity of the producer and *it is often on this basis that they are sold.* Products in this category contain more than just the results of human labor; they also embody individual human ideas, insights, and creativity. In the case of many commodities, producers own the products of their labor only until they release them for sale on the market. When they let it go, it becomes a product with no producer, a product whose creator no longer has any bearing on its value or meaning, an alienated product.[38] But music and other cultural forms (art, literature, dance) are products of human labor that retain, to a greater extent, the identity of the producer. Music, unlike other commodities, constantly reminds us of who made it. When we listen, we imagine not only the singer's words, but also the singer. This is particularly true with music of the African diaspora, which often contains elements of self-reference or "authoring" (Rose 1994, 86).[39]

But what underlies this conception of "cultural" commodities? It is difficult to avoid the trap of trying to agree on a satisfactory definition of the term "commodity." Definitions that focus on "exchangeability" seem incomplete since they fail to account for key concepts such as Marx's formulation of alienation or Polanyi's emphasis on goods that are produced with the market in mind. In this discussion, however, I have attempted to bypass the debate about what a commodity is or is not (the conference that inspired this volume clearly showed that many things can be seen and analyzed as commodities) and focus instead on what commodities do—or to go one step further, what people do with commodities. The distinction between commodity as "thing" and commodity as "process" is essential to understanding the transactions and meanings attached to musical forms such as *soukouss*, which are often unproblematically labeled "world music" (Erlmann 1996). That is, a particular product is a commodity not simply because it is exchanged. It becomes a commodity as it becomes more integrated into commercial networks, travels greater distances, is sold in larger quantities, and is subjected to structural or stylistic changes in order to be sold. Examining commodities in motion, not only over space but also over time, can reveal valuable information about the processes and consequences of commodity exchange in non-Western societies.

In this analysis I have examined the relationship between transactions in the commercialization process and meanings associated with cultural performance and practice. By exploring how local forms of cultural expression are transformed through the (sometimes incomplete and uneven) process of commodification, not only are we able to glimpse ways capitalist development operates in the margins, but we also learn something about the peculiar position of Africans and African cultures in a globalizing world economy (cf. Burke 1998). Although we tend to define commodity exchange as a process in which the producer is progressively alienated from his or her product, the case of African "world music" provides an example of how African identities—both individual and national—are reinserted into products intended for sale in global markets. But the reinsertion of identities can be problematic, since it covers up processes of cultural construction and objectification that increasingly occur on Western terms and on Western turf. New meanings are created, but they are just as easily romanticized or essentialized (Erlmann 1996).

Also important is the extent to which African producers perceive "cultural" commodities as a means of obtaining access to foreign markets. Painfully aware of Africa's marginal position in the global economy and haunted by the history of Western exploitation of African resources—both human and natural—many Congolese see cultural forms of expression (and the products that result from them) as their only means of acquiring much-needed foreign exchange. Attempts to commercialize such products are sometimes quite successful (such as the Baule *colon* figures in Steiner's 1994 account of art traders). At other times, however, the result is partial or cottage commodification (as in the case of *soukouss*). Through live performances and interactions with audiences, *soukouss* musicians have the distinct advantage of being able to read and influence global consumer demand for their product, but because they depend financially on music sponsors and promoters in order to practice their trade, they have little or no control over how the product is actually marketed or distributed on a larger scale. As a result, they tend to view production (i.e., live performance)—rather than the sale of the product—as their source of livelihood (as several contributors to this volume demonstrate is true for other types of commodity production as well). In the case of African music, however, the producer and the consumer often relate to one another face to face.[40]

As this chapter's opening epigraph suggests, cultural identity for many Congolese is not necessarily sacred or immutable, but instead a potential strategy to open doors to an entirely different world of goods and power:

> In terms of the local market [for music], it's good to satisfy the local market, but you also have to be able to export yourself. To export yourself you have to have a certain number of ideas in order to do work that will be well-received. Don't forget that we live in a very sophisticated world and you have to know how to sell yourself. (Sam Mangwana in Ntondo 1997, 41, my translation)

Indeed the sale of "cultural" goods in Africa depends precisely upon some form of identity ("traditional," "authentic," "African") (Steiner 1994; Meintjes 1990). This observation, however, should not suggest that people in Africa are "selling out" their culture, or worse yet, their selves. African ideas of personhood are not necessarily based on the Western model of an essential "true" self that is opposed to a world external to the self, or that is necessarily compromised by exposure to the forces of the market.

NOTES

Most of the data for this chapter are based on preliminary field research, but some insights were gained from fieldwork conducted in Brazzaville and Kinshasa (1995–1996) with the help of the following organizations: the Centre for the Study of Society, Technology and Development (STANDD), McGill Associates, McGill Graduate Faculty, and the Zeller Family Foundation. In researching this chapter, I have benefited from conversations with Thierry Banza-Matulu, Gilles Bibeau, T. K. Biaya, Gerard Buakasa, Ellen Corin, John Galaty, and Eric Worby. In its early stages the chapter was fortunate to have been looked at by Liz Fajber, Regina Harrison, and Peter Johnson. Cory Kratz and Blair Rutherford offered crucial commentary on later drafts of the chapter, as did Angelique Haugerud, Ingrid Monson, Priscilla Stone, and Peter Wade. I am especially grateful for the valuable input of Bogumil Jewsiewicki and Dave Macaulay. Despite the seemingly collaborative nature of this chapter, I take full responsibility for the particular construction (or mutation) of the ideas presented.

1. John Rockwell, "The New Colossus: American Culture as Power Export," *New York Times* 30 January 1994, sec. 2, pp.1, 30–31.

2. In recent years, there has been an increase in the production of Christian-based religious music. Although religious music has not displaced *la musique moderne,* it represents a significant portion of the music commonly heard in public in Kinshasa (see Ndaywel è Nziem 1993). Elsewhere (White 1998) I have discussed how this genre borrows from "modern" dance music in order to appeal to a larger, increasingly youthful audience.

3. Where I have used the term "Zaire" it refers to Congo-Kinshasa after independence but before the ousting of Mobutu in 1997. Where I use the term "Congolese" it is intended to refer to Congo-Kinshasa. Although the musical style discussed here evolved in the Pool region between the two capitals, I am primarily interested in Congo-Kinshasa since it is generally considered to be the capital of contemporary Central African dance music. It is true that a number of very important musicians from the early period were originally from Congo-Brazzaville (see Bemba 1984), but as the industry began to develop, their numbers in comparison to Zaireans decreased rapidly. Over recent years, Brazzaville has become home to several important music promoters, primarily in the domain of distribution.

4. Surprisingly little academic research has been done on Congolese popular music. Monographs by Michel Lonoh (1969) and Sylvain Bemba (1984) serve as important historical resources on the subject. Onyumbe has written extensively on thematics in the music (see 1994 for one example) and Nkashama's (1979) and Gondola's (1992) articles on music and youth culture deserve special mention. Manda Tchebwa's work (1996) is a compelling look at Kinshasa through the lens of Congolese popular music, and is the only book-length study of the Kinshasa music scene and urban culture in the region.

5. Christopher Steiner challenges us to view the penetration of capitalism in Africa "as a series of personal linkages, forged one at a time by different individuals each with their own motives, ambitions and set of goals," rather than as an "impersonal force which arrives full-sail like a ship to shore" (1994, 164).

6. Such an approach is by no means novel. Bruce Kapferer (1976) originally used the terms "transaction" and "meaning" in a series of publications he edited in the mid-1970s, focusing on symbolism and exchange. Marcus and Fischer's (1986) discussion of attempts to embed rich ethnographic accounts within larger systems of political economy gives several excellent examples of work in this area. More recently, I have also drawn some inspiration from the methodologies implicit in the work of Arjun Appadurai (1995) and Lila Abu-Lughod (1990). Drawing from these various writings, I would argue that a transaction and meaning framework should account for not only the production of things, but also the production of ideas and sounds.

7. Peter Wade (1998) has made the point that all commodities are cultural, but certain types of commodities are more easily identified with certain places or cultures "because of their more communicative, text-like nature which makes it easier to decipher their biographies" (personal communication). Where I use the term "cultural" commodities, I am referring to goods (such as music, art, and literature) that can be distributed and sold as commodities, but which retain to some extent visible signs of the producer's identity, be it national, cultural, or individual.

8. Ingrid Monson has raised the very important question of exactly what music Congolese took to be *rumba*. Although I plan to do more thorough research on the historical relationship between Congolese and Afro-Cuban musical styles, my preliminary findings on this subject suggest that Afro-Cuban recordings of various types were available and extremely popular by the time Congolese started composing and performing nontraditional music of their own (see Martin 1995). More research is required to determine why the label *rumba* in particular became associated with these styles, but it does seem that Afro-Cuban music in general constituted for many Congolese an expression of their modern, urban lifestyle. It is interesting to compare this account with Wade (1998), who has shown that in 1930s Colombia, *rumba* music was associated with a racialized ethnicity of African origin, and

therefore considered by some to be a threat to the formation of a coherent national identity.

9. Kazadi (1979) raises the question of whether the style emerged only in the Kinshasa-Brazzaville region and then spread to other urban centers, or if it emerged in a number of different places at the same time. What is certain is that Congolese music has been, from its inception, an urban phenomenon. Many musics of the African diaspora (reggae, rap, blues) began as urban folk forms and became hugely successful as commercialized genres. A comparison of these forms in the early stages may prove to be interesting.

10. On nightlife, music, and male-female relations in the creation of Congolese urban culture, see Biaya (1994).

11. During Mobutu's nationalization campaign in the mid-1970s (*zaïrianization*), management of the large recording studios and record-pressing factories was handed over to Zairean nationals and in some cases Zairean musicians. The artists who benefited most from these programs were those who had already allied themselves with Franco, Verckys and Tabu Ley, who by this time had formed a loosely organized "music cartel" in Kinshasa, making and breaking careers and exerting control over local networks of production and distribution (Tchebwa 1996).

12. It must be emphasized that Congolese music was fully commercialized within Africa before the development of *soukouss,* but as I will discuss below, *soukouss* extended the process of commercialization even further by altering certain stylistic aspects of the music (such as song structure and rhythm) in order to market the music to non-Congolese audiences abroad.

13. The term originally comes from a dance of the same name that became popular in Brazzaville in the late 1970s. According to guitarist Lokassa ya Mbongo, foreign audiences, upon hearing the name of the dance shouted on the microphone, confused the dance with the musical style and that is how *soukouss* came to be named (interview with author, 17 January 1998).

14. For the purposes of this discussion, I view commercialization as a process that is analogous but parallel to the process of commodification. In most cases, I use the term "commercialization" to talk about specific aspects of material and economic processes, while "commodification" (following the writings of Marx) refers not only to economic processes but to social and political processes as well.

15. In the mid-1990s an original, locally produced cassette cost approximately $5 and compact discs, where available, somewhere around $25. Pirated or homemade cassettes could be found for the equivalent of about $1. On the unofficial, informal economic activity that has now come to characterize economic and political descriptions of Congo, see MacGaffey (1991).

16. Music sponsorship has come from other industries as well (especially local airlines and tobacco companies), but breweries have been the most active in this area. This is probably no coincidence given the complementarity of these two leisure products and their tendency to occupy the same time and space.

17. I am grateful to Mr. Bomboro from the marketing division of Unibra Breweries in Kinshasa for this information.

18. It is important to distinguish between corporate and patron sponsorship. In Kinshasa, both forms exist side by side, although the latter is becoming more and more common (cf. endnote 30).

19. An increase in the number and quality of historically minded studies of African popular music (e.g., Christopher Waterman's *Juju* [1990] and *Nightsong* by Veit Erlmann [1996]) suggests the possibility of comparative research on the development of local recording industries and industry-performer relations. Blewett and Farley's (1998) preliminary research on musical entrepreneurship in Kenya has made some tentative comparisons with Congo-Kinshasa.

20. Previously (White 1998) I looked at how the hierarchical organization of music groups in Kinshasa tends to concentrate power in the hands of bandleaders and administrators, and how this keeps younger musicians in a state of subordinate poverty.

21. Author's interview with Lokassa ya Mbongo, 30 June 1997.

22. Verckys has since left music and now operates a bakery in downtown Kinshasa, as well as a glossy weekly newspaper on culture and current events in the capital. Several promotion and production houses were organized in the late 1980s, the most notable of which was Yoshad Productions, a company run by Mobutu's late son Kongolo (alias "Saddam Hussein"), who was known to use his position as a high-ranking military officer in his father's army to strong-arm the local music scene in Kinshasa.

23. Lingala is the language used in most popular music in Congo. In Kinshasa, French is very common, especially in government and institutional settings where this former colonial language has official status. Apart from French, the Congolese government recognizes four regionally based African languages (Kikongo, Swahili, Chiluba, and Lingala), although Lingala historically has enjoyed a privileged status, not only through music but as the predominant language of Mobutu's military.

24. Martin Sinnock, a leading chronicler of Congolese popular music, has compared the pace of this Paris-style *soukous* to that of an "amphetamine gazelle" (*The Beat* 16(3): 1997, 30).

25. "Now *that's* good. That's *real* African music." On the notion of authenticity in African cultural production see Jewsiewicki (1996) and Steiner (1994). Compare with Averill (1997) on authenticity and popular music under the Duvalier regime in Haiti, and Kapalanga (1989) for Zaire under Mobutu.

26. "Ivoirian woman, my dear / I can't stop thinking about you, oh-oh / I can't stop thinking about you, my love / I'm all yours, oh-oh . . ." (Aurlus Mabele and his group Loketo, 1998. "*La femme Ivoirienne*," undocumented cassette.)

27. Compare, for example, gangster rap with message rap (Allen 1996) or dancehall with roots reggae (Macaulay 1998).

28. The same is true of popular music within the Congo, where the threat of political persecution is more immediate. Nonetheless, at several points in the history of modern Congolese music, "politics" has entered into the lyrics of the musical style, especially in the years leading up to independence and later in the form of political praise singing. Political rallies (*l'animation politique*) sponsored by Mobutu's one-party state combined pro-party rhetoric with the promotion of "Zairean culture" by showcasing traditional dance and song from various regions of the country (for a more detailed description, see Kapalanga 1989).

29. One well-known Congolese musician, when approached about participating in a series of concerts to raise awareness for human rights, responded by saying: "No, no. I don't do political events. My fans expect me to play romantic music" (personal communication, John Grinling).

30. The importance of patrons in Congolese music points to the very conservative nature of this seemingly libertine musical style. Elsewhere (White 1997) I have discussed how musicians become entangled in the common practice of singing or "throwing" the names of important local politicians and businesspeople in the hopes that such gestures will win them financial protection or political favor.

31. "Tamdriya" (Ninga des Comores), Paris: SACEM NG1.92. (See also note 37.)

32. And this trend is not unique to the Comoros. Many parts of sub-Saharan Africa have produced groups that either borrow from or directly imitate Congolese music: The Bundu Boys (Zimbabwe), Savan'Alla, Meiway, Monique Seka (Côte d'Ivoire), Virunga (Kenya), Roger Wango, Zaksoba (Burkina Faso), and Nico Mbarga (Nigeria), to mention only a few. There is also a market for *soukouss* in urban centers in Japan. In addition to the Congolese groups that have been there on tour, there are several locally based *soukouss* bands that are made up exclusively of Japanese musicians.

33. Peter Wade, in an article about race, music, and nationality in Colombia, writes that "Costeño music can constitute the nation as an imagined community when people dancing and listening to it imagine others doing so all over the country" (1998, 16). Within Congo-Zaire, music has obviously played an important role in the elaboration of an imagined national identity (see Fabian 1998; Kapalanga 1989).

34. Author's interview with Lokassa ya Mbongo, 17 January 1997.

35. Author's interview with M. Socrates, 21 December 1995.

36. For an overview of the "world music" phenomenon, especially the distinction between "world music" and "world beat," see Feld (1994).

37. The role of foreign brokers in African music (the most well-known examples being Paul Simon and Peter Gabriel) is a hotly debated topic, with some viewing their efforts as a form of cultural appropriation and others as a way of promoting local artists and culture. Feld's (1994) discussion of the album he produced in Papua New Guinea (*Voices of the Rainforest,* Rykodisc RCD 10173, 1991) is a good example of the latter. On Paul Simon's controversial *Graceland* album, see Louise Meintjes' (1990) description of the social and political meanings associated with multiracial musical collaboration in 1980s South Africa.

38. I take "alienation" to mean both the separation of the product from the producer and the psychological state that results from this separation. Alienation has been the implicit motivation of NGOs working in the "fair trade" movement (for example Bridgehead, a nonprofit arts and crafts marketing cooperative affiliated with Oxfam Canada), whose mission is to reinject producers' identities into indigenous products marketed in the West.

39. There is already a rich literature on how personhood and identity are condensed in ritual forms of expressive culture in an African setting (see Kratz 1994 for a recent example). In this chapter I have attempted to show how notions of identity are related to commercial or popular forms of cultural expression as well (see also Waterman 1990).

40. The presence of nationally based, internationally recognized organizations for the protection of intellectual property (beginning with the formation of the U.N.'s Organisation Mondiale de la Propriété Intellectuelle in 1967) means that artists of various kinds can earn income from the duplication, sale, and broadcast of their products. Copyright payments, if properly managed, might offer African musicians extra protection from the unpredictability of global markets for their music, especially given the widespread practice of cassette piracy in many parts of Africa. In reality, however, very few musicians can benefit from copyright

payments since copyright bureaus in most African countries are barely functional, and since membership in foreign bureaus requires citizenship or residence status in the particular country where membership is sought.

REFERENCES

Abu-Lughod, Lila. 1990. Shifting Politics in Bedouin Love Poetry. In Lila Abu-Lughod and Catherine Lutz, eds., *Language and the Politics of Emotion*. Cambridge: Cambridge University Press.

Allen, Ernest, Jr. 1996. Making the Strong Survive: The Contours and Contradictions of Message Rap. In William Eric Perkins, ed., *Droppin' Science: Critical Essays on Rap Music and Hip Hop Culture*. Philadelphia: Temple University Press.

Anderson, Benedict. 1983. *Imagined Communities*. New York: Verso.

Appadurai, Arjun. 1995. Playing with Modernity: The Decolonization of Indian Cricket. In Carol Breckenridge, ed., *Consuming Modernity: Public Culture in a South Asian World*. Minneapolis: University of Minnesota Press.

————, ed. 1986. *The Social Life of Things*. Chicago: University of Chicago Press.

Averill, Gage. 1997. *A Day for the Hunter, A Day for the Prey: Popular Music and Power in Haiti*. Chicago: University of Chicago Press.

Barber, Karin. 1987. Popular Arts in Africa. *African Studies Review* 30(3): 1–78.

Bemba, Sylvain. 1984. *Cinquante ans de musique du Congo-Zaire: (1920–1970): De Paul Kamba à Tabu Ley*. Paris: Présence Africaine.

Biaya, Tshikala K. 1994. Mundele, Ndumba et Ambience. Le vrai "Bal blanc et bal noir(e)." In Gauthier de Villers, ed., *Belgique/Zaire: Une histoire en quête d'avenir*. Institut Africain-CEDAF. Paris: L'Harmattan.

Blewett, Robert A., and Michael Farley. 1998. Institutional Constraints on Entrepreneurship in Kenya's Popular Music Industry. In Anita Spring and Barbara McDade, eds., *African Entrepreneurship: Themes and Realities*. Gainesville, Fla.: University of Florida Press.

Bourdieu, Pierre. 1984. *Distinction: A Social Critique of the Judgement of Taste*. Cambridge: Harvard University Press.

Braudel, Fernand. 1979. *Civilization and Capitalism 15th–18th Century: The Wheels of Progress*, Vol. 2. Paris: Librairie Armand Colin.

Burke, Timothy. 1998. Cannibal Margarine and Reactionary Snapple: A Comparative Examination of Rumors about Commodities. *International Journal of Cultural Studies* 1(2): 253–270.

Chernoff, John Miller. 1979. *African Rhythm and African Sensibility: Aesthetics and Social Action in African Musical Idioms*. Chicago: University of Chicago Press.

Cheyney, Tom. 1989. Loketo: Shake Your Hips. *Beat* 8(6): 36–40.

Clifford, James. 1994. Diasporas. *Cultural Anthropology* 9(3): 302–338.

de Certeau, Michel. 1984. *The Practice of Everyday Life*. Berkeley: University of California Press.

Erlmann, Veit. 1996. The Aesthetics of the Global Imagination: Reflections on World Music in the 1990s. *Public Culture* 8: 467–488.

Ewens, Graeme. 1990. *Africa O-ye!* London: Guiness Books.

Fabian, Johannes. 1978. Popular Culture in Africa: Findings and Conjectures. *Africa* 48(4): 315–334.

———. 1998. *Moments of Freedom: Anthropology and Popular Culture.* Charlottesville: University Press of Virginia.

Feld, Steven. 1994. From Schizophonia to Schismogenesis: On the Discourses and Commodification Practices of "World Music" and "World Beat." In Steven Feld and Charles Keil, eds., *Music Grooves: Essays and Dialogues.* Chicago: University of Chicago Press.

Gandoulou, Justin Daniel. 1989. *Dandies à Bacongo: le culte de l'élégance dans la société congolaise contemporaine.* Paris: L'Harmattan.

Geschiere, Peter, and Michael Rowlands. 1996. The Domestication of Modernity: Different Trajectories. *Africa* 66(4): 552–554.

Gilroy, Paul. 1993. *The Black Atlantic: Modernity and Double Consciousness.* Cambridge, Mass.: Harvard University Press.

Gondola, Charles Didier. 1992. Ata Ndele . . . et l'independence vint: musique, jeunes et contestation politique dans les capitales congolaises. In Catherine Coquery-Vidrovitch and Hélène d'Almeida-Topor, eds., *Les Jeunes en Afrique.* Paris: Harmattan.

Gregory, Chris A. 1982. *Gifts and Commodities.* New York: Academic Press.

Gudeman, Stephen. 1986. *Economics as Culture: Models and Metaphors of Livelihood.* Boston: Routledge and Kegan Paul.

Guilbault, Jocelyne. 1993. *Zouk: World Music in the West Indies.* Chicago: University of Chicago Press.

Hebdige, Dick. 1979. *Subculture: The Meaning of Style.* New York: Methuen.

Jewsiewicki, Bogumil. 1991. Painting in Zaire: From the Invention of the West to the Representation of Social Self. In Susan Vogel, ed., *Africa Explores: Twentieth Century African Art.* New York: Center for African Art/Munich: Presto.

———. 1996. De l'art africain et de l'esthétique: valeur d'usage, valeur d'échange. *Cahiers d'Etudes africaines* 36(1–2): 257–269.

Jules-Rosette, Bennetta. 1984. *The Messages of Tourist Art: An African Semiotic System in Comparative Perspective.* New York: Plenum Press.

Kapalanga, Gazungil Sang'Amin. 1989. *Les Spectacles d'animation politique en République du Zaire.* Louvain-la-Neuve: Cahiers théâtre Louvain.

Kapferer, Bruce. 1976. *Transaction and Meaning: Directions in the Anthropology of Exchange and Symbolic Behavior.* Philadelphia: Institute for the Study of Human Issues.

Kazadi, Wa Mukuna. 1979. The Origin of Zairean Modern Music: A Socio-Economic Aspect. *African Urban Studies* 1979–80(6): 31–39.

Kratz, Corinne. 1994. *Affecting Performance: Meaning, Movement, and Experience in Okiek Women's Initiation.* Washington, D.C.: Smithsonian Institution Press.

Kurin, Richard. 1997. *Reflections of a Culture Broker: A View from the Smithsonian.* Washington, D.C.: Smithsonian Institution Press.

Lonoh, Michel B. 1969. *Essai de Commentaire sur la Musique Congolaise Moderne.* Kinshasa: SEI/ANC in collaboration with the Zairian Ministry of Arts and Culture.

Macaulay, David. 1998. The Poetics and Politics of Cultural Identity in Jamaican Popular Music. Ph.D. diss. in progress, McGill University, Montreal.

MacGaffey, Janet, ed. 1991. *The Real Economy of Zaire.* Philadelphia: University of Pennsylvania Press.

Manuel, Peter. 1993. *Cassette Culture: Popular Music and Technology in North India*. Chicago: University of Chicago Press.

Marcus, George, and Michael Fischer. 1986. *Anthropology as Cultural Critique*. Chicago: University of Chicago Press.

Martin, Phyllis. 1995. *Leisure and Society in Colonial Brazzaville*. New York: Cambridge University Press.

Mbembe, Achille. 1992. The Banality of Power and the Aesthetics of Vulgarity in the Postcolony. *Public Culture* 4(2): 1–30.

Meintjes, Louise. 1990. Paul Simon's *Graceland*, South Africa, and the Mediation of Musical Meaning. *Ethnomusicology* 43(1): 37–74.

———. 1994. Mediating Difference: Politics in the Production of Zulu Music in Johannesburg. Paper Prepared for the African Studies Association meeting, Toronto, November 4–7.

Middleton, Richard. 1990. *Studying Popular Music*. Philadelphia: Open University Press.

Mintz, Sidney. 1985. *Sweetness and Power: The Place of Sugar in Modern History*. New York: Viking Press.

Ndaywel è Nziem, I. 1993. La Société Zaïroise dans le Miroir de son Discours Religieux (1990–1993). *Cahiers Africains/Afrika Studies* 6: 1–95. Brussels: CEDAF/ASDOC.

Nkashama, P. Ngandu. 1979. Ivresse et Vertige: les nouvelles danses des jeunes au Zaire. *L'Afrique littéraire et artistique* 51: 94–102.

Ntondo, Ladji. Interview by Sam Mangwana, 1997–98. La piraterie c'est le SIDA de la musique en Afrique centrale. *Afro-Vision* (Dec.–Feb.): 44–45.

Onyumbe, Tshonga. 1994. Urban Music and Public Rumor: Popular Expression Against Political Authority in Zaire. Seminar presentation at the Institute for Advanced Study and Research in the African Humanities, Northwestern University, Evanston, Illinois.

Ortner, Sherry. 1984. Theory in Anthropology Since the Sixties. *Comparative Study of Society and History* 26(1): 1–26.

Paine, Robert. 1971. A Theory of Patronage and Brokerage. In Robert Paine, ed., *Patrons and Brokers in the Arctic*. St. John's: Memorial University.

Polanyi, Karl. 1957. *The Great Transformation*. Boston: Beacon Press.

Radio France International (RFI). 1992. "Rumba Cha-Cha: Musiques des deux Congos (1950–1960)." Compact disc liner notes. Paris: RFI.

Rose, Tricia. 1994. *Black Noise: Rap Music and Black Culture in Contemporary America*. Hanover, N.H.: Wesleyan University Press, University Press of New England.

Santoro, Gene. 1994. Manu Dibango. *The Nation* 259 (October 24): 469.

Sinnock, Martin. 1997. Zaire Roundup, Part Deux. *The Beat* 16(3): 30.

Socrates, M. 1995. Interview with author. Kinshasa, 21 December.

Steiner, Christopher. 1994. *African Art in Transit*. Cambridge: Cambridge University Press.

Taussig, Michael. 1980. *The Devil and Commodity Fetishism in South America*. Chapel Hill: University of North Carolina Press.

Tchebwa, Manda. 1996. *La Terre de la Chanson*. Brussels: Duculot.

Troupe, Quincy. 1995. Salif Keita: Beat King. *New York Times Magazine*, 29 January.

Wade, Peter. 1998. Music, Blackness and National Identity: Three Moments in Colombian History. *Popular Music* 17(3): 1–20.

Wallerstein, Immanuel. 1974. *The Modern World System*. New York: Academic Press.

Waterman, Christopher. 1990. *Juju: A Social History and Ethnography of an African Popular Music*. Chicago: University of Chicago Press.

White, Bob W. 1997. *Singing the Sponsor: Popular Music and Micropolitics in Mobutuland and After*. CAAS Working Paper Series, no. 44: 1–30. Ann Arbor: Center for Afroamerican and African Studies, University of Michigan.

———. 1998. Modernity's Spiral: Popular Culture, Mastery, and the Politics of Dance Music in Congo-Kinshasa. Ph.D. diss., McGill University.

Wilk, Richard. 1993. Local Producers and Global Consumers: Emerging Linkages in the World System as a Challenge to Economic Anthropology. Paper presented at SEA annual conference, Durham, New Hampshire.

Wolf, Eric. 1982. *Europe and the People Without History*. Berkeley: University of California Press.

3

What It Means to Be Restructured: Nontraditional Commodities and Structural Adjustment in Sub-Saharan Africa

Peter D. Little and Catherine S. Dolan

INTRODUCTION

Fifteen kilometers south of Banjul, the West African capital city of The Gambia, a woman gardener stoops in the blistering sun to harvest the last of her green chili peppers. Her produce will fulfill a contract with a large export company. On the other side of the continent, 50 kilometers north of Nairobi, Kenya, a similar scenario unfolds. A peasant farmer is busily sorting her recent harvest of French green beans, packing the highest quality produce into cartons labeled "Marks and Spencer," the trademark of the popular London-based retailer. The less attractive produce is stuffed in plastic bags destined for the hotel markets of Nairobi, or ferried back to smallholder farms and fed to livestock. As in The Gambia and other African countries, the exportable produce from Kenya will go to an international airport, and then be shipped more than 5,000 kilometers to Europe, where within twenty-four hours it will embellish the shelves of grocery stores and produce stands. This process embodies a complex set of global power relations, institutional actors, and consumer demand(s) that is ambiguously labeled the "nontraditional" commodity trade.

What is a nontraditional commodity (NTC)? Barham and his colleagues, in their study of nontraditional agricultural exports in Latin America, offer a threefold typology for examining commodity types and markets:

First, an export can be nontraditional because it involves a product that has not been produced in a particular country before, such as snowpeas in Guatemala. A second type of nontraditional export is a product that was traditionally produced for domestic production but is now being exported, like various tropical fruits. Finally, the term can refer to the development of a new market for a traditional product, such as exporting bananas to the Soviet Union. (1992, 43)

As the authors demonstrate, however, the definition encompasses larger social and political contexts, of which the physical product is merely one element. The classification process and its language reflect global changes that are closely associated with neoliberal trade policies and the structural adjustment programs of the past decade. In short, a definition cannot be divorced from the power relations embedded in the World Bank and other investment groups that largely determine what is classified as a nontraditional commodity. The taxonomic exercise has considerable consequences, since millions of dollars of third world development funds now chase NTC programs in hopes of diversifying exports, increasing trade revenues, and enhancing the private sector (Barham et al. 1992; Meerman 1997; World Bank 1989). Part of what it means to be restructured, therefore, is played out through the discourse and power relations that designate some peasants as nontraditional commodity growers and others as traditional commodity farmers.

In practice, the NTC concept is rife with contradictions and uncertainties because what constitutes a nontraditional export changes both within and across national boundaries. For example, under the U.S. Agency for International Development (USAID) trade program in Ghana, the yam, a tuber crop with a lengthy history in West Africa, is classified as a nontraditional export while cocoa, an industrial commodity introduced by the British in the past century, is considered a traditional export product. The contradictions are even more striking in East Africa; in Uganda coffee and cotton are labeled as traditional products, but maize and some local bean varieties qualify as nontraditional commodities because they have not been exported to overseas markets in the past. The whole range of so-called specialty crops the World Bank (1989) has strongly endorsed—including "exotic" produce (e.g., mangoes), high-value horticultural products (e.g., French beans and cut flowers), and spices— fall mainly into the nontraditional category. The distinctions are often blurred, however; business entrepreneurs and politicians have been known to petition the government (usually an export promotion unit established by the World Bank or another outside agency) to have a certain product reclassified as a nontraditional export in order to receive a subsidy or credit. Thus, with one stroke of a pen, a banker or planner can reclassify an entire commodity regime, its farmers, and its traders into a grouping worthy of investment and promotion, potentially instigating agrarian changes and struggles that have widespread implications (as discussed below).

This chapter examines nontraditional commodity production and trade in Africa, addressing both the ideology (discourse) and practice (farming) of this activity. It goes beyond work such as that by Barham and his collaborators (1992), by arguing that the nontraditional commodity business creates opportunities for private capital (both international and domestic) to reconfigure African agriculture. Although the local impact of this phenomenon has been documented in some Latin American countries, with unsettling results (Paus 1988; Stonich 1991; Carter, Barham, and Mesbah 1994), the topic is relatively new for economic anthropologists working in Africa (see Dolan 1997; Little and Watts 1994). Using a recent case study of nontraditional exports in The Gambia, this chapter explores what it is like for a group of farmers to be restructured under an economic reform program that emphasizes NTCs.

THEORY AND CONCEPTS

To theorize about NTCs, we draw on the work of scholars such as Friedland (1984), whose research on commodity systems examines the social and economic relations of NTC production, trade, and consumption. His approach recognizes that each commodity is associated with specific conditions of labor, processing, and marketing from the point of production to consumption. International capital enters particular commodity systems at different points in the chain, reconfiguring their technical requirements. Such interventions might include investment in new forms of refrigeration and processing. Commodity-specific characteristics influence the nature of particular commodity systems, since labor, processing, and marketing demands are not universal. For instance, green tea must be processed within eight hours after harvest, sugarcane requires a moisture threshold for crushing, and vegetables must meet certain standards (quality, size, and taste) to be exportable. The advantages of the commodity systems framework are that it recognizes commodity-specific differences and provides a straightforward means of focusing on a particular point in a commodity chain. In this chapter, we draw on insights of Friedland and others (Friedmann 1987; McMichael 1994; McMichael and Myhre 1991; Watts 1994) who have used a commodity systems approach to examine recent changes in global agricultural trade.

From a nonmaterialist perspective, Appadurai's (1986) work is helpful in conceptualizing the cultural dimensions of commodities. The introduction to his book, *The Social Life of Things: Commodities in Cultural Perspective*, includes three points that are useful to analysis of NTCs. First, he shows that the values attached to certain commodities reflect power relations that often circumscribe local communities producing for global markets; local producers and consumers "are intimately tied to larger regimes of value defined by large-scale polities" (Appadurai 1986, 30). Although his analysis emphasizes European monarchies' valuation of commodities, the ways medieval European monarchs and courts shaped production by defining goods such as silk rugs as "royal" items are similar to international capital's influence on what types of commodities (e.g., specialty produce) third world producers emphasize.

Second, Appadurai's schema highlights the importance of larger—often hidden—knowledge relations that characterize commodities. In our case an NTC embodies substantially more than the particular knowledge of an agricultural commodity; it carries with it a set of knowledge relations about private sector investment, the restructuring of state policies in the South, and neoliberal trade philosophy. This knowledge is not shared between the point of consumption (the North) and the workplace (the South) of commodity production, since what is "read into the commodity" varies sharply across positions in global trade (Appadurai 1986, 41). Without necessarily comprehending the nonlocal context of her actions, the Gambian gardener mentioned earlier is part of a larger agenda that aims to fundamentally restructure African economies.

A third significant element of Appadurai's discussion is the notion that, like all social things, commodities experience distinct life cycles. These sequences reflect complex historical and political relations that go beyond changing conditions of supply and demand. As Mintz (1985) has so eloquently demonstrated, even sugar was at one time an exotic commodity that only graced the tables of royalty and rich merchants. As sugar became more widely available and culturally acceptable to the masses, it was transformed into a necessity. There are myriad examples of the conversion of a nontraditional or exotic commodity into a common or "humble" one (the latter term is Appadurai's 1986, 40). Illustrations include bananas and pineapples; both are important tropical export products that have been transformed from exotic to common commodities during this century.[1] Some vegetables categorized as exotic, such as French beans and chili peppers, are now so widespread in European markets that they might be destined for relabeling.

While this chapter acknowledges the power of symbols and discourse, they can only account for part of the NTC production story. The rest emerges from the farm fields and often harsh labor conditions and relationships that characterize this activity.

HISTORICAL CONTEXT

The 1980s witnessed a rapid increase in low-income farmers' participation in NTC production. As prices of classical export crops such as sugar and cocoa declined during that decade, many farmers, who were actively encouraged by governments and development agencies, pursued high-value, "niche" crops such as spices and certain vegetables. In The Gambia, for example, the share of groundnuts in total foreign exchange earnings fell from 45 percent in the early 1980s to 12 percent in 1991–1992 (Hadjmichael, Rumbaugh, and Verreydt 1992). Confronted with declining incomes from traditional export commodities, governments and international development agencies initiated campaigns to diversify export production among smallholders and other producers. The campaigns entailed significant alterations in the organization of smallholder production and marketing, including the promotion of agribusiness and contract farming (see Little and Watts 1994). Such changes are part of larger transformations in global commodity systems and trade; high-value exports and foods have partly compensated for declining traditional export incomes in much of the third world, including Africa.[2] Many policymakers view these structural changes in agriculture as optimal solutions for resolving agricultural and trade dilemmas faced by the poorest countries (World Bank 1989).

Growth in nontraditional exports during the past fifteen years is best illustrated by examining the global fresh fruit and vegetable (FFV) industry, which has involved strong participation by both agribusiness firms and smallholders. Growing demand for fresh produce in northern countries, particularly Japan, as well as technical innovations in refrigerated storage and transportation (Watts 1994, 37) have increased fresh fruit and vegetable trade, which grew annually by more than 9 percent from 1965 to 1985 (Islam 1990, cited in Watts 1994, 37). According to Watts (1994, 37), when processed fruits and vegetables are included, the global fruit and vegetable trade represents "the fourth most important commodity group in world agricultural trade." Although a few key countries such as Mexico and Thailand account for most of the growth in horticultural exports, African agriculture is affected nonetheless by the boom. Watts (1994, 39) remarks on the continent's surge in exports:

> Between 1976 and 1988 sub-Saharan Africa's horticultural exports doubled. . . . By the 1990s they were third in value, in excess of tea, cotton, and tobacco and only trailing coffee and cocoa. South Africa, Kenya, and Côte d'Ivoire dominated the trade. Other newcomers such as Senegal have also performed quite respectably and made important gains in the EEC green bean import trade. . . . In all of these cases, contracting and subcontracting arrangements were central to the dispersion and growth of the horticultural industry worldwide.

Most of Africa's horticultural produce goes to Europe, where demand for African produce is especially strong in the winter months when the region's own production of fruits and vegetables is limited. Countries such as South Africa and Kenya, whose air connections to Europe are frequent and generally reliable, have a significant advantage over most other African nations where international air traffic is minimal. Trade statistics demonstrate South Africa's and Kenya's overwhelming dominance in African horticultural exports.

Growth in nontraditional exports has accompanied changes in the economic policies of developing countries and international donor agencies. During the 1980s, when African governments confronted threats of national bankruptcy and depleted foreign exchange reserves, a radically different approach to development emerged (or reemerged, some might say). The new paradigm advocated private-sector development with an emphasis on export-led growth, monetary and fiscal reform, and government deregulation in agricultural production and marketing. Structural adjustment programs (SAPs) imposed by the International Monetary Fund (IMF) and the World Bank became part of the new development agenda, and nontraditional export activities were central to reforms that promoted export diversification. These programs included expansion of niche-market exports such as spices, flowers, and specialty fruits and vegetables. The need for production and marketing flexibility[3]

Table 3.1   Attributes Associated with Nontraditional and Traditional Export
Commodities

Nontraditional Commodities	Traditional Commodities
Private Sector	Government
Progressive	Backward
Global market-driven	Government monopoly
Assist economic reforms	Can hinder economic reforms
Pro-transnational corporations	Pro-parastatal corporations
Wave of the future	Wave of the past

and perceived failures of the state in agricultural export ventures became justifications for a private-sector–led strategy (see World Bank 1981, 1989).

In Africa, the notion of a nontraditional commodity took on powerful associations. Table 3.1 lists hidden attributes of NTCs that strongly reveal themselves in imposed economic reforms. While production and trade in traditional export commodities symbolize the old statist policies and "backward-looking" programs of agriculture, the NTC business is seen as progressive, export-driven, and entrepreneurial. In short, NTC production signifies the necessary replacement of Africa's previous parastatal-controlled agriculture by market-savvy private actors (including transnational companies), fiscally conservative budget reformers, and true believers in the benefits of global commerce.

The International Finance Corporation (IFC) and other international and bilateral donors have been important sources of funding for export diversification projects. USAID alone now supports more than twenty-five export diversification programs.[4] In sub-Saharan Africa, where structural adjustment programs exist in more than 80 percent of the countries, the promotion of NTC exports is tied closely to austerity measures that often provoke political instability. The Economic Recovery Programme (ERP) introduced in The Gambia in 1985, one of the most far-reaching programs on the continent, included strong fiscal and other incentives to encourage both private firms and farmers to invest in niche-market activities. Here, as elsewhere, government helped to establish an export promotion council within the country and has promoted international trade shows to solicit markets for the country's exports. The Gambian export promotion council planned to depict a ripe mango and eggplant on its brochures, with the caption: "The Gambia means more than beautiful beaches and friendly people."[5]

NONTRADITIONAL COMMODITIES IN THE GAMBIA

The Gambia is a small country of just 1.1 million people on the West African coast (Kakoza et al. 1995). Its annual per capita income of less than US$300 places it among the twenty poorest countries in the world. It inherited a British colonial structure centered on control of the Gambia River, a wedge in French-controlled Senegal. At independence, The Gambia's private sector included mostly Europeans and other non-Africans. As in so many newly independent states, the government quickly moved to gain control over lucrative export commodities that had benefited Africans very little. Before the ERP, The Gambia adopted a policy of direct intervention in agricultural production and trade of groundnuts, the country's main export crop, and established a state marketing board to ensure government profits from this commodity.

Under the ERP, donor aid was to transform The Gambia into the "Gateway to West Africa" (Kakoza et al. 1995, 3). By the 1980s, The Gambia had become one of the largest recipients of foreign aid in the world (averaging US$80 per capita, per year from 1975–1985). From 1985 to 1989, the international community provided The Gambia with approximately SDR 232 million in grants and concessional loans, an amount nearly unprecedented in Africa (Radelet 1995). Foreign aid accounted for more than 50 percent of the operating budgets of many Gambian government ministries,[6] and one product (groundnuts) accounted for more than 40 percent of agricultural export earnings. Given such high dependence on foreign aid, it is not surprising that The Gambia became one of the first African countries to succumb to World Bank and IMF structural adjustment programs. Indeed, by the end of the 1980s it was heralded as one of the most successful cases of structural adjustment on the continent, with a reduced budget deficit, a growing export portfolio, and an environment conducive to private foreign investment (Jabara 1990; Radelet and McPherson 1995). The rationale for the 1994 coup, however, included public disenchantment with corruption and poor results of the privatization program, which incited public demonstrations.

Before the coup, President Sir Dawda K. Jawara and his party were very committed to economic reform. As Grindle and Roemer note:

> The nature of The Gambia's leading political party, and its regular recourse to elections, also eased the introduction of reform. The party, with a strong base in the country's rural area, provided widespread legitimacy to the president's leadership and helped carry the message about the importance of the reforms to its membership. (1995, 315)

By the early 1990s, however, the country faced a major budget deficit and unprecedented corruption. The Jawara government's failure to address corruption "increased the public perception that ordinary Gambians were being asked to sacrifice in the name of reform, while Jawara allowed his colleagues to reap the benefits" (Grindle and Roemer 1995, 315).

THE NONTRADITIONAL COMMODITY DRIVE

By the mid-1980s NTC promotion had taken hold in The Gambia as the country attracted transnational investment and emerged as an important regional exporter of horticultural produce to Europe. (Table 3.2 shows the strong growth in horticultural exports from 1984 to 1992.) The Gambia exported horticultural products before the 1980s as well, but the volume was minimal. Investment in NTCs was partly a response to decline in the world price of groundnuts, historically the mainstay of The Gambian economy. Despite widespread official enthusiasm for the NTC subsector (see *Task Force* 1993), annual earnings remained below US$10 million in 1994.

Horticultural exports have received considerable attention from the Gambian government and international development agencies; they are prominent in the state's export diversification program (*Task Force* 1993, 17–18). Horticultural exports, however, are almost entirely under the control of a few private companies and individuals. The government has eliminated export taxes on horticultural produce and tariffs on certain inputs and, with donor funding, has subsidized infrastructure and marketing services for export firms. Some of the NTC export farms received funding from the IFC, the Commonwealth Development Corporation (United Kingdom), and the African Development Bank (the latter is financed by the World Bank, USAID, and several other Western institutions). Nonetheless, exporters believe that the government and international aid donors have done very little for them.[7]

The Gambia's most important horticultural exports, in order of importance, are eggplant, mangoes, chilies, okra, green beans, a range of Asian vegetables (e.g., kerela and dudhi), and flowers. Most Gambian produce exports go to the United Kingdom, though other European countries import these products as well. The Gambia's export trade has particularly targeted the United Kingdom's ethnic markets that serve the growing Southeast Asian immigrant community. The United Kingdom accounted for 93 percent of the total market for Gambian produce in 1990–1991, and this figure rose to 96 percent in 1991–1992.

Table 3.2   Horticulture Exports from The Gambia, 1984–1992

Year	Volume (metric tons)	Value (000 Dalasis)[a]	Value per ton
1984–1985	32	163	5.09
1985–1986	24	177	7.38
1986–1987	137	584	4.26
1987–1988	814	3,458	4.25
1988–1989	1,168	7,787	6.67
1989–1990	1,145	8,658	7.56
1990–1991	1,747	10,951	6.27
1991–1992	2,280	16,258	7.13

Sources: Ministry of Trade, Industry, and Employment, The Gambia, n.d.; Ministry of Agriculture, The Gambia, 1992.
[a]U.S. $1 = 9 Dalasis (D) in 1994.

The Gambian export trade comprises three seasons. The main season (November to April) accounts for more than 60 percent of trade and corresponds with the peak of the winter vegetable market in Europe. The "mango season" (May to July), or mango harvest period, accounts for about 20 percent of export volume. It is especially important to certain firms that focus on tropical fruits, though at least 20 percent of export farms do not export any fruits, and depend on sales of vegetables during this period. Finally, during the low season (August to October) exports drop to less than 30 percent of high season volumes, and both fruit and vegetable sales are very low.

The productive and institutional arrangements of export horticulture incorporate Gambian farmers into international agro-food systems. Export horticulture trade and production systems are quite diverse, ranging from discrete traders to large-scale corporations. Market concentration is increasing; since 1989 the proportion of total horticultural exports accounted for by the two largest firms has grown by an estimated 30 percent.[8] Exports from these enterprises increased by more than 300 percent from 1989 to 1992, a rate well above the average for the sector. Estimated 1992 sales indicate that the two largest farms accounted for approximately 75 percent of the country's total horticultural exports; the largest farm alone contributed more than 50 percent of the country's total.[9]

REALITY AT THE WORKPLACE

> The supermarket chains in Europe know nothing about farming or the needs of farmers. They only want a certain size and color of vegetable and think that a farmer should be able to produce this every time. They think our farms are like factories where we can turn out a bean of 10 centimeters every time. Farming is not like factory work. (Gambian farmer and exporter, 4 May 1994)

> The exporters ask us to grow chilies and to harvest them when they are green. Then they don't come to pick them up and pay us. We have a lot of problems with these exporters. There is no local market for green chilies so we will not grow them unless we have a written contract. (Gambian gardener, 18 February 1993)

Who is involved in the production and export of horticultural products? What realities underlie an industry so many organizations have praised? When horticultural exports began to take off in the mid-1980s, policymakers hoped that village smallholders and members of communal gardens,[10] especially women growers, would benefit from this boom. Even some local nongovernmental organizations (NGOs) jumped on the NTC bandwagon: it has been assumed "that vertical integration by vegetable producers is more desirable than other market interventions" (Sumberg and Okali 1987, cited in Daniels 1988, 32).

The concept of "vertical integration" is central to the discourse of market reformers and agribusiness advocates. Some local villagers do grow produce for export firms, but their numbers have declined since the 1980s. Although most NGO investment in local vegetable gardens was based on the assumption that locals would participate actively in the export business (see Food and Agricultural Organization, 1992), more than 90 percent of export produce is grown directly on export farms, using hired laborers, rather than by small-scale gardeners. Until the 1994 coup, however, official rhetoric stressed the importance of small farmers in NTC activities and suggested that they benefited immensely from export diversification and market reforms.[11]

Horticultural export production in The Gambia is practiced in several types of production units: communal or village gardens, household or "backyard" gardens, and export or large farm units. A fourth category of vegetable producer recently emerged in sizable, peri-urban villages, where the small export producer (owner of two to six irrigated hectares) is typically a male who also has an urban job. These farms are referred to as "small commercial farms" and should be distinguished from both the larger export (commercial) farms and the smaller local gardens (communal or household). While they represent a relatively small percentage of total producers (less than 1 percent), they are favored by some horticultural firms who contract them for production and provide a means to participate in the export trade.

Most communal and household vegetable producers are women who engage in such production after the rice growing season ends in November. Communal gardens are operated by groups of individuals who usually have been allocated land by the *alkalo* (chief), and who have received assistance from an international donor or an NGO. The schemes have officeholders who allocate individual plots to local women for growing vegetables. Communal gardens, found in most peri-urban settlements around the capital city of Banjul, are usually 2 to 15 hectares, with approximately 5 hectares per communal garden allocated to vegetable production.

Export farms range in size from about 10 to 400 hectares, but most of their owners control additional uncultivated land. They rely almost solely on laborers hired from neighboring countries or nearby villages and urban centers. Field and farm managers supervise this labor. Most of these farms use motorized boreholes, and some have recently introduced sprinkler irrigation systems. They also depend on improved seed varieties, fertilizers, and pesticides, and incur much higher capital costs per land unit than do other farms.

In 1993 there were about fifteen export farms in the peri-urban areas, as was the case in 1988 (Daniels 1988). The average size of export farms, however, was much larger in the early 1990s than it was in the late 1980s. The aggregate area devoted to export horticultural production rose from 150 to 200 hectares in 1989 (Landell Mills Associates 1989, 2) to an estimated 723 hectares in 1993 (Little and Dolan 1993). This expansion further diminished the smallholder sector and ignited local resentment. Among current export farms, at least 20 percent did not export at all during the 1992–1993 season, while another 20 percent exported only minimally (about twice per month). This pattern, coupled with a dropout rate of about 25 percent between 1988 and 1993, highlights the risks associated with export activities (particularly among small exporters).

Approximately 20 percent of Banjul's peri-urban export farms are vertically integrated into the marketing and investment operations of larger overseas companies, which allows the firms to substantially reduce production costs in the fresh produce trade. These firms include subsidiaries of parent companies operating in Europe that provide financial, technical, and marketing services. Since most of these companies already have import and, in some cases, wholesale operations in Europe, their Gambian subsidiaries have a guaranteed outlet for their produce. Large exporters that have long-term relationships with European importers are better equipped to overcome severe market impediments and invest in value-added operations that remain prohibitively expensive for small-scale exporters. The largest export farm in the country is fully integrated into a transnational company, and the newest farm in the region is linked to a UK-based producer and importer of Chinese vegetables and fruits. This firm markets horticultural products throughout the United Kingdom using an elaborate distribution network of wholesalers and grocery retailers. Although these large farms confront some of the same problems that other horticultural enterprises encounter (such as air cargo and storage constraints), they hold a competitive advantage over most producers, as confirmed by their better trade and financial performances.[12]

Labor recruitment is critical to the operation of export farms, as well as to smaller-scale producers of horticulture. An important institutional mechanism in The Gambia for acquiring labor is contract farming, a phenomenon that has strong roots in neoliberal economic policies (see Little and Watts 1994). The next section of this chapter explores contract farming and its relationship to NTC production and trade.

LABOR RELATIONS AND CONTRACT FARMING

Contract farming involves at least three types of production arrangements: communal gardens, small commercial growers, and export farmers. Peasants are involved in the NTC export trade as contracted outgrowers (a form of "waged" labor) or by working directly for export farms or firms. As mentioned, their role as contract farmers has declined in recent years; as a result, some peasants now work as unskilled laborers (for minimal wages) for large export farms.

Contracting with Communal Gardens

Many exporters we interviewed in 1993 relied initially on communal gardens for procuring export produce while they were developing their own farms. In the mid-to late-1980s, when investment in communal gardens was at its peak and many of the current export farms were first establishing themselves, the use of outgrowers in the NTC business was higher than it was in 1994. As the farm sector grew in the late 1980s and early 1990s—aided by liberal land policies and concessions (Roth, Carr, and Cochrane 1994)—attention shifted from small-scale gardeners to large export farms.[13] For instance, in 1988, 45 percent of export farms were contracting with communal gardens. In 1994 the figure dropped to 25 percent. Communal gardens in 1994 figured heavily in the export strategies of only one major firm that contracts out for all of its export produce.

Data from communal gardeners point to a similar trend. The most common contracted crops were eggplants and chilies (a few gardeners had also grown French beans for a limited time). Exporters prefer to use communal gardens to grow labor-intensive crops, such as chilies, and to use small commercial growers for other crops, such as Asian vegetables.

Exporters usually do not deal directly with individual members of communal gardens; rather, they work through the scheme management committee. An agreement, which usually does not entail a written contract, is made with the scheme committee itself and specifies the amount of land to be allocated to each contracted crop and the inputs the exporter will supply. For example, an exporter might agree to buy all chilies from 0.8 hectares and all eggplants from 0.6 hectares of garden land. The scheme committee then selects individual growers and designates plot sizes for each crop. Plot owners who want to grow a particular crop are often allowed to do so, and allocations are usually distributed equitably. Each female gardener may produce contracted crops on less than 0.02 hectares of her plot with the remainder allocated for local vegetable production. The exporter provides seeds, fertilizer, and technical advice and these costs are subtracted from the final payout. Payment typically occurs after the exporter is reimbursed, which means farmers may wait four to six weeks for compensation. In practical terms, then, gardeners actually provide credit and subsidize large-scale exporters.

In addition to payment delays, exporters frequently reject gardeners' produce, leaving the scheme with crops it cannot sell locally. As noted previously, growers often have to pick chilies when they are green. Unlike mature red chilies, the local market for green chilies is minimal. Women growers also complain about low prices and the labor intensity of growing many of the contracted crops. They argue that the local market—especially sales to tourist hotels—is more reliable and lucrative than growing for export.

Exporters, however, explain the decline of contract growing very differently. Their most frequent complaint about contracting with communal gardens is the problem of convincing growers to begin work on their gardens before December; most communal gardeners do not start work on export crop production until after they have harvested their rice in November. By the time they harvest their first vegetable crop in late January or February, the winter export season is well under way. A related difficulty is that of coordinating harvest schedules to meet export market demands. Exporters frequently complain that despite agreements to harvest at a certain date, gardeners may be delinquent because of other agricultural demands or social obligations, such as funerals or weddings. On more than one occasion in 1993 exporters contended that they could not fill orders or meet commitments for air cargo space because vegetables were not harvested on time.

Finally, exporters complain about the need to work through scheme committees to reach agreements on crops and prices. Although some would prefer to contract directly with individuals, many farmers prefer the current arrangement because it reduces their own liability under the contract and they do not want to work directly with exporters. Exporters rarely mention lack of high-quality vegetable production as a reason for not relying on communal gardens. Nevertheless, as long as export farms can acquire large tracts of land in peri-urban areas and the cost of farm labor remains relatively low, communal gardeners' participation in the export business is likely to diminish further.

Contracting with Small Commercial Growers

In recent years a small but important class of commercial growers who concentrate almost exclusively on market production has emerged. In contrast to other vegetable growers, most of these producers are males who have significant sources of nonfarm income, including government positions in Banjul. They usually have small farms of 1 to 3 hectares in the Sukuta and Sinchu areas near Banjul and often invest in mechanized boreholes for irrigation. These small commercial producers contract with export farms to grow crops such as eggplants, French beans, and Asian vegetables. In return for selling their produce at an agreed price, exporters provide them with seeds, fertilizer, and, in some cases, diesel fuel.

In contrast to communal gardens, this category of contract farming appears to be increasing in importance. While there are probably fewer than twenty small commercial growers in peri-urban areas, their numbers have increased considerably in recent years and they now are integral to the operations of certain export firms. In some respects they operate like mini-export farms, relying on hired farm managers and labor, and using expensive farm inputs. But rather than exporting directly, they grow under contract for large export firms that sell the produce overseas.

Contracting with Other Export Farms

In addition to exporting their own produce, more than 40 percent of all export farms—especially the small enterprises—grow export crops, usually under contract, for the two largest export farms. Nearly one-third of export farms sell most of their export-quality produce through one large farm in The Gambia that is owned by a transnational firm with an import subsidiary in the United Kingdom. This trend is increasing as smaller firms find it difficult to establish viable overseas market contacts and to secure air cargo space. At least two export farms, which are in serious financial difficulty, now produce all of their export-quality vegetables under contract for a large farm. Production under contract minimizes their initial financial outlays and allows them to maintain some minor export activity. One of the smaller export farmers recalled in 1993 a recent instance when they had to "feed their cattle French beans" because they could not secure adequate cargo space and the local market was unable to absorb the produce.[14] Acquiring cargo space often involves a series of "rent payments" to airport employees. Small export farmers are willing to sell produce at lower prices under contract to avoid these transport and marketing problems.

WAGED LABORERS

Employment on large farms often is tied to the original land agreements between owners and village authorities. Because NTC activities are concentrated in the Banjul region, where population and land values are highest, "surplus" land is not easy to acquire. With government intervention, large farmers either acquired land by having it officially "titled" by local government authorities or by leasing it from villages. Land titling—especially in export agricultural zones—was encouraged under the structural adjustment program. Not coincidentally, those who acquired titles for large plots often held important political positions. When an exporter approached a village to acquire land for NTC activities, he or she frequently arranged with the *alkalo* (chief) to employ local laborers in return for use of the land. Interviews with several *alkalo* suggested that the hiring of villagers was the main reason that they agreed to these transactions.[15] At least one-quarter of such informal arrangements became an integral part of land acquisitions. In return for hiring villagers, a company was allowed access to landholdings that in some cases exceeded 100 hectares.

The employment-for-land deals, however, did not always produce stable relationships. Disputes over land both in the horticultural and coastal tourist areas were frequent and on more than one occasion villagers vehemently protested to the government about land deals. Indeed the issue was so controversial in 1993 that very few officials wished to discuss it, and there was widespread coverage of land conflicts in local newspapers. In addition, villagers and chiefs complained that skilled, higher-paying positions on export farms were usually allocated to outsiders, particularly Senegalese, and that exporters often trucked in their own laborers rather than hire locals. "We have let the large farmers use our land to grow their crops, but they have not hired our people as they promised. When they do so they pay us wages that are lower than we can earn working on a local farm."[16] Outside laborers are brought in for a number of reasons: (1) they are not "involved with local politics" and do not complain to local chiefs; (2) local peasants—who have their own farms—sometimes refuse to work on export farms, or do not reliably adhere to a rigid work regime; and (3) outside laborers are willing to work for very low wages, thereby deflating compensation levels for other laborers.

On large farms, hired labor is usually reimbursed at a rate of D 10 per day (1 dalasi equaled approximately US$0.11 in 1994), although workers are occasionally compensated on a piece-rate basis during harvest periods. Payment can range from D 0.20 to D 1.00 per kilogram depending on the type of produce harvested. Wages are no higher than payments on local food farms and in some cases they are lower. Horticultural employment is seasonal, with most unskilled laborers being laid off during the summer months. Since employment on large farms tends to be a strategy of last resort for local laborers, other options, such as small-scale gardening and trading, are more lucrative.

Our survey data on wage laborers and employment show that most employment involves casual, low-paying positions at or below the minimum wage; skilled positions tend to go to non-Gambians. Of an estimated 1,806 employees on twelve large farms in 1993, only 168 involved any skilled work. Most of the skilled positions concerned operation and maintenance of the irrigation infrastructure. Many unskilled laborers, in turn, work only six to seven months per year on average; during nonpeak months when exports to Europe decline, casual laborers are fired.

There is a salient gender division of labor on export farms. Women are hired for the more exacting tasks of planting, weeding, and picking; men engage in field preparation, irrigation work, and packing—tasks that hold less significance for the final product. Some farm managers indicated that "women are more reliable and diligent vegetable pickers."[17] They are particularly favored for harvesting chilies and French beans. Work conditions are very difficult and shifts of up to ten hours are not uncommon in peak months. Harvesting activities, for example, entail the back-breaking chore of stooping in the hot sun and picking minuscule vegetables at a breakneck pace. In 1993 women accounted for about 70 percent of unskilled farm labor, but less than 10 percent of skilled or management positions.

There are virtually no time-series data for employment on export farms, but some changes seem to have occurred since the 1980s. First, employment has been increasingly concentrated among the two largest horticultural companies, which in 1993 accounted for about 76 percent of total employment in the sample. The growth of these two companies since the late 1980s, coupled with the demise of a number of smaller horticultural firms, probably accounts for this concentration.

The lack of alternative employment opportunities in rural and peri-urban areas and the displacement of small farmers (potential laborers) by the expansion of export farms may help to explain low wages. Export farm owners and managers do not complain of labor shortages, nor of the need to adjust operations because of a lack of casual farm labor. Some farm owners transport laborers from Serekunda town (approximately 10 kilometers from Banjul city), where unemployed and underemployed workers are readily available, to their farms, which are usually located within 10 to 20 kilometers of Serekunda. Other owners rely on migrant laborers from drought-affected areas of the Sahel (such as eastern Gambia and Senegal). Compensation levels and work arrangements further confirm the adequate supply of casual labor. Under conditions of severe labor constraints we would expect to find the following patterns: (1) wage rates on export farms above local farm wages; (2) labor incentives such as the provision of housing or land for growing food crops; (3) greater use of outgrowers or contract farming to shift the labor and production burden onto smallholders; and (4) the use of labor tenancies or a "stranger farmer" (sharecropping) system to maintain farm laborers during the production season. In each instance, however, this was not the case. As noted, casual labor is not compensated any better by large farmers than by small farmers or gardeners, and in some cases wages are lower. There are very few added incentives to labor recruitment, except provision of meals and transport in certain cases. Furthermore, the use of outgrowers is actually decreasing as large farms increasingly rely on hired workers. Labor tenancies, share-cropping, and other institutional means of acquiring farm labor are virtually absent in the horticultural sector. In short, low levels of compensation suggest it is unlikely that living standards of most employees on NTC enterprises improved during the boom years.

Under one donor agency's program the consulting firm of a well-known transnational agribusiness firm studied the Gambian horticultural subsector and made recommendations on how to improve it (Cargill Technical Services, Ltd., 1994). The firm recommended that no export farm with less than US$1.5 million in start-up costs and 100 hectares of irrigated NTCs should be encouraged, which would effectively eliminate all but one of the country's exporters. The study also suggested ways to modernize production techniques and labor relations on the export farms. Noting that most labor in The Gambia is employed on a daily basis, the report states that "It would significantly improve productivity if piecework payment was introduced" (Cargill Technical Services, Ltd., 1994, 65). Most local chiefs have resisted piece-rate payment ("it is not the local custom"), a form of labor relations that can be highly exploitative in the competitive horticultural market. (For a case of this in Kenya, see Little 1994.) Caught up in the NTC fever and its expectations, the Gambian government did not dispute the international consultants' conclusions, although many local entrepreneurs strongly contested their findings about farm size and capital requirements.

CONCLUSION

This chapter has combined economic and cultural analyses of nontraditional commodities by examining the social, symbolic, and material relations that embody the nontraditional export trade. The wide disparity between the official discourse of NTC production and its actual practice should not be surprising to most who have studied commodity relations in poor countries. NTCs are a powerful symbol of European hegemony, suggesting images such as cut flowers gracing the tables of an affluent couple. NTCs in The Gambia, however, have done little to improve the material welfare of farmers; NTC activities involve fewer farmers, yield smaller incomes, and incur greater risks than development agencies would like us to believe. As we have illustrated here, something as small as an "exotic" vegetable entails a set of global relations, symbols, and labor processes that encompass bankers, peasants, and large bureaucracies. The process discussed in this chapter is merely one example of a historical pattern described by Appadurai (1986) in which the affluent define the conditions and values of commodities produced by the poor.

The practice of NTC production in The Gambia cannot be directly linked to the country's recent coup, but it was a prominent part of a larger development agenda that was perceived as corrupting and as benefiting only the wealthy and politically connected. During the military regime's first year (1995) in power, there was little change in most ERP policies, including the floating exchange rate, flexible interest rates, and privatization of the Gambia Produce Marketing Board. The decision to reintroduce rice subsidies, however, courted the support of urban consumers and marked a sharp reversal of one essential ERP reform. The most profound impact of the coup on economic recovery has been the withdrawal of donor aid from the country (Radelet 1995). It remains to be seen whether the government will sustain earlier reforms as donor support wanes.

NOTES

This chapter is based on the authors' field research in The Gambia between August 1992 and June 1993. Dolan spent about four months in the field and Little was there for two and a half months. We wish to acknowledge the support of our colleague, Ms. Isatou Jack, in the Gambian study. Ms. Jack assisted us with data collection and supervision in the field (a team of research assistants gathered data throughout the period from August 1992 until June 1993). We also thank the following colleagues who collaborated with us on a larger comparative study of peri-urban economies in Africa: Drs. Benjamin Carr, Douglas Graham, Geetha Nagarajan, and Michael Roth. The Gambian research reported here was carried out in association with the Peri-Urban Economies in Africa project, a joint undertaking of the Institute for Development Anthropology (Binghamton, N.Y.), the Land Tenure Center (University of Wisconsin), and the Rural Finance Program (Ohio State University), which was funded by the U.S. Agency for International Development. The authors of course take full responsibility for the contents of the chapter, and the views expressed here should not be attributed to institutions and individuals named above.

1. A significant doctoral thesis could be built on the social history (life cycle) of the yam, which we have noted is now classified by international agencies as an NTC export in Ghana. It first came to North America from West Africa more than 300 years ago via the Atlantic slave trade. One irony is that current demand for yams in the United States and Europe comes mostly from African and West Indian immigrant communities, while cocoa (a nonindigenous crop introduced to Africa by the British in the nineteenth century) has been downgraded to a "traditional" export commodity.

2. The promotion of NTCs includes manufacturing as well as agricultural products. In Kenya, for example, both clothing and leather sectors have diversified. In Mauritius, clothing, jewelry, watches, and leather products are considered to be nontraditional exports. In The Gambia, the production and export base has diversified through increases in tourism, a nontraditional earner of foreign exchange, and trade services. Tourism doubled between 1985–1986 and 1991–1992, replacing groundnut exports as the most important source of foreign exchange (Hadjmichael, Rumbaugh, and Verreydt 1992).

3. The markets for many of these niche commodities are highly seasonal and volatile and usually require considerable flexibility in production and trading operations. They also are strongly associated with private-sector firms and merchants.

4. Personal communication with USAID official, The Gambia, 9 May 1994. From Peter Little's field notes.

5. Author's interview with Gambian government officials involved in export promotion. From Peter Little's field notes.

6. This is not an uncommon feature in debt-ridden African states.

7. Peter Little's field notes.

8. Figures in this sentence and the one that follows are drawn from Peter Little's field notes.

9. This figure may be slightly overstated because it was not possible to account for all the exporters of fruits. It is based on Peter Little's interviews with larger-scale exporters. Little interviewed 80 percent of exporters in the country. In 1993–1994 there were only fifteen large-scale horticultural export farms in the country (those with irrigated farms greater than 20 hectares).

10. These are irrigated gardens that have been established on communal land allocated to a group of farmers (usually women) by a chief. They have been the "favorite project" of many NGOs and some development agencies who have invested considerable funds in them.

11. In a recent study of Gambian traders we found that even these quintessential private-sector actors feel they have benefited very little from market reform programs (Little and Dolan 1993).

12. It was very difficult to gather financial data from large farms because of their operators' reluctance to reveal the profitability of their enterprises. In comparing the economics of different firms, we often had to rely on indirect indicators, such as level of exports and size of landholdings, and qualitative information based on interviews.

13. This same phenomenon has been documented in Guatemala (Carter, Barham, and Mesbah 1994) and Kenya (Mukumbu 1995); both are countries where small-scale growers initially played important roles in NTC exports. For discussion of reasons for this change, see Carter, Barham, and Mesbah (1994) and Little and Watts (1994).

14. Gambian exporter. Interview by Peter Little, Serekunda, The Gambia, 16 February 1993.

15. Most large farm owners did not consider insecure land rights to be a problem, probably because they knew that the state could be invoked in cases where chiefs tried to repossess land on behalf of villagers.

16. Local elder. Interview by Peter Little, Pirang village, The Gambia, 19 May 1993.

17. Gambian exporter. Interview by Peter Little, Serekunda, The Gambia, 15 February 1993.

REFERENCES

Appadurai, Arjun. 1986. Introduction: Commodities and the Politics of Value. In Arjun Appadurai, ed., *The Social Life of Things: Commodities in Cultural Perspective*. Cambridge: Cambridge University Press.

Barham, Bradford, Mary Clark, Elizabeth Katz, and Rachel Schurman. 1992. Nontraditional Agricultural Exports in Latin America. *Latin American Research Review* 27(2): 43–82.

Cargill Technical Services, Ltd. 1994. Farm Strategies Study: Fruits/Vegetables and Flowers in The Gambia: Interim Report. Oxfordshire, U.K.: Cargill Technical Services.

Carter, Michael, Bradford Barham, and Dina Mesbah. 1994. Agroexport Booms and the Rural Resource Poor in Chile, Guatemala, and Paraguay. Unpublished manuscript. Department of Agricultural Economics, University of Wisconsin at Madison.

Daniels, Lisa. 1988. The Economics of Staggered Production and Storage for Selected Horticultural Crops in The Gambia. Master's thesis, Department of Economics, University of Wisconsin at Madison.

Dolan, Catherine. 1997. Tesco Is King: Gender and Labor Dynamics in Horticultural Exporting, Meru District, Kenya. Ph.D. diss., Department of Anthropology, State University of New York, Binghamton, N.Y.

Food and Agricultural Organization (FAO). 1992. *Horticultural Improvement Project: Project Findings and Recommendations, The Gambia.* Prepared for the Government of The Gambia by FAO/United Nations Development Programme. Rome: FAO.

Friedland, William. 1984. Commodity Systems Analysis. *Research in Rural Sociology* 1: 221–235.

Friedmann, Harriet. 1987. The Family Farm and the International Food Regimes. In Teodor Shanin, ed., *Peasants and Peasant Society.* Oxford: Blackwell.

Grindle, Merilee, and M. Roemer. 1995. Insights from the Economic Recovery Program for Sub-Saharan Africa. In Steven Radelet and Malcolm McPherson, eds., *Economic Recovery in The Gambia: Insights for Adjustment in Sub-Saharan Africa.* Cambridge, Mass.: Harvard University Press.

Hadjmichael, Michael T., Thomas Rumbaugh, and Eric Verreydt. 1992. *The Gambia: Economic Adjustment in a Small Open Economy.* International Monetary Fund (IMF) Occasional Paper 100. Washington, D.C.: IMF.

Islam, Nurul. 1990. *Horticultural Exports of Developing Countries: Past Performances, Future Prospects, and Policy Issues.* Research Report No. 80. Washington, D.C.: International Food Policy Research Institute (IFPRI).

Jabara, Cathy. 1990. *Economic Reform and Poverty in The Gambia: A Survey of Pre- and Post-ERP Experience.* Washington, D.C.: Cornell University Food and Nutrition Policy Program.

Jaffee, Steven M. 1991. Marketing Africa's Horticultural Exports. Paper presented to the Workshop on Globalization of Fresh Fruits and Vegetables, University of California, Santa Cruz, December.

Kakoza, J., R. Basanti, T. Ehrleck, and R. Prem. 1995. *The Gambia—Recent Economic Developments.* IMF Staff Country Report No. 95/123. Washington, D.C.: IMF.

Landell Mills Associates. 1989. *A Market Survey for Gambian Horticultural Crops in the UK, Sweden, The Netherlands and the Federal Republic of Germany: Final Report.* Commissioned by the Export Market Development Division of the Commonwealth Secretariat. Bath, U.K.: Landell Mills Associates.

Little, Peter D. 1994. Contract Farming and the Development Question. In Peter Little and Michael J. Watts, eds., *Living under Contract: Contract Farming and Agrarian Transformation in Sub-Saharan Africa.* Madison: University of Wisconsin Press.

Little, Peter D., and Catherine Dolan. 1993. *Horticultural Production and Trade in the Peri-Urban Area of Banjul, The Gambia.* Binghamton, N.Y.: Institute for Development Anthropology.

McMichael, Philip, ed. 1994. *The Global Restructuring of Agro-Food Systems.* Ithaca, N.Y.: Cornell University Press.

McMichael, Philip, and David Myhre. 1991. Global Regulation versus the Nation-State: Agro-Food Systems and the New Politics of Capital. *Capital and Class* 43: 83–105.

Meerman, Jacob. 1997. *Reforming Agriculture: The World Bank Goes to Market.* Washington, D.C.: The World Bank.

Ministry of Agriculture. 1992. *Statistical Yearbook of Gambian Agriculture: 1991.* Department of Planning, Ministry of Agriculture, Banjul, The Gambia.

Ministry of Trade, Industry, and Employment. n.d. Statistical Data. Banjul, The Gambia.

Mintz, Sidney. 1985. *Sweetness and Power.* New York: Basic Books.

Mukumbu, Mulinge. 1995. Impact of Export Horticultural Production on Rural Income Growth and Poverty Alleviation in Kenya. Paper presented at the Workshop on Poverty Alleviation through International Trade, January 10–13, Santiago, Chile.

Paus, Eva, ed. 1988. *Struggle Against Dependence: Non-Traditional Export Growth in Central America and the Caribbean.* Boulder, Colo.: Westview Press.

Radelet, Steven. 1995. Donor Support for the Economic Recovery Program. In Steven Radelet and Malcolm McPherson, eds., *Economic Recovery in The Gambia: Insights for Adjustment in Sub-Saharan Africa.* Cambridge, Mass.: Harvard University Press.

Radelet, Steven, and Malcolm McPherson. 1995. Epilogue: The July Coup d'Etat. In Steven Radelet and Malcolm McPherson, eds., *Economic Recovery in The Gambia: Insights for Adjustment in Sub-Saharan Africa.* Cambridge, Mass.: Harvard University Press.

Roth, Michael, Ben Carr, and Jeff Cochrane. 1994. *Land Rights and Intra-Household Employment and Resource Use in the Peri-Urban Area of Banjul, The Gambia.* Madison, Wisc.: Land Tenure Center.

Stonich, Susan. 1991. The Promotion of Non-Traditional Exports in Honduras. *Development and Change* 22: 725–755.

Sumberg, James E., and Christine Okali. 1987. *Workshop on NGO-Sponsored Vegetable Gardening Projects in The Gambia: A Report and Summary.* Banjul, The Gambia.

Task Force on the Formulation of a National Industrial Policy. 1993. Banjul, The Gambia: Ministry of Trade, Industry, and Employment.

Watts, Michael J. 1994. Life Under Contract: Contract Farming, Agrarian Restructuring, and Flexible Accumulation. In Peter D. Little and Michael J. Watts, eds., *Living under Contract: Contract Farming and Agrarian Transformation in Sub-Saharan Africa.* Madison: University of Wisconsin Press.

World Bank. 1981. *Accelerated Development in Sub-Saharan Africa: An Agenda for Action.* Washington, D.C.: The World Bank.

———. 1989. *Sub-Saharan Africa: From Crisis to Sustainable Growth.* Washington, D.C.: The World Bank.

4

The Globalization of Agricultural Commodity Systems: Examining Peasant Resistance to International Agribusiness

Lois Stanford

INTRODUCTION

With the passage of the General Agreement on Trades and Tariffs (GATT) in 1986 and the North American Free Trade Agreement (NAFTA) in 1994, global trade now integrates local agricultural economies into international markets as never before. The concept of a commodity system offers a useful methodological framework for social scientists to examine vertical linkages across levels of an international economic system and to consider how conditions at particular levels impinge upon local communities and producers. Agricultural economists have long employed the agribusiness commodity system as a methodological framework for studying all participants in the production, processing, and marketing of a single agricultural commodity. Recent studies by anthropologists and rural sociologists demonstrate the usefulness of a commodity systems approach for exploring the historical, social, and political structures of specific commodity systems (Friedland 1984; Friedland, Barton, and Thomas 1981).

Although the global economy integrates local economies, many social scientists have expressed reservations about the deterministic nature of political economy models, turning instead toward models of individual agency and action. Drawing on Scott's (1985; 1990) discussions of resistance, this chapter examines local action, response, and resistance within a single agricultural export commodity system. By placing local agency within an international commodity system, I credit poor peasants' capacity to take action and to resist, without losing sight of the constraints and dangers they face in doing so.

In the Mexican case examined here, national policy changes from 1988 to 1994 reduced state-dominated development and integrated peasant producers more directly into an international market. In this Mexican case, export commodity systems historically have structured the regional agricultural economy, thereby influencing the political and social organization of rural society. My particular focus is the state of Michoacán on Mexico's western coast, which was traditionally a major commercial agricultural region for both domestic and U.S. export markets. In Michoacán, the tropical lowlands of the valley of Apatzingán benefited from irrigation, as well as infrastructural and social development through Mexico's River Basin Development Programs (Barkin and King 1970). As the cultivated area expanded from 42,000 to 205,000 hectares, export production of cotton, limes, cantaloupe, and watermelon increased from 8 percent to 56 percent of the valley's cultivated area (Fernández, Gil, and Singuín 1986, 111). Infrastructural development was accompanied by aggressive agrarian reform programs that directed irrigated land of high quality toward peasants. By the late 1970s, *ejidatarios,* or land reform beneficiaries, comprised 88 percent of farmers and controlled 76 percent of the land within the irrigation district, situated within Michoacán's tropical lowlands (Barajas 1979, 54). As president of Mexico from 1934–1940, and later as the administrative director of the Río Balsas Commission, Lázaro Cárdenas personally intervened (on behalf of peasants of this region) in government-initiated programs of land redistribution, commercial agriculture, and peasant organization. Other Michoacán peasants, particularly those in the highlands, viewed the *ejidatarios* of the valley of Apatzingán as the "spoiled grandchildren of Lázaro Cárdenas."[1]

In spite of active peasant involvement in commercial agriculture from 1930 to 1995, export commodity systems were structured to allow state control over production; as a result, the system limited peasant influence on, and knowledge of, market operations. The region experienced boom-and-bust cycles of commercial crops, including limes and rice (1930–1950), cotton (1955–1970), cantaloupe (1970–1990), and, currently, mango and limes. During each such period, producers shifted into specific commercial or export crops that dominated the irrigation district. These commodity systems possessed vertical linkages to international markets that transcended *ejido* boundaries. Such systems organized production, channeled inputs and credit, and commercialized operations, thereby creating a system of social, economic, and political relations that cut across existing community and *ejido* boundaries. Although most *ejidatarios* pursued multiple economic activities, those who grew export crops depended more heavily on them for their annual household incomes than on other activities. As a result, *ejidatarios* in the irrigation district came to be socially and politically associated with the export commodity system in which they participated. Thus, in the Tierra Caliente, a farmer who grew cotton was called an *algodonero;* a mango producer, a *manguero;* and a melon grower, a *melonero.* Through their participation in commodity-specific peasant unions, producers of a single crop organized, demonstrated, and actively attempted to defend their common interests within a single export commodity system.

In the case of all commodities (cotton, lime, mango, cantaloupe, and honeydew melon), the agricultural industries operated as monopsonistic economic systems. An alliance of government agencies and agribusinesses controlled the purchase of the commodity and market access; and producers could not enter other markets (Ferguson and Gould 1975, 407–416). In the case of cantaloupe, the monopsonistic export system was dominated by U.S. companies (primarily in McAllen, Texas) that controlled access to U.S. markets. Mexico's federal government, at various times, required peasants to join legally registered agricultural organizations in order to obtain necessary planting and irrigation permits. U.S. companies contracted these local organizations to deliver the agricultural product and financed production by channeling credit and chemical inputs to them. In alliance with foreign companies, Mexican state agencies regulated planting permits in order to restrict production and to maintain high local prices for the final product. The system that channeled financial support, permits, information, and export market access through the U.S. companies and local organizations was rife with corruption. Through long experience with commercial and export crops, and with the accompanying financial malfeasance and abuse of power, peasants in this region developed a cynical attitude toward the economic opportunities of export agriculture. Although they lacked influence over international market conditions, peasants' consciousness of their own exploitation became the basis for an ideology and practice of resistance toward the more powerful government authorities and U.S. agribusiness representatives.

James Scott's landmark book (1985) shifted the focus of social science research on peasants away from infrequent instances of overt peasant rebellion and toward the more common, individual, less visible acts of "everyday" resistance. Drawing on Antonio Gramsci's and others' works on hegemony, Scott argues that peasants are fully conscious that they are exploited and recognize the inevitability of their situation, but do not accept it as legitimate (1985, 304–350). Their everyday acts of resistance, hidden from the dominant elite, express their consciousness and desire to retain some autonomy over their own lives. In a later book, Scott (1990) analyzes the discourse or "art" of resistance, exploring power and social relations in highly structured systems of domination such as slavery, serfdom, and caste-based societies. Here he examines three different kinds of transcripts, including the public discourse, the "hidden" transcript of the powerless, and the private discourse of the powerful, demonstrating how the persistence of these often conflicting discourses allows room for limited negotiation and "space for a dissident sub-culture" (1990, 108–135). By comparing these "arts" of resistance across societies, Scott contends that "structurally similar forms of domination will bear a family resemblance to one another" (1990). Although Scott's study provides critical insights into subordinated peoples' struggles under slavery and in other settings, it does not focus on expressions of resistance in capitalist economies.

In this chapter, I extend Scott's discussion to contemporary capitalist systems by examining the case of peasant resistance in the Tierra Caliente of Michoacán, Mexico, from 1968–1990. Exploring peasant resistance within a fresh fruit and vegetable export commodity system provides an opportunity to further develop Scott's ideas. This particular case is important for several reasons. First, both small, private land-holders and *ejidatarios* in this region entered into commercial agriculture during the 1940s and, through peasant unions, actively participated in a capitalist, export agricultural economy. Contrary to Scott's earlier work (1976), these peasants did not fight back in an attempt to reject capitalism but rather as a strategy to defend their interests in a capitalist system. In light of increased international agricultural trade, Michoacán peasants and their forms of resistance are similar to those of other contemporary third world peasants (Paige 1975; Brockett 1990).

Second, the timing of these resistance activities allows us to examine resistance within the context of major socioeconomic and political changes. Peasant resistance in the Tierra Caliente emerged under, and as a response to, Mexico's state-dominated capitalism from 1940 to the 1980s. Since 1988, Mexico has been privatizing the national economy, a program initiated under President Carlos Salinas and continued under President Ernesto Zedillo. Restructuring Tierra Caliente's agricultural economy has undermined the ability of peasants to resist in a privatized capitalist economy.

Third, Tierra Caliente *ejidatarios* historically established a national and international reputation in the fresh fruit and vegetable export industry for open confrontation and local action. Through public demonstrations, they manipulated the capitalist system in a limited manner to serve the interests of local producers and entrepreneurs. Scott notes the difference between the "public" transcript, in which the powerless allow their oppressors to see, and the "hidden" transcript, in which the oppressed privately express their frustration and anger. In the Tierra Caliente, the public transcript was always one of open defiance, in which local entrepreneurs and leaders of peasant organizations publicly expressed their hostility toward the state and foreign agribusiness. This public discourse obscured the peasant leaders' corruption and informal alliances with state officials and agribusiness representatives, a situation characteristic of economic systems incompletely integrated into a capitalist system. This case fits Scott's definition of an "ideological contradiction" in which the "economic behavior is increasingly based on the logic of the new market opportunities, while their [political elites'] social authority has been based on traditional forms of domination" (1985, 311). Elites' political control over local peasants is based on a traditional system of patron-client relations, and patrons' power and legitimacy depend on their ability both to protect clients and deliver expected services.

Finally, as Mexico recently has privatized its agricultural economy, peasant resistance has shifted from a public transcript of confrontation to the passive resistance of hidden, individual acts depicted in Scott's earlier work (1985). In his recent work as well, Scott continues to highlight the trajectory from private to public confrontation, citing that first moment of public expression, in which, "the open declaration of the hidden transcript in the teeth of power is typically experienced, both by the speaker and by those who share his or her condition, as a moment in which truth is finally spoken in the place of equivocation and lies" (1990, 208). As concerned social scientists, we sympathize with dramatic and public confrontations in which the powerless reject domination by elites. The case of *ejidatarios* from the Tierra Caliente suggests that the strength of local agency or action also must be measured in its economic impact, and, unfortunately, in the type of retaliation these acts of resistance incur.

This chapter examines three specific acts of resistance (in 1968, 1980, and 1988) within the structure of a fresh fruit and vegetable export industry. I compare these events in terms of type, arena, target, level, impact, and retaliation that resulted from each historic act of resistance. In contrast to Scott's findings about resistance under slavery, I find that this case, as representative of a peasantry's long experience with capitalism, does not demonstrate a progression from private, passive resistance to public confrontation. Instead peasants who are frustrated with the inability of public mobilizations to transform capitalist systems increasingly retreat into the private, hidden acts that eventually erode agribusiness profits. As discussed in the conclusion, this shift undermines small producers' ability to defend their interests in today's open economy.

1968: WITHHOLDING THE PRODUCT

By the late 1960s, facing increased production costs and low international prices for cotton, Mexican state officials searched for crop alternatives. The Mexican Ministry of Agriculture encouraged expansion of export fresh fruit production, primarily cantaloupe and honeydew melon. In 1967, the U.S. Environmental Protection Agency precipitated political confrontations when it identified Endrin, a pesticide commonly used in cotton production, on Michoacán melon shipments arriving at the U.S. border. At the time, local newspapers claimed the blockade was arbitrary, and that the United States had other reasons for rejecting Mexican fruit.[2] Interviews with local producers and peasant leaders suggested more conspiratorial explanations, such as the notion that the United States was rejecting the April and May harvest because Texas had started production, and the United States did not welcome competition with Mexican producers. Other interviewees cited rumors of a war between two major agribusinesses (in McAllen, Texas) that were responsible for buying most of the region's harvest, and still others contended that the United States was retaliating against Mexican producers because the national government refused to break political relations with Cuba.[3]

State agencies and local producers concurred that if producers were organized, they would be better able to defend their interests against foreign agribusinesses. The representative of the National Confederation of Horticultural Producers (CNPH) contended that local producers needed to organize themselves in order to eliminate the "personal interests" of the foreign companies.[4] That year producers acquired state support to establish the first local agricultural association, the AAL Apatzingán, which unified all regional producers of a single commodity—cantaloupe. From the start, farmers publicly expressed their anger and intent to use their organization to confront U.S. agribusinesses. As one *ejidatario* commented in 1968 to a local newspaper: "This year, the *meloneros* will be vindicated. 1968 will be the year of our unification, our liberation from those coyotes, and our real conquest of the great North American markets."[5]

During the 1967–1968 season, the AAL Apatzingán bypassed brokers representing U.S. companies and sold fruit by commission to U.S. wholesalers for U.S. dollars, rather than selling in Mexican pesos to local buyers. The association contracted refrigerated cars to ship fruit by rail to the U.S. border and enlisted the support of local icehouses to produce ice to coincide with the shipments.[6] By 3 March 1968 U.S. wholesalers began to remit commissions from the U.S. market; local newspapers reported market prices at $7.20 per crate, the highest price in export history.[7]

A few local producers sold their harvests to commercial packinghouses in the valley instead of delivering the harvest to the association's packinghouse, as agreed to at the beginning of the season. In response, members called a special assembly to attack publicly and reprimand the twenty producers who had betrayed their association. Angry members knew who the transgressors were and called for the traitors' names to be revealed publicly at the meeting. The board of directors hedged, claiming that if the names were revealed, there would be "personal problems" among the producers. In response, one *ejidatario* stood up and addressed the assembly as follows: "If our own leaders are afraid to act, then give us producers the names of those turncoats, and we'll take care of them ourselves."[8] He sat down amid thundering applause. During successive weeks, producers with the regional association met and continued to denounce publicly any producer who sold directly to U.S. brokers' private packinghouses, instead of delivering their fruit to the association's packinghouse for commission sale to U.S. wholesalers. In later interviews, U.S. brokers recalled acts of hidden sabotage by the *ejidatarios*; these included slashing truck tires at night, in order to evict commercial operations in the Tierra Caliente. For the *ejidatarios*, this first season brought a heady rush of success in confronting gringo brokers. (Whether the U.S. businesses retaliated for this initial confrontation remains a hotly debated topic locally.)

During the first season, the association successfully bypassed the brokers and sold fruit by commission. By demonstrating their capacity to confront U.S. businesses, producers gained politically, and they profited financially from higher product prices. In the assemblies *ejidatarios*, private producers, and their leaders clearly targeted U.S. agribusinesses and their local representatives as enemies, specifically stating how these brokers prevented local access to the winter fresh fruit and vegetable market in the United States. In contrast, in newspaper articles and interviews, *ejidatarios* never identified their own leaders as part of the problem. The united front against the gringos also served the interests of the state. From 1968 to 1970, government political support and subsidized credit facilitated local associations' takeover of the commercial packinghouses.

Unfortunately, these temporary gains were offset by events during the following season (1968–1969). By November 1968, other associations were being established in Tierra Caliente municipalities, thus undermining the united front presented the previous season. According to a local newspaper editor:

> Pessimism reigns among the *meloneros* because the state has given the green light to a new association in Nueva Italia. This will only serve the interests of the gringos. At the initial meeting, there were only fourteen people attending, the majority of them *ejidatarios* who have never grown cantaloupe before. This association is only a front, a front for the likes of Jack Simmons and Othal Brand.[9]

Some interviewed later assigned responsibility to U.S. agribusinesses for financing new associations and packinghouses in Tierra Caliente towns. Others blamed their own compatriots, who sold out the collective in favor of individual, personal gain. Within the first year after the successful confrontation, the *meloneros'* collective identity vis-à-vis the international agricultural industry was eroding. Efforts to continue direct sales to U.S. wholesalers were further undermined by local U.S. brokers who actively pursued contracts with the newer associations. These associations sold their product locally at lower prices to U.S. agribusiness brokers, and the increased competition meant that the original association could not continue selling by commission. In a 1988 interview, one of the original leaders sadly remembered the experience:

> We organized to sell directly. Then, the companies worked with some of the associations. It's a tragedy that I just can't tell you about because I would be a very bad Mexican. I can't tell you what really happened because I can't speak badly of my own people.

By 1969, even the AAL Apatzingán was selling locally to U.S. agribusinesses, and for the next twenty years, few organizations attempted to sell by commission. Although this historic act of resistance failed to transform the monopsonistic structure of the export commodity system, it convinced *ejidatarios* of their ability to confront powerful brokers and foreign businesses if they acted collectively. They also learned that confrontational acts bring retaliation. For these peasants, the international market system was not a vague and impersonal universe; rather, it included organized individuals who sought to undermine any efforts by regional producers to improve their own economic conditions. Local elites, particularly the leaders of agricultural organizations, exploited local perceptions of U.S. agribusiness as the enemy in their efforts to downplay their own role in undermining collective organizations. Conflicts occurred at various levels of the system: between regional producers and foreigners and, within the region, between producers and their leaders. Conflicts between leaders resulted from competition over access to credit, production contracts, and producer support. Furthermore, consciousness was never an issue. In interviews and newspaper accounts, producers freely identified the names of "collaborators," generally attaching obscene adjectives to express fully their opinions. As political and economic conflicts developed in this export commodity system, producers also identified and attacked their own leaders.

1980: SEIZING THE UNION OFFICES

During the 1970s, the Ministry of Commerce collected an ad valorem tax of 7 percent from all Mexican fruit exports to the United States. Under the Echeverría administration, however, the federal agrarian reform law included an article that forbade the federal government from taxing *ejidal* production. In 1979, the director of the CNPH discovered this error and used the law to collect a reimbursement for *ejidal* sector production for all regional unions belonging to the CNPH.[10] An estimated 12 million pesos due to AAL Apatzingán producers was returned to the CNPH, which, in turn, returned the money to the regional union. The regional union, however, did not distribute the money among its member producers, nor did it notify them of the reimbursement. Only after the *ejidal* unions filed a legal injunction against the president of the regional union did it acknowledge receipt of the money.[11]

By July 1980, the union president's actions were public knowledge, and both private producers and *ejidatarios* called for his impeachment and urged legal pressure to make the regional union return the money. A public letter was printed in the local newspaper and signed by a group of *ejidatarios;* they accused Juan Aguirre, the regional union president, of lying to them. The letter also stated that Aguirre could not argue that the money was intended for a social fund, to benefit all melon producers, since he could not produce the legal paperwork to support the claim.[12] In a 1990 interview, an *ejidatario* activist recalled,

> Juan told us that the social fund would provide credit for all melon producers, not just *ejidatarios,* but also private producers, investors, and renters. Then, he said that the fund would be used as credit to buy inputs, that they would loan the money to us with interest. Well, if the money belonged to *ejidatarios,* how is it possible to lend us money that is rightfully ours? The regional union was not a credit union. How could he say that he was going to lend me my own money?[13]

On 26 August 1980, 306 *ejidatarios* invaded the offices of the Regional Agricultural Union, "Jose Maria Morelos," denouncing the union's president for failing to return the estimated 12 million pesos that had been improperly collected and later returned to the regional union in 1979. Those who participated in this public confrontation remember painting signs, traveling to the *ejidos* to hold assemblies, and busing in *ejidatarios* to storm the union's offices. Local organizers have fond memories of their successful confrontation with local elites.[14] The lawyer who represented the *ejidatarios* later explained:

> This action did not represent an invasion, as Juan claimed. The *ejidatarios* were occupying the local offices where they had a legal right since they were the ones paying the rent. We had tried all other means to solicit the money. We had exercised our legal rights of petition to the tax applied to the harvests of 1977–1978, 1978–1979, and 1979–1980. We originally petitioned the CNPH and they informed us that they had

already sent the money to the regional union. We tried all other means to solicit the money from the regional union. Nothing else worked. The president forced us to take this action.[15]

From 26 August to 12 September 1980, in groups of thirty to fifty men, *ejidatario* members of seven agricultural associations continuously occupied the offices. On 12 September, leaving some members at the regional office, fifty *ejidatarios* traveled by bus to Mexico City to the national headquarters of the Ministry of Agriculture and Water Resources (SARH) to demand that the government force the union president to return the money.[16] When SARH officials claimed they lacked the authority to intervene, the *ejidatarios* continued to occupy the office. On 24 September 1980, an estimated 1,000 *ejidatarios* held an assembly outside the regional union to voice their demands.[17] In retaliation, the union hired airplanes to drop leaflets throughout the valley that had been signed by the union president and other members of the regional union's board of directors. The leaflets alleged that the *ejidatarios* and lawyers involved in the occupation were members of the Communist party.

Facing the threat of continued occupation, Juan Aguirre succumbed to the pressure and arranged to have the money redistributed evenly among the organizations. The union required, however, that the associations legally file for the reimbursement. The lawyer representing the AAL Nueva Italia filed for his association, but none of the other associations did, nor did they ever receive any form of financial compensation. Following the public shame of incarceration, Aguirre resigned his presidency and never again served in office at the regional level, although he served in the CNPH. Despite this public shame, he eventually forgave the lawyer who filed the charges against him. As one informant recounted:

> You know that David [the lawyer] now serves as the legal advisor for the AAL Chilatan and for Juan. Juan forgave David for putting him in jail. Juan just thought that he had everything under control, and then David caught him. He has a lot of respect for David because David is even more cunning than he is. Why, Juan even sent mariachis for David's daughter's birthday.[18]

In this instance, the public confrontation over collective funds forced the regional union to comply with *ejidatario* demands; private, hidden acts would not have produced the timely response needed. Peasant occupation of association offices also reminded regional officials of the line they should not cross. Most *ejidatarios* were fully conscious of the numerous ways in which their own leaders cheated them in this commodity system. Although local elites presented themselves as defenders against foreign agribusiness, most *ejidatarios* were aware of, and talked among themselves about, the deals the leaders cut for themselves with U.S. brokers. *Ejidatarios* tolerated corruption, but they also used the public arena to confront their leaders if they felt the latter had overstepped "corruption" boundaries. Furthermore, in occupying union offices and traveling to the national SARH offices, the *ejidatarios* demonstrated their capacity to bypass local political officials and take their problems to the national level. In turn, national officials pressured local leaders to comply with *ejidatario* demands because they were more concerned about bad publicity than about financial resources. Through their successful political mobilization efforts, Tierra Caliente *ejidatarios* solidified their national reputation as being politically combative and savvy. Furthermore, businesses remained unaffected and outside the local fray. Union leaders who lost this political battle could not retaliate directly against the producers given the public nature of the mobilization and local support for producers' actions.

Conflicts within the region had costs as well. Through public meetings and newspapers, peasants could challenge corrupt leaders and vent their frustrations, but most leaders continued to hold important political and economic positions—despite temporary setbacks—and the corruption continued unabated. New producer organizations continued to form, forcing more battles over limited planting and export permits. In addition, new packinghouses undermined the collective solidarity of producer organizations. Corrupt managers and leaders cheated their own producers without getting caught. As demonstrated in the quotes above, the *ejidatario* describes the 1980 office seizure as almost a personal conflict between the union president and the lawyer. The president expressed no regrets for his actions, only admiration for the cunning lawyer and his political maneuvers. This ideology of competition and underlying respect for trickery further undermined producers' loyalty to their own organizations.

1988: INDIVIDUAL SABOTAGE

During the 1980s, political mobilization became more difficult to organize and less effective as a means of confronting local elites or foreign agribusinesses. In 1970, there were five producer organizations. By 1980, thirty organizations were registered and, by 1987, there were forty-three, consisting of more than 2,500 farmers, *ejidatarios* and private producers in the irrigation district. The numerous organizations undermined local efforts to confront collectively either U.S. agribusinesses or regional leaders. *Ejidatarios* and small farmers more often turned to passive, hidden acts of resistance in an effort to retain some autonomy and profits in an increasingly corrupt and combative commodity system. Expanded numbers of producers and organizations also undermined efforts to limit production and preserve product quality. Overproduction and poor product quality led U.S. companies to reduce seasonal prices paid to local producers and to complain bitterly about the "decline" of the region as a cantaloupe-producing area.

As the number of producers and parcels increased, agricultural technicians, hired by the organization to which each producer had to belong, could visit a particular farmer's field only once per week. Lack of direct supervision allowed *ejidatarios* to sell the insecticides or fertilizer they received and to divert to other crops chemicals and credit received for cantaloupe production. Others overplanted their allotments, spreading credit and inputs over larger parcels. In addition, *ejidatarios* used credit obtained for capital expenses to hire local labor (often their relatives) from landless households within the *ejido*. Given the volatility of export prices, a producer was never sure of the income he would earn until the end of the agricultural cycle. Thus, many *ejidatarios* viewed the production process rather than final products as their income source.

Local and regional authorities complained bitterly about declining yields and poor fruit quality and responded to individual peasant resistance with increased regulation that failed. Legal statutes restricted total production and staggered production permits in two-week intervals throughout the planting season. In 1987, local authorities and peasant leaders signed public documents agreeing that producers would abide by technical recommendations that called for the postharvest destruction of crop residue and for planting in large, compact areas (rather than in individual parcels) for more effective pest control and management (Banco de Crédito 1987). In addition, the regional union contracted a private company to police production and commercialization by inspecting farmers' fields, supervising the distribution of agricultural inputs and credit, and periodically making unannounced visits to the associations' packinghouses during the harvest (Compañía Impulsora 1987).

The 1987–1988 melon season was marked by increased resentment and frustration on the part of *ejidatarios*. They were incensed over the regional authorities' efforts to collectivize farming in compact areas, believing it was a tactic to enable technicians to supervise more closely their production activities. All production stages provided income opportunities for farmers, as long as they retained individual control over the production process. As unequal partners in an export commodity system, *ejidatarios* only controlled production within their own parcels. If authorities shifted production to compact areas, the farmers would lose their limited access to export income. They particularly resented the regional union's efforts to police them, since these costs were covered by an ad valorem tax on the *ejidatarios'* own harvests.

In early January 1988, with the harvest well under way, U.S. buyers dropped melon prices to an average of $3 per crate, followed by $2 per crate, a price that did not even cover Tierra Caliente production costs.[19] Given the low prices, U.S. businesses pressured packinghouses to restrict their export volume. In an effort to cut their own losses, associations restricted agricultural inputs and credit to producers—and, in some cases, even dropped certain fields—based on assessments that the fields' yield would not cover production costs. In these cases, an association official would issue the *ejidatario* a "letter of freedom," stating that he would receive no more credit and that he was free to sell his harvest to any commercial packinghouse. *Ejidatarios* never received any prior notice and were left standing in their fields, holding their papers. As the director of one association drove off in his pickup truck, a devastated *ejidatario* turned to me and said, "Those double-crossers. . . . They abandoned me. They left me to fail on my own."

In response to their leaders' betrayal, *ejidatarios* brought their fruit to private, commercial packinghouses. Even those *ejidatarios* who still had credit contracts recognized that they too could be abandoned any day. Furthermore, they could not earn any income if they delivered their fruit to their association's packinghouse and honored their credit obligations. The cumulative impact of these individual acts of resistance devastated the local agricultural economy. Packinghouse data indicate that each *ejido* association lost 270 tons of melon in a two-week period from 20 March to 20 April 1988 (Stanford 1991). Locals said that they had never seen such chaos in the entire history of melon production in the Tierra Caliente.

Ejidatarios now crossed the line from passive resistance to active revolt. They were frustrated by the dominant classes' failure to deliver the support or resources due them according to the dominant ideology (Scott 1985, 311–312). They tolerated their leaders' corruption as long as export agriculture remained profitable. Still, these actions did not resemble the public confrontations of earlier days. *Ejidatarios* communicated about prices and export volumes at certain commercial packinghouses, but each farmer delivered his or her fruit independently. The resistance did not constitute a collective, organized confrontation with local directors, since each *ejidatario* delivered his or her own fruit. Individual decisions, however, were based on informal group consensus, because no *ejidatario* would take action that risked ostracism from fellow community members.

CONCLUSION: CHALLENGES TO RESISTANCE IN THE NEW PRIVATIZED ECONOMY

Mexico's 1988 to 1994 economic privatization devastated Tierra Caliente's agricultural economy (Stanford 1994). U.S. agribusinesses prefer to plant cantaloupe, honeydew melon, and cucumber in other regions, where they do not have to contend with independent, confrontative *ejidatarios*. State reduction of agricultural credit has decreased agricultural production. During both rainy and dry seasons in the Tierra Caliente, many fields in the irrigation district lay abandoned. As one *ejidatario* told me in 1994:

> So, when it's planting time, there's no money for planting. The ones who are fortunate, well, they can grow corn. Some agribusinesses come here in the winter to plant cucumber, but that has never amounted to more than 3,000 hectares. The other possibility is mango; there's 7,000 hectares and most of it belongs to us, *ejidatarios*. But, there's no agricultural extension now, it's all growing wild.
>
> The globalization, the economic opening, and all this, it's good for manufacturing and for industry. . . . But, we're farmers, we are *ejidatarios*. We are losing everything.

A symbolic separation of political and economic arenas emerged in Tierra Caliente's commodity system. By allowing *ejidatarios* and peasant leaders to vent their frustrations and anger publicly at various times throughout the history of this crop, a corrupt and exploitative economic system could continue. Local entrepreneurs and leaders publicly expressed allegiance with their followers who criticized the transgressions of foreign companies but continued to steal from their own organizations. Scott (1990, 206–212) describes that moment of "electricity" in which the powerless first stand up to the powerful. In the Tierra Caliente, the institutionalization of this confrontation, through public expressions of resistance, converted it to a farce. These *ejidatarios* not only were aware of their leaders' transgressions, they also recognized that public pronouncements of "solidarity" were mere rhetoric. Increasingly frustrated with a lack of improvement in their economic situations, *ejidatarios* turned to the individual acts of sabotage that Scott (1985, 1990) describes as passive resistance.

In other regions of Mexico, particularly Chiapas, peasant frustration with state-initiated *campesino* organizations led to the emergence of more autonomous associations dedicated to social reform and political mobilization (Moguel, Hernández, and Botey 1992). By 1992, *campesino* organizations in Chiapas already had demonstrated against the economic and political reforms of the Salinas administration. The passage of NAFTA and Mexican constitutional reforms created the final abuses to emergent organizations of indigenous, landless peasants and smallholders. The 1994 Zapatista uprising granted a political space to indigenous peasants to renegotiate the government's political reforms (Harvey 1998).

In contrast, *ejidatarios* in the lowlands of Michoacán already held land through agrarian reform. Dependent on commercial agriculture, however, they lacked access to finance capital. In adopting strategies of passive resistance and sabotage, *ejidatarios* engaged in the financial malfeasance that made them unattractive to private investors once the government reduced subsidized credit programs. *Ejidatarios'* experiences with demonstrations and office invasions increased their cynicism about the potential accomplishments of political activities. Instead of turning their frustration toward government officials, Tierra Caliente residents expressed their sense of futility against one another, leading to a rapid rise in rural violence.

The evolution of a dissident "subculture," or a culture of resistance, reflected a complex and ambivalent relationship between peasants and the state. Mexico's federal government played a critical role in the establishment of *ejidal* associations in the Tierra Caliente by providing political support, subsidized credit, and legal restrictions that forced U.S. agribusinesses to work with the local associations. Without such institutional support, it is unlikely that local *ejidatarios* would have exerted the economic and political force they exhibited in Michoacán. Once the institutional structure was established, however, the state confounded *ejidatarios'* efforts to operate independently. State support accompanied paternalistic control over financial decisions, marketing efforts, and credit repayment. *Ejidal* organizations emerged under the tutelage and domination of the state; as a result, *ejidatarios* defended their economic interests against U.S. agribusinesses through public confrontations and, later, individual acts of sabotage. Through these different forms of resistance, *ejidatarios* shaped their organizations in terms of both their external relations and internal structures. As *ejidatarios* shifted from active confrontation in the 1960s and 1970s to individual acts of passive resistance in the 1980s, they undermined their own economic well-being. As a means of retaliating against their own leaders and U.S. agribusinesses, *ejidatarios* adopted strategies such as siphoning credit or reneging on credit contracts. In a privatized agricultural economy, the persistence of such confrontation, combined with a pattern of reneging on contracts, further undermines efforts to organize regional production and commercialization.

This culture of resistance also fostered hostile relations between the local agrarian elite and *ejidal* unions and their members. In 1994, interviews with leaders of some of the newer agricultural associations revealed the elite's resentment of Tierra Caliente *ejidatarios*. Private producers and the agrarian bourgeoisie now openly express their hostility toward *ejidatarios*. In group interviews, cotton producers stated that they would never support the involvement of *ejidal* organizations in cotton production. The few organizations who continue to plant melon are led by private producers and local entrepreneurs; no *ejidal* organization actively functions in the export industry.

In an open privatized system, peasants cannot demand that the government grant them access to the international market; Mexico no longer exerts that kind of economic control. The culture of resistance that emerged in response to an export commodity system dominated by an alliance between the state and foreign agribusiness now precludes *ejidatario* participation in a privatized economy. The institutional arrangements of Mexico's neoliberal economy do not facilitate small farmer participation. In addition, agribusiness representatives remember the political confrontations of earlier years and take their business elsewhere.

Without the presence of local or regional organizations, *ejidatarios* who enter into commercial agriculture are increasingly drawn into international commodity systems. Changes in global conditions directly impinge on farmers' incomes and their ability to retain control over their land. Furthermore, these commodity systems respond to their own conditions and changes. Thus, local efforts to plan or effect policy are cross-cut by separate, vertically integrated commodity systems that connect local *ejidos* and producers to separate international systems. Indigenous entrepreneurs and producers searching for commercial agricultural opportunities bypass local authorities and establish their own contacts and buyers in the private sector. Private producers interviewed in 1994 see themselves as independent entrepreneurs whose survival depends on their own initiative and contacts with external financiers. They actively attempt to establish market contacts, obtain commercial marketing information on the U.S. fruit and vegetable industry, and link themselves directly with private U.S. companies. They clearly perceive the privatization of the export fruit and vegetable commodity system as both a danger to them (because they are not wealthy like the west Mexican producers from Sinaloa or Sonora) and an opportunity that requires them to move quickly to establish direct personal and economic ties with U.S. businesses.[20]

Ejidatarios in the Tierra Caliente of Michoacán have long been involved in commercial agriculture. Despite the promises of privatization and international market opportunities, *ejidatarios* are skeptical about the entire process. Never having trusted the state's agenda, they do not believe in the promised opportunities that supposedly await them under joint ventures with national and foreign companies. *Ejidatarios* fight a long legacy of state intervention and domination. Previously, they successfully negotiated limited influence and temporary spaces of power by direct confrontation with foreign businesses and state authorities under the state-dominated economy. Their sense of collectivity, however, was based on opposition, both to outsiders and to the government. In a few cases, these agricultural associations did develop an autonomous identity in which internal mechanisms linked their identification and obligations toward one another. Although they lack the necessary historical and practical experiences, peasants, entrepreneurs, and private farmers now recognize the need for new forms of association to defend their common regional interests in an open, market economy (Stanford 1998).

NOTES

I wish to thank Angelique Haugerud, Peter Little, and Priscilla Stone for their comments on an earlier version of this chapter. This analysis is based on key informant interviews conducted in Apatzingán, Michoacán, from 1988 to 1992 and on newspaper articles from the *Epoca: Voz del Valle*, a local newspaper that has reported on agricultural and political news since 1962. From June through July 1988, Hortensia Toscano, owner and founder of the newspaper, granted access to her personal archives. This chapter draws on newspaper accounts on agricultural production, organizations, and commercial marketing. From 1990 to 1992, the author conducted follow-up interviews with key informants who remembered the documented events. Taped interviews were transcribed in Spanish and then translated into English by the author. In both the translated and newspaper accounts and interviews, actual names have been altered to provide anonymity. In addition, residents of the Tierra Caliente, known for their forthrightness and directness, often employ obscenities in describing their political adversaries; in these cases, an approximate English translation has been chosen that may downplay the vehemence of their emotions.

The research upon which this chapter is based was funded by the U.S. Department of Education Fulbright-Hays Dissertation Research Abroad Fellowship (1987–1988), and by a New Mexico State University minigrant (1990).

1. The *ejido* is a communal landholding held by a community of peasant farmers, known as *ejidatarios*. After the Mexican Revolution (1910–1917), the government redistributed land to peasant communities, granting members usufruct rights while retaining the land titles. Unlike many regions of Mexico where peasants invaded land, in the Tierra Caliente of Michoacán, the government assumed primary responsibility for land redistribution. Under

his presidential administration (1934–1940), Lázaro Cárdenas established many new *ejidos* in the Tierra Caliente for both lowland and highland Michoacán peasants, as a means of rewarding peasant political support (see Barajas 1979; Barkin and King 1970).

2. *Epoca: Voz del Valle,* 2 April 1967.

3. *Epoca: Voz del Valle,* 2 April 1967.

4. This information is based on a 1988 interview conducted by the author with the former director of Affiliate Organizations and Promotion, National Confederation of Horticultural Producers (CNPH).

5. *Epoca: Voz del Valle,* 14 January 1968.

6. *Epoca: Voz del Valle,* 11 February 1968.

7. *Epoca: Voz del Valle,* 3 March 1968. Producers were paid in pesos, 90 pesos/crate, at the exchange rate of 12.5 pesos/US$1.

8. *Epoca: Voz del Valle,* 17 March 1968.

9. *Epoca: Voz del Valle,* 24 November 1968.

10. This information is based on a 1988 interview conducted by the author with the former director of Affiliate Organizations and Promotion, National Confederation of Horticultural Producers (CNPH). According to this CNPH representative, the CNPH never intended that the money be redistributed to individual *ejidatarios;* rather it was to be placed in a social fund to be used for collective benefit. The representative stated that he himself had written the rules for the collective fund, rules that were never implemented because the local lawyer started "agitating" the *ejidatarios.*

11. This information is based on interviews the author conducted in 1990 and 1991 with the local lawyer who served at that time for one of the plaintiff *ejidal* organizations in this legal case.

12. *Epoca: Voz del Valle,* 18 July 1980.

13. Interview with *ejidatario,* Apatzingán, Michoacán, July 1988.

14. *Epoca: Voz del Valle,* 29 August 1980.

15. Interview by author, Uruapon, Michoacán, June 1990.

16. *Epoca: Voz del Valle,* 12 September 1980.

17. *Epoca: Voz del Valle,* 26 September 1980.

18. Local producer, interview by author, Apatzingán, Michoacán, July 1988.

19. *Epoca: Voz del Valle,* 8 January 1988. Export crates of cantaloupe were graded by fruit size. For example, "12s" hold 12 cantaloupe, "15s" hold 15 cantaloupe, "18s" hold 18 cantaloupe and "23s" hold 23 cantaloupe. Prices refer to prices for the entire crate. Although U.S. dollar prices were quoted in local newspapers and among local producers, *ejidatarios* were paid in peso equivalents, based on the daily exchange rate.

20. Comparative analysis of different fruit and vegetable regions demonstrates a stratification between northern Mexico, which is expanding rapidly, and central Mexico, where export fruit and vegetable production has stagnated during the initial years of privatization (Stanford 1996).

REFERENCES

Banco de Crédito Rural del Pacífico Sur (BANRURAL). 1987. Reordenamiento de los organismos de productores de melón y pepino en el valle de Tierra Caliente. Reportes de mesas de trabajo número uno, dos, y tres. BANRURAL, Apatzingán, Michoacán. Unpublished report.

Barajas M., J. Encarnación. 1979. Breve historia del Distrito de Riego: Cupatitzio-Tepalcatepec. *Epoca: Realidad Política, Económica, y Social de Michoacán* 2(19): 52–56.

Barkin, David, and Timothy King. 1970. *Regional Economic Development: The River Basin Approach.* Cambridge: Cambridge University Press.

Brockett, Charles P. 1990. *Land, Power, and Poverty: Agrarian Transformation and Political Conflict in Central America.* Boston: Unwin Hyman.

Compañía Impulsora y Supervisora Agrícola de Michoacán (CISAM). 1987. *Contrato de servicios.* Apatzingán, Michoacán. Unpublished Document, financial contract.

Ferguson, Charles E., and James P. Gould. 1975. *Microeconomic Theory,* 4th ed. Homewood, Ill.: Richard D. Irwin.

Fernández, María Teresa, Francisco Javier Gil, and Evelyne Singuín. 1986. El monopolio de la producción rural: la Unión Agrícola Regional de Apatzingán. In Evelyne Durán et al., eds., *Las productores rurales y sus problemas en el occidente de México.* Mexico City: Facultad de Economía.

Friedland, William H. 1984. Commodity Systems Analysis: An Approach to the Sociology of Agriculture. In Harry K. Schwarzweller, ed., *Research in Rural Sociology and Development: A Research Annual.* Greenwich, Conn.: JAI Press.

Friedland, William H., Amy E. Barton, and Robert J. Thomas. 1981. *Manufacturing Green Gold: Capital, Labor, and Technology in the Lettuce Industry.* New York: Cambridge University Press.

Harvey, Neil. 1998. Rural Reforms and the Question of Autonomy in Chiapas. In Wayne Cornelius and David Myhre, eds., *The Transformation of Rural Mexico: Reforming the Ejido Sector.* La Jolla: Center for U.S.-Mexican Studies, University of California, San Diego.

Moguel, Julio, Luis Hernández, and Carlota Botey, eds. 1992. *Autonomía y los nuevos sujetos sociales en el desarrollo rural.* Mexico City: Siglo Veintiuno.

Paige, Jeffrey. 1975. *Agrarian Revolution: Social Movements and Export Agriculture in the Underdeveloped World.* New York: Free Press.

Scott, James C. 1976. *The Moral Economy of the Peasant: Subsistence and Revolution in Southeast Asia.* New Haven, Conn.: Yale University Press.

———. 1985. *Weapons of the Weak: Everyday Forms of Peasant Resistance.* New Haven, Conn.: Yale University Press.

———. 1990. *Domination and the Arts of Resistance: Hidden Transcripts.* New Haven, Conn.: Yale University Press.

Smith, Gavin. 1989. *Livelihood and Resistance: Peasants and the Politics of Land in Peru.* Berkeley: University of California Press.

Stanford, Lois. 1991. Peasant Resistance in the International Market: Theory and Practice in Michoacán, Mexico. *Research in Economic Anthropology* 13: 67–92.

———. 1994. Transitions to Free Trade: Local Impacts of Changes in Mexican Agrarian Policy. *Human Organization* 53(2): 99–109.

———. 1996. Ante la globalización del tratado de libre comercio: el caso de los meloneros de Michoacán. In Sara María Lara Flores and Michelle Chauvte, eds., Vol. 1, *La inserción de la agricultura mexicana en la economía mundial.* In Hubert Carton de Grammont and Hector Tejera Gaona, eds., *La sociedad rural mexicana frente al nuevo milenio,* 4 vols. Mexico City: Plaza y Valdéz.

————. 1998. Commercial Opportunities for *ejidatarios* in the International Market: Comparative Analysis of Commodity Systems in Michoacán. In Wayne Cornelius and David Myhre, eds., *The Transformation of Rural Mexico: Reforming the Ejido Sector*. La Jolla: Center for U.S.-Mexican Studies, University of California, San Diego.

5

Tracing Social Relations in Commodity Chains: The Case of Grapes in Brazil

Jane L. Collins

INTRODUCTION

This chapter's focus is the commodity chain that links producers and consumers of grapes. I demonstrate that even in the case of such a "simple" (that is, unprocessed) product, consumer demand and consumer culture shape production and distribution practices in powerful ways. Analyses of global food systems have emphasized the growing homogeneity of the consumer environment (Friedmann and McMichael 1989; Raynolds, Myrle, and McMichael 1993; Kloppenburg, Hendrickson, and Stevenson 1996). First world consumers now can purchase foods of standard quality throughout the year nearly anywhere in the industrialized world. How does this imperative to homogenize, standardize, and ensure year-round access to fresh produce at the point of consumption affect social relations at the point of production, as well as along the distribution chain? Susan Willis has said that if, as Marx suggests, commodities are the containers of hidden social relationships, then these relationships are all the more concealed by the movement of production to the third world (1991, 52). The example of grapes provides an opportunity to make visible some of the relationships hidden in a globally integrated, late-twentieth-century commodity.

A substantial literature on commodity chains now exists. Many scholars believe that the commodity chain is a particularly useful unit of analysis for our post–Cold War, post–nation-state world. Recent advocates of commodity chain analysis, such as Gary Gereffi and Miguel Korzeniewicz, argue that since the 1960s, "major breakthroughs in communications and transportation technologies have shrunk the world dramatically in terms of time and space, permitting manufacturers and retailers . . . to establish transnational production and trade networks that cover vast geographical distances" (Gereffi 1994, 14). These authors also argue that economic activities that formerly took place within nations are being reorganized in globally integrated commodity chains and complex regional divisions of labor. Earlier proponents of commodity chain analysis, such as Friedland (1984) and Hopkins and Wallerstein (1986), made more modest claims, simply suggesting that studying the commodity chain is a useful way to trace connections among complicated production and distribution systems and to organize information on processes that cross national boundaries. Hopkins and Wallerstein also suggested that such an approach is valuable in linking the local and the global through its emphasis on process. The method is particularly useful, they argue, for tracing connections between producers and consumers without "losing the thread" at the level of global markets and international regulatory practices.

Several important case studies have relied on commodity chain analysis. For example, Sidney Mintz's book, *Sweetness and Power* (1985), details relationships between the growth of Caribbean sugar plantations and increasing sugar consumption among the working classes in Europe. Mintz uncovers the powerful interests, laws, policies, and regulatory mechanisms that connected such dispersed developments, creating a mass market for sugar where it had not existed before. Another such case study is Harriet Friedmann's 1990 essay, "Family Wheat Farms and Third World Diets," which performs a commodity systems analysis of the international grain trade. Friedmann examines how grain farming practices in the first world and the increased consumption of wheat in third world diets are linked through the institutions of the grain trade. She demonstrates how policies designed to support the "family farm" in the United States (including P.L. 480—the Food for Peace Bill) undercut grain farming in the third world, and she traces ramifications of the Fordist bargain with U.S. workers for grain to cheapen and pacify labor in Latin America and elsewhere. By focusing on production and global distribution of a single commodity, Friedmann tells a new story about how U.S. family farming in the post–World War II period was built successfully on the increased proletarianization and food dependency of the third world. Tracing the circulation of commodities in this way can reveal previously unseen connections between production and consumption regimes in places widely separated by distance and culture.

CONSUMING GRAPES

What features of grape consumption are significant for social relations along the commodity chain? First, grape consumption is rapidly expanding in the world's industrialized nations. U.S. imports of this crop grew from about 14,000 metric tons in 1970 to nearly 400,000 metric tons in 1990—an increase of about 2,800 percent (Food and Agricultural Organization 1985–1993). Horticultural trade overall has expanded as a proportion of world agricultural exports. At 13 percent of world totals, fruits and vegetables now rank third (after grains and oil seeds), and they have become more important than either agricultural raw materials or sugar. While Western Europe is the largest import market, the United States and Japan have been the fastest-growing markets over the past twenty years (Islam 1990, 9). In addition, the growth in grape trade is linked to a trend that began in the 1970s toward the consumption of more fresh—as opposed to canned and frozen—fruits and vegetables.

A second important aspect of grape consumption is that people no longer eat grapes seasonally; rather, they have become accustomed to having year-round access to their favorite fruits and vegetables. This year-round availability requires global sourcing, with different locations contributing their produce to first world markets at varying times of the year. The U.S. market for grapes, for example, is supplied by California producers during the summer and by Chilean producers during the winter. European demand is met through southern European production from July through September, Chilean and South African production from January through March, and Brazilian production from October through December and April through June. Southern Hemisphere grape exports fill "windows"—or gaps—in the availability of first world grapes for first world markets.

Third, because grapes require highly specific agroecological conditions, they are frequently traded across longer distances than most commodities. The average food product consumed in the United States travels 1,300 miles and changes hands a dozen times (Kloppenburg, Hendrickson, and Stevenson 1996). Given the long distances grapes travel, transport must be refrigerated, and this cost is a high proportion of retail price.

Fourth, grapes are what Philip McMichael (1990) calls a "luxury crop." Luxury crops are those destined for upscale consumers, who emphasize quality, not bulk. These products are not dietary staples; rather, they make the diet healthier or more interesting. Thus consumption of luxury crops is directly tied to quality; because these items are not staples, consumers simply will not buy them if they do not meet their standards. Quality standards vary from country to country (Japan's are the highest, followed by northern Europe and the United States). Individual purchasing agents also demand different grades of produce for the specific market segments they serve within countries.

In her series of essays on commodities, Susan Willis has described the encounter between consumers and "luxury" fruits in U.S. supermarkets as follows:

> Stepping through the automatic sliding door and leaving behind a dreadful winter slush . . . you pick up your shopping cart and proceed along the prescribed course which invariably leads to the Land of Oz: a wonderland of brightly colored fruits . . . and vegetables . . . whose only acceptable attribute of tropicality is color. Air conditioning . . . swaddles the product in First World antiseptic purity and severs its connection with the site of its production. The shopper who enters the air-conditioned supermarket and chooses between its papayas, mango, pineapples, bananas; its winter supply

of peaches, nectarines, plums and grapes from Chile, is as unaware of the factors and labor force behind their production as the tourist whose experience of Mexico is an air-conditioned hotel lobby. (1991, 50–51)

What are the implications of the consumption pattern just described? How do the freshness and quality demanded by first world consumers shape the ways that grapes are produced and shipped, and ultimately the social relationships entailed in production and distribution? The next section explores these questions by presenting the results of research conducted on export grape production in the São Francisco river valley of northeastern Brazil in March 1991 and the summer of 1993.[1] First, evidence from this location suggests that the demands of shipping highly perishable produce for fresh consumption has limited the opportunities for small-scale grape producers to enter the market, despite their lower production costs and their higher quality product.[2] Second, this case reveals that rigid quality standards—because of the kind and amount of careful, skilled labor grapes require—have shaped labor recruitment practices in third world production sites, leading producers to hire women in export grape enterprises.

POSTHARVEST COSTS LIMIT SMALL FARM COMPETITIVENESS

Grape production in Brazil has begun relatively recently. Although Brazil's grape exports are minuscule compared with those of a country such as Chile, they have expanded from about 1,200 metric tons in 1987 to 12,000 metric tons in 1993 (a 1,000 percent increase in five years). In the lower middle São Francisco valley, encompassing parts of the northeastern states of Bahia and Pernambuco, farmers planted their first grapevines in the early 1980s and exported their first crops in 1987. Between 1970 and the early 1990s, this part of the São Francisco valley was transformed from a zone of low-input cattle ranches to one of intensive fruit and vegetable production—from a drought-stricken zone of *fazendas* (large, traditionally organized farms) employing servile labor to a zone of multinational investment and highly capitalized irrigated production. This transformation required huge investments on the part of foreign capital and the Brazilian state. In 1973, Brazil's military government began building a large hydroelectric dam on the São Francisco River at Sobradinho. Supported by the World Bank and other bilateral and multilateral donor agencies, the dam was designed to provide cheap hydropower in a period of increasing oil prices, to regularize the flow of the São Francisco River, and to make irrigated agriculture possible in the region. The dam was completed in 1979, creating a reservoir of 4,150 square kilometers and forcing the relocation of 65,000 people.

Irrigation was initiated by the Brazilian state, which purchased or expropriated lands near the reservoir and organized them into irrigation districts under the supervision of the São Francisco Valley Development Company (CODEVASF). Each district included a mixture of large, medium, and small enterprises. By 1993, nearly 50,000 hectares were being farmed within the irrigation districts, and nearly an equal amount of private land had been irrigated. New enterprises were growing more than twenty different crops in the region; the most important were tomatoes, mangoes, and grapes.[3] Irrigation and climate allowed both tomato and grape farmers in the region to harvest two crops per year.

In 1993, the São Francisco valley had 4,000 hectares in vineyards. Three thousand hectares were controlled by eighteen large firms (averaging a little over 150 hectares per enterprise); the remaining 1,000 hectares were distributed among some 300 small farms of under 6 hectares. State programs offered credit for grape production to both small and large farms, and both had access to at least minimal technical support through CODEVASF. Both small and large farms have succeeded in growing grapes that meet export standards. Indeed small farms have a slightly better record: an average of 45 percent of their grapes were exportable in 1993, compared with 40 percent for larger farms (Collins 1995a). Farmers sold unexportable grapes on the domestic market for one-third to one-half the export price.

Producing grapes on farms of any size is labor intensive, and even more so when grapes are destined for export. Export grapes must meet standards for features such as bunch size, grape size, weight, sugar content, absence of blemish, and absence of pesticide residue. Tasks involved in producing grapes to meet these standards include removing old growth from vines; tilling; fertilizing; securing new growth to arbors; trimming nonproducing branches; monitoring for rate of growth, blemishes, and signs of disease; applying pesticides biweekly; selecting the two best bunches on each branch and culling the rest; trimming bunches to export size; harvesting; grading; packing; and transporting to refrigerated warehouses.

Small farmers would seem to possess several advantages in export grape production. Economists have noted that small farms have a cost advantage for producing crops with high interactive labor intensity—that is, crops that are highly responsive to constant and careful manipulation and monitoring (Carter et al. 1993). This advantage occurs largely because family labor performs the crucial (and expensive) supervision tasks that ensure such careful, interactive labor. Indeed overall production costs for small grape farms in northeastern Brazil were 45 percent lower than those of larger farms, and the labor bill for small farms was 70 percent lower.[4] Grapes are among those "nontraditional" exports, which would seem, on the basis of production characteristics, to present good opportunities for small farmers who wish to enter export markets.

Labor costs for large farms were high for two reasons. First, in order to reduce labor turnover and retain skilled workers large farmers invested in on-farm housing and services. Second, they were forced to implement a system for controlling and monitoring work in the vineyards. Firms with the highest percentage of exportable grapes used a three-tier system. For every twenty workers there was a monitor who constantly checked task performance. For every five monitors (100 workers) there was a supervisor who oversaw both efficiency and technical aspects of production.

One manager estimated that this three-tiered monitoring system cost his firm 25–30 percent of gross returns. In addition to this monitoring, many firms provided incentives for productivity, rewarding workers for high yields and high levels of exportability. Managers sought to combine skilled, almost "artisanal," care of grapes and vines with piece-rate compensation, monitoring and control. Managers who spoke about the need to standardize procedures, at the same time referred to their workers as artisans—emphasizing the care required in the execution of tasks.

Although small farms had lower labor and production costs, they could not necessarily continue to participate in exports. This uncertainty arose because small farmers were at a disadvantage in obtaining access to the postharvest services necessary to export. Grapes depend on the maintenance of an elaborate "cold chain," from packing shed to final destination. The fruit must be refrigerated within a few hours of harvest and, once cooled, the cold chain cannot be broken without damaging the produce. Small farmers are at a disadvantage in negotiating access to refrigerated warehouses at the point of production and on the docks, as well as to refrigerated trucks for ground transport and the refrigerated tankers that carry the fruit to Rotterdam. Operating on their own, small farmers cannot guarantee sufficient quantities of produce to make it worthwhile for shipping companies to show up at the right time, or to justify competitive shipping rates. Small farmers must also gain entry into foreign markets through foreign buyers or agents. Gaining entry is itself a complex task that involves, at a minimum, finding such a partner, negotiating terms of exchange, transferring goods, monitoring terms, and enforcing the contract.

Accomplishing all of these tasks is not only expensive, but requires access to banking and legal systems, and often some political influence as well. As Carter and his colleagues (1993) suggest, small farms are often at a significant disadvantage in performing many of these tasks. In the São Francisco valley, small producers' lower production costs were offset by the higher prices they paid for some materials (such as boxes) and services (such as technical assistance for setting up and regulating irrigation and drainage systems). Additionally, they were unable to export grapes directly, relying instead on intermediaries.

One such intermediary was the Brazilian Grape Marketing Board (BGMB), an association of seven of the valley's largest grape farmers. Large farmers organized BGMB in 1992 with two goals in mind: first, to overcome the high cost of shipping by bulking produce and, second, to avoid competition among producers. In this sense, BGMB functioned as a sort of cartel, setting a common price and working to manage supply. As long as production in the valley was not yet meeting European demand during the market "windows," BGMB members were willing—indeed eager—to buy export quality grapes from small producers; they then sold these fruits together with their own produce. BGMB members also offered technical assistance to small growers, supervised harvest and packing, and assumed responsibility for transport and for locating the produce on the market. These services allowed them to "regularize throughput" (Watts 1994) in the event of production problems on the estate, as well as to expand exports once their own vineyards had reached the maximum feasible size.

The other export option for small farmers was to sell grapes through the export firm Cacique, which was owned and run by the French government. Although the firm originally specialized in tobacco products, it began to diversify into veterinary supplies and fruit exports approximately fifteen years ago, when significant public health campaigns against smoking began. Cacique's fruit operations relied on the marketing infrastructure of the original tobacco firm. It began operations in the São Francisco valley in 1990, providing export services to large firms. As these firms began to develop the contacts and infrastructure necessary to export on their own (culminating in the establishment of the BGMB), Cacique turned its attention to small producers, buying their grapes and handling refrigerated transport, quality control, shipping, export papers, and so on.

Because both BGMB and Cacique were operating in 1993, small farmers benefited from the competition between them. Were either of these two marketing channels to disappear, however, small producers would face significantly higher charges for postharvest services. If both were to disappear, they would lose access to markets altogether. Small farms possess advantages in *producing* fresh fruit, but the cost and complexity of the distribution infrastructure work against them. The high cost of the refrigerated infrastructure has led to the relative monopolization of the distribution system. Such monopolies appear wherever perishable fruit is shipped for fresh consumption. Thus consumer demand for a year-round supply of fresh fruit—particularly delicate or tree-ripened fresh produce—requires access to a distribution system that is rarely available to small producers. It is therefore unlikely that small-scale producers can participate in this export market.

QUALITY PRODUCE AND FEMALE LABOR

Aspects of consumer demand—particularly the rigid quality standards applied to grapes—have also structured production and the labor process. Export grapes are evaluated according to dozens of attributes, and an immense number of tasks must be performed during each production cycle. Some firms in the São Francisco valley reported labor-intensity quotients in irrigated grape production (with two crops each year) as high as 1,500 person days per hectare each year, compared with approximately 500 person days per hectare each year in mango production, and even less for most field crops.

Such a labor-intensive process is quite costly for three reasons: (1) the absolute number of labor hours required; (2) the large amount of high-cost supervisory labor required; and (3) the preference for a skilled, relatively fixed labor force. Labor reductions have an immediate impact on the quality of grapes produced. The largest export grape producer in the São Francisco valley said that his two "secrets" were maintenance of the cold chain and having plenty of well-monitored labor. He employed a variety of the three-tiered monitoring system described in the previous section.

Today there is no technology available to reduce labor inputs. Seedless grapes are hardier and thus require significantly less labor, but they have not yet been successfully adapted to the region. In the absence of such technology, large exporters have responded to high labor costs by turning to women, who can offer skills and low turnover at a lower price than traditional workers. Large exporters have employed women for most tasks in vineyards and packinghouses (Collins 1995b; 1995c). In 1993, 65 percent of the workers in export grapes were women. Men did tilling, irrigating, and carrying. Women selected, culled, trimmed, harvested, and packed— performing tasks that had most significance for the product's final quality.

Hiring women reduced the cost of labor in four ways. First, as evidence from many parts of the world has shown, the very fact that work is performed by women tends to reduce the skill level attributed to it (Glenn and Feldberg 1977; Compton and Jones 1984). What would ordinarily be construed as skill (including grafting of grapevines) is coded instead as manual dexterity, delicacy, and nimbleness of fingers. These attributes, while valued, are considered mindless and manual and thus do not increase women's wages. Men who operated rototillers in vineyards of the São Francisco valley received one and a half times the minimum wage in 1993, while women who grafted vines received the minimum.

Second, the notion that women have primary responsibilities in the home, and thus require "flexible" schedules, provides firms with a justification for hiring them on a series of temporary contracts. Such temporary hiring releases firms from the obligation to comply with a number of state labor regulations and to provide certain benefits. Of course "flexibility" is always defined from the perspective of the firm and may entail women working twenty hours per day during harvest, a practice that is hardly consistent with child care and other home responsibilities.

Third, because rural unions have discriminated against women, firms perceive women as less likely to participate in union activities. Hiring women supplies firms with a stable, skilled, controllable, and nonunion labor force at a lower cost than they would face if they hired men.

Finally, women are more desirable employees in export grape production because firms perceive them to be less likely to chafe under the heavy supervision implied in three-tier monitoring systems. Thomas, describing labor control practices in the California lettuce industry, quotes a male worker as saying, "to a man, that [treatment] would be a challenge to a fight. To a woman, it's not right, but women are treated that way" (1985, 180). The gender relations and gender ideologies implied in this remark also operate in northeastern Brazil, and the supervision of work in grapes is much more intensive than that in lettuce.

For most women who work in fruit and vegetable production in the São Francisco valley, that labor is their first experience with waged work outside the home. Since women have very few alternatives in the local labor market, firms can draw "advantages from women's disadvantages" (Arizpe and Aranda 1981). For some women the wages earned in fruit production supplemented family income, but for others these earnings substituted for income lost when a family's formerly share-cropped lands were flooded by the dam at Sobradinho, or when owners converted such land to irrigated production.

Hiring women for export fruit production is not unique to the São Francisco valley, but is characteristic of many parts of the world. Over half of the labor force in fruit and vegetable production in Mexico is female (Barrón 1992; Roldán 1982). In Chile, where the fruit industry contributes almost 20 percent of national exports, the labor force is predominantly (and increasingly) female (Lago 1987; Rodríguez 1987; Rodríguez and Venegas 1989; Goldfrank 1992, 3; Gómez 1992, 17). Female labor is also important in fruit and vegetable production in the Dominican Republic (Mones and Grant 1987; Raynolds 1992, 18), in Senegal (Mackintosh 1989), and in the export flower industry throughout the Southern Hemisphere (Gruhn 1992, 20; Medrano 1980; Silva and Corredor 1980). A recent Del Monte advertisement in *The Packer,* the trade magazine for fruit and vegetable growers and distributors, referred to labor as its "secret ingredient"; smiling laborers portrayed in the ad were women. If commodities are the containers of hidden social relationships, this is a rare instance where the firm allows us a peek inside. Del Monte is telling us that the quality we demand in our supermarkets is linked significantly to their employment of third world women workers.

CONCLUSION

What we eat is not naturally determined (although there are some natural limits and boundaries). Rather, as Sidney Mintz's (1985) classic treatise on sugar has taught us, our consumption is a product of historically situated and shifting cultural preferences and economic interests. Chilean agronomists argue that "the essential new fact" accounting for the Chilean agroexport boom is dietary change in the first world, particularly the current emphasis on health, fitness, low fat, and freshness, which opens a new space for fresh fruits and vegetables (Gómez 1992, 10; Goldfrank 1994, 269).

As Kloppenburg, Hendrickson, and Stevenson have observed, however,

> The distance from which [our] food comes represents [our] separation from the knowledge of how and by whom what [we] consume is produced, processed and transported. . . . Provided with a cornucopia of continuously available foods, few consumers have much knowledge of the biological, social or technical parameters and implications of food production in the global village. (1996, 123)

Few of us realize, for example, that the *homogeneity* of quality and supply that we experience in our supermarkets, as a product of global procurement strategies, depends on the creation of new forms of *differentiation* in the labor force in other parts of the world—that is, on the creation of new forms of gender segmentation in the agricultural labor force. Few of us consider that fresh consumption requires access to transport technology that puts export strategies beyond the reach of small producers.

During the past two decades, the fruit and vegetable industry has become more global, more vertically integrated, and more concentrated. Highly capitalized industry leaders such as Dole and Del Monte tend to set quality standards and adopt packaging and labeling practices that provide consumers with brand recognition. Although negotiations at the World Trade Organization and other international venues have raised issues of whether states can impose consumer safety standards (such as regulating pesticide residues) or industry health standards (such as testing for presence of pests on imported fruits), vertically integrated retailers can define whatever standards they wish when they purchase from local producers. Standards associated with luxury foods of high value, as Stanford's chapter in this volume also demonstrates, have implications for how food is produced, and by whom.

As the introductory chapter, as well as other chapters in this volume, points out, the value we attach to particular commodities is partly cultural, but it also reflects power relations. Some groups can make their cultural preferences or values felt through the market or by other means. Northern consumers, in constituting a market for a year-round supply of flawless fresh fruit and vegetables, underwrite the displacement of existing cropping systems by production regimes that are complex, irrigated, and highly technical. As Friedmann (1990) describes, wheat produced on North American farms, distributed through food aid in the 1960s and 1970s, undercut production of basic grains (wage foods) in the developing world. In the 1980s and 1990s, demand for luxury foods such as year-round fresh fruits and vegetables has become a new force that supplants both self-provisioning and the production of wage foods for local consumers.

Berry (1992); Friedmann (1990); Kloppenburg, Hendrickson, and Stevenson (1996); and others have suggested that one response to this situation would be to "draw in our economic boundaries and shorten our supply lines." Berry suggests that "the closer we live to the ground, the more we will know about our economic life, and the more able we will be to take responsibility for it"(1992, 35). These scholars' works provide a powerful justification for the Community Supported Agriculture movement and the regionalization of consumption patterns. Another—and perhaps complementary—response to growing distances between point of production and point of consumption is to develop new analytical tools that will allow us to uncover connections between production and consumption practices in different parts of the world. As the example of grapes suggests, such approaches would allow us to move past models of local communities connected to abstract global forces and to conceptualize relations between producers and consumers linked through humanly produced institutions of regulation and trade. Like "shortening our supply lines," such analysis would enable us to break open the "black box" of the commodity to see the social relations it entails and to make informed choices about how and what we will consume.

NOTES

1. Research was funded by the National Science Foundation and affiliation and support were provided by the Federal University of Pernambuco. The author thanks collaborators Andrea Melo and Jose Ferreira Irmão for their participation in the research.

2. See Lois Stanford's chapter on Mexican melon producers in this volume.

3. These crops included acerola, alfalfa, asparagus, banana, beans, cantaloupe, chili peppers, citrus, cotton, grapes (table and wine), guava, hybrid seed, mango, maracuja, onions, papaya, rice, squash, sugarcane, sweet peppers, tamarind, tomato, and watermelon.

4. These figures are drawn from a detailed analysis of accounts of fifty-two fruit farms in the São Francisco Valley, conducted by the author in 1993.

REFERENCES

Arizpe, Lourdes, and Josefina Aranda. 1981. The "Comparative Advantages" of Women's Disadvantages: Women Workers in the Strawberry Export Agribusiness in Mexico. *Signs* 7(2): 453–473.

Barrón, Maria Antonieta. 1992. The Impact of Globalization on the Mexican Labor Market for Vegetable Production. Working Paper no. 11. Fresh Fruit and Vegetables Globalization Network, University of California, Santa Cruz.

Berry, Wendell. 1992. Conservation Is Good Work. *Amicus Journal* (Winter): 33–36.

Carter, Michael R., Bradford B. Barham, Dina Mesbah, and Denise Stanley. 1993. *Agro-exports and the Rural Resource Poor in Latin America: Policy Options for Achieving Broadly-Based Growth*. Agricultural Economics Staff Paper Series no. 364. Madison: University of Wisconsin.

Collins, Jane L. 1995a. Farm Size and Non-Traditional Exports: Determinants of Participation in World Markets. *World Development* 23(7): 1103–1114.

———. 1995b. Gender and Cheap Labor in Agriculture. In Philip McMichael, ed., *Food and Agrarian Orders in the World-Economy*. Westport, Conn.: Praeger.

———. 1995c. Transnational Labor Process and Gender Relations: Women in Fruit and Vegetable Production in Chile, Brazil, and Mexico. *Journal of Latin American Anthropology* 1(1): 78–99.

Compton, Rosemary, and Gareth Jones. 1984. *White Collar Proletariat: Deskilling and Gender in Clerical Work*. Philadelphia, Penn.: Temple University Press.

Food and Agricultural Organization (FAO). 1985–1993. *Trade Yearbook*, vols. 39–47. Rome: Food and Agricultural Organization of the United Nations.

Friedland, William H. 1984. Commodity Systems Analysis: An Approach to the Sociology of Agriculture. *Research in Rural Sociology and Development* 1: 221–235.

Friedmann, Harriet. 1990. Family Wheat Farms and Third World Diets: A Paradoxical Relationship Between Waged and Unwaged Labor. In Jane L. Collins and Martha Gimenez, eds., *Work Without Wages*. Albany: State University of New York Press.

Friedmann, Harriet, and Philip McMichael. 1989. Agriculture and the State System: The Rise and Decline of National Agricultures, 1870 to the Present. *Sociologia Ruralis* 29(2): 93–117.

Gereffi, Gary. 1994. Introduction. In Gary Gereffi and Miguel Korzeniewicz, eds., *Commodity Chains and Global Capitalism*. Westport, Conn.: Praeger.

Glenn, Evelyn N., and Roslyn L. Feldberg. 1977. Degraded and Deskilled: The Proletarianization of Clerical Work. *Social Problems* 25: 52–64.

Goldfrank, Walter. 1992. Chilean Fruit: The Maturation Process. Working Paper no. 16. Fresh Fruit and Vegetables Globalization Network, University of California, Santa Cruz.

———. 1994. Fresh Demand: The Consumption of Chilean Produce in the United States. In Gary Gereffi and Miguel Korzeniewicz, eds., *Commodity Chains and Global Capitalism*. Westport, Conn.: Praeger.

Gómez, Sergio. 1992. La uva chilena en el mercado de los Estados Unidos. Working Paper no. 19. Fresh Fruit and Vegetable Globalization Network, University of California, Santa Cruz.

Gruhn, Isebil V. 1992. Say It with Flowers. Working Paper no. 27. Fresh Fruit and Vegetables Globalization Network, University of California, Santa Cruz.

Hopkins, Terence K., and Immanuel Wallerstein. 1986. Commodity Chains in the World Economy Prior to 1800. *Review* 10(1): 157–170.

Islam, Nurul. 1990. *Horticultural Exports of Developing Countries: Past Performances, Future Prospects and Policy Issues*. Washington, D.C.: Food Policy Research Institute.

Kloppenburg, Jack, Jr., John Hendrickson, and G. W. Stevenson. 1996. Coming in to the Foodshed. In William Vitek and Wes Jackson, eds., *Rooted in the Land: Essays on Community and Place*. New Haven, Conn.: Yale University Press.

Lago, Maria Soledad. 1987. *Rural Women and the Neo-Liberal Model in Chile*. In Carmen Diana Deere and Magdalena León, eds., *Rural Women and State Policy: Feminist Perspectives on Latin American Agricultural Development*. Boulder, Colo.: Westview Press.

Mackintosh, Maureen. 1989. *Gender, Class and Rural Transition: Agribusiness and the Food Crisis in Senegal*. London: Zed Books.

McMichael, Philip. 1990. Class Diets and Trajectories in World Agriculture. Paper presented to Fernand Braudel Center, Binghamton, N.Y., 3 March.

Medrano, Diana. 1980. El caso de las obreras de los cultivos de flores de los municipios de Chía, Cajica y Tabio en la sabana de Bogotá, Colombia. Rural Employment Policies Branch, International Labour Organization, Research Paper.

Mintz, Sidney. 1985. *Sweetness and Power*. New York: Viking.

Mones, Belkis, and Lydia Grant. 1987. Agricultural Development, the Economic Crisis, and Rural Women in the Dominican Republic. In Carmen Diana Deere and Magdalena León, eds., *Rural Women and State Policy: Feminist Perspectives on Latin American Agricultural Development*. Boulder, Colo.: Westview Press.

Raynolds, Laura T. 1992. Forces of Instability in Caribbean Participation in International Fresh Produce Systems: Lessons from the Dominican Republic. Working Paper no. 21. Fresh Fruit and Vegetables Globalization Network, University of California, Santa Cruz.

Raynolds, Laura T., David Myhre, and Philip McMichael. 1993. The "New Internationalization" of Agriculture: A Reformulation. *World Development* 21(7): 1102–1121.

Rodríguez O., Daniel. 1987. Agricultural Modernization and Labor Markets in Latin America: The Case of Fruit Production in Central Chile. Ph.D. diss., University of Texas, Austin.

Rodríguez O., Daniel, and Sylvia Venegas L. 1989. *De praderas a parronales: Un estudio sobre estructura agraria y mercado laboral en el Valle de Aconcagua.* Santiago: Grupo de Estudios Agro-regionales.

Roldán, Marta. 1982. Subordinación genérica y proletarización rural: Un estudio de caso en el Noroeste Mexicano. In Magdalena León, ed., *Debate sobre la mujer en América Latina y el Caribe: Las trabajadoras del agro.* Bogotá: Asociación Colombiana para el Estudio de la Población.

Silva de Rojas, Alicia E., and Consuelo Corredor de Prieto. 1980. La explotación de la mano de obra femenina en la industria de las flores: Un estudio de caso en Colombia. Rural Employment Policies Branch, International Labor Organization, Geneva. Research Paper.

Thomas, Robert J. 1985. *Citizenship, Gender and Work: Social Organization of Industrial Agriculture.* Berkeley: University of California Press.

Watts, Michael. 1994. Life Under Contract. In Peter Little and Michael Watts, eds., *Living Under Contract: Contract Farming and Agrarian Transformation in Sub-Saharan Africa.* Madison: University of Wisconsin Press.

Willis, Susan. 1991. *A Primer for Daily Life.* New York: Routledge.

Part II

The Circulation and Revaluation
of Commodities

6

Profit Markets and Art Markets

Stuart Plattner

This chapter examines producers (artists) and consumers (collectors) in a capitalist arena, namely, the contemporary avant-garde local art market. I argue that the diverse goals and values of artists and the risky position of collectors have produced economic behavior that seems paradoxical at first glance. Avant-garde artists, who are akin to petty commodity producers, often act in direct contradiction to reasonable sales practices by ignoring the preferences of their potential customers. Commodity marketers—contemporary avant-garde art dealers—have such market power that they can receive remuneration for sales of art they have never seen to buyers they have never met. In a classical market situation, small-scale producers who ignored their customers' preferences would soon be without customers, and would eventually go out of production. Monopolistic dealers would tend to represent ever fewer producers than dealers who were more flexible, and would also go out of business. In true anthropological style, this chapter shows how the behavior's historical context explains the anomalies: the growth of wealth in the United States during this century and the current postmodern state of aesthetic theory combine to cause an extraordinary market weakness of artists, strength of dealers, and high risk for buyers. The contribution of this chapter is not to advance new theory, but to extend existing theory to cover a case that may have seemed exempt from socioeconomic regularities. While the analysis is meant to be general, the examples are based on ethnographic research in a local Midwestern art world in St. Louis, Missouri.

TYPES OF MARKETS

This section distinguishes between sellers who work primarily for money and those who dream more of glory, and between buyers who are capable judges of art quality and those who cannot recognize good art without substantial help.[1] My purpose is to situate the local art market in a conceptual space to highlight causes of the unexpected economic behavior observed.

To understand art as a commodity, we must first appreciate its unique cultural status:

> The art community, producers and informed audiences, believes that aesthetically successful new imagery pushes the horizons of reality away from us all, expanding civilized consciousness. Should the process of creating new vision cease, should the fine art challenge go unmet, then the world would become visually finite. It would be as if civilization, having trod a path inscribing reality, were to confront again its own footprints and the realization of the closed nature of that reality. (Simpson 1981, 6)[2]

As melodramatic as this may sound to those unconnected to the art world, it is a realistic figure of speech for people involved in fine art. The cultural status of art justifies the hype and high prices, since expanding our cultural capital is as important as providing food and shelter—more important, some would argue, since art gives meaning to material survival. Fine art is similar to religion, then, as an institution that counteracts the crassly commercial search for advancement in a capitalist world. At the same time, these objects of supposedly sublime vision are bought and sold as commodities. But art is a strange commodity; aesthetic excellence does not necessarily make for marketability. Art that experts agree is of high quality and significantly avant-garde does not always command high prices and often is not salable at all. This paradox underlies behavior in the art market.

A second crucial characteristic of art commodity markets is that they are structured into rigid hierarchies reflecting the hegemony of elite taste. A small set of elite dealers, critics, collectors, and institutions in New York dominates the contemporary art world. A few art stars earn fabulous amounts—hundreds of thousands of dollars for each piece, millions in the aggregate—for their work. But the overwhelming majority earn barely a pittance from the sale of their fine art.

PRODUCERS

Most producers who bring goods to market work mainly for money, designing their production so as to sell the appropriate type and quantity of goods to achieve their expected income. Other producers, or the same producers in different situations, pursue nonmonetary aims as well. These other (social or psychological) goals explain why production styles and levels seemingly contradict commercial interests.

For example, commissioned portrait painters are business artists or profit-oriented (petty commodity) producers. Their goal is to generate enough work to make a living, and, if possible, to raise their prices so that their standard of living can increase. As a successful portrait painter in St. Louis said:

> To be a good portrait painter, you have to be sensitive to what the sitter has in mind, because there's one thing that commercial art taught me, was to get paid. And whereas in fine arts they try to not get too much involved with money and all that, it's not that way at all if you are going to try to make it as a portrait painter. Getting paid is very important. So that means you have to at least listen to what the sitter has in mind, or what the people who are commissioning the painting have in mind. (fifty-six-year-old father of three grown children, interview by author, no. 43)[3]

In contrast to business artists, self-described fine-art painters, working speculatively without commissions, do not set their production to maximize income. The goals of "museum-quality" artists may be to advance the aesthetic avant-garde (as artists would say, "extending the edge" of visual art imagery), or to increase the likelihood that they will be considered significant artists in art history's long term, in addition to, or above the goal of, making a living.[4] A young sculptor put it this way:

> The worst kind of sellout is [artist X], his work is horrendous, shiny, slick, devoid of personality, how can it not be for anything but to sell? It is void of any kind of personality of the artist. Slickness, you sacrifice yourself to anything just to sell. . . . None of my work was ever made with the possibility that I might sell it. I tried it once, I made a series of pieces that would be sellable, but they didn't sell. I sold a couple for around $200. (thirty-one-year-old single woman, interview by author, no. 133)

This artist's words show the tension felt by most contemporary avant-garde artists between their interest in income from sales and their commitment to create valid aesthetic value. She receives a salary from her full-time faculty position and has no expectation of earning any significant income from her artwork. Her life is totally committed to making art. She lives in rudimentary accommodations in the rear of her storefront studio (1,500 square feet), which is filled with the found and purchased objects from which her sculptures are made.

CONSUMERS

Buyers usually do not care about producers' goals as much as they do about the attributes of goods. When buyers have adequate information they base their consumption decisions on qualities of the goods that are apparent to their inspection. For example, buyers of pottery (or clothing, or automobiles) base their choices on size, shape, color, material, price, payment options, and so on. Consumers usually cannot worry about the life goals and constraints of the producers of every item they buy, since life is complex enough without all those additional concerns.[5] Buyers' consideration of the seller's life concerns would raise transaction costs and therefore limit the possibilities for exchange. On the other hand, when lack of information raises consumer risk to unacceptable levels, higher transactions costs are justified since the alternative is no exchange at all. Conditions under which high-transaction cost exchange occurs are summarized below.

What does one have to know to buy art? The physical attributes of the work—including its material, size, shape, and appearance—are usually far less significant in determining value than the social history of the piece and the overall standing of the artist in the national or international art market. High value correlates with elite provenance (when either the piece itself or similar work by the artist has appeared in elite collections), status in the hegemonic art centers (primarily by elite gallery and museum representation of the artist's work in New York City or, secondarily, representation by elite places in other major centers), and an investment-quality biography (records of auction sales in elite houses such as Sotheby's and Christie's, prizes in major international and national shows, and so on). Some buyers feel satisfied that they have all the information needed to determine the value of the art they purchase. A dealer in St. Louis talked about buying art:

> I generally buy prints by nationally important artists that have an actual value that I can determine; in other words, if I don't sell it here, I can send it to New York and somebody there will pay at least what I did for it, so I can't really lose. (fifty-five-year-old single male dealer, interview by author, no. 10)

Other buyers are equally confident in their ability to assess art, but more daring in their purchases:

> The museum will buy a few very expensive pieces, art that is so expensive that they can't lose. I prefer to take the risk of buying a $10,000 painting. (forty-five-year-old married male collector, interview by author, no. 17)

The individuals just quoted are experts; the former is a professional dealer and the latter is a wealthy collector who devotes his life to art activities and has curated art shows. (The risk he mentioned refers to the chance that the art—paintings in this case—will not become more well known and significant over the next decade or so in the art world, and thus will not increase in aesthetic or monetary value.) Experienced and knowledgeable buyers can actually add value to an artist's work by including it in their collections. Recognition by a well-known connoisseur adds commercial value to an artist's products by validating their aesthetic status through their association with other high-status work in the collection.

The average collector is more challenged to assess value. A St. Louis banker, for example, who occasionally bought art but was not a sophisticated buyer, remembered purchasing his first painting while on vacation in Michigan during the 1950s. The gallery was asking $500, a serious price at that time (equivalent to almost $3,000 today). He went so far as to call the Guggenheim Museum in New York City to ask "if they knew of this artist." The person with whom he spoke recognized the artist's name and said that he was a "legitimate artist." The banker explained:

> It makes common sense. I'm buying the painting because I like it, but I don't want to be had. I don't like making mistakes. It would be different if I went to [X, a local dealer] where I know the gallery. If I'm buying a diamond, I want to be sure the diamond is flawless. I can't see that, I have to rely on the dealer. I bought the painting because I liked it, and my ideas were supported by the fact that he [the artist] had some recognition, he had legitimacy. . . . I wanted to be sure I was doing the right thing. (fifty-one-year-old investment banker, interview by author, no. 42)

Legitimacy means status in a nonlocal market, so that the buyer's interest in the work is shared by a larger set of collectors (the significance of this is discussed below, in the section "Markets for Stars"). Potential buyers are reassured by the knowledge that a work is sold and written about in a social context wider than the local scene.

Other buyers simply ignore the issue of legitimacy. A wealthy, self-employed investor who collected books as well as ancient and contemporary art discussed his purchases of local art in these terms:

> I figured when we bought the pictures by [local artists X and Y] that they were not being bought for investment. . . . It would be very nice if they achieved the distinction which I believe they deserve, but I'm not counting on it. We bought them from local painters, local galleries at . . . shows where they had just been painted. And we expect to keep them all our lives. We are not really concerned that they are not, to our knowledge, major elements in the national or international, the New York-dominated market. For all I know, they may be but I don't keep track of that. I know that they are not major and I know that neither [artist X or Y] has attempted to compete actively in the rat race of New York art reputations. (sixty-one-year-old investment counselor, interview by author, 66)

In short, art buyers range from those with supreme self-confidence in their "eye," to professional dealers or persons who should be so confident, to those who do not trust themselves to assess enduring value and who either get additional information to minimize their risk (the banker) or who simply ignore the whole issue, treating the art purchase as a simple consumable and not asking whether the price is justified in any larger sense (the investment counselor).

A MODEL OF LOCAL ART MARKETS

The main parameters of the model I wish to discuss now have been introduced; these include the goals of producers and the information constraints of consumers. In the standard, profit-oriented market situation producers offer things for sale primarily because they want income, and buyers have adequate information to assess the value of the things they seek (see table 6.1, upper-left quadrant). The market for most manufactured commodities, such as new cars, is a good example. The producer is in it for the money with no pretense of building culture. The buyer knows fairly well why a Mercedes costs more than a Mercury—better engineering, finer materials, and more expensive manufacturing quality overall. In the art world, the market for crafts and purely decorative art (work with no pretense of high aesthetic quality) fits the classical standard economic market with adequate information. Price differences reflect materials, size, and form, with no premium for the artist's position in art history.

Markets where producers are involved mainly for money but where consumers do not know the product's value—either because of structural features or because the rules of value are confused, contested, or unclear—are also familiar to us (see the lower-left quadrant of table 6.1). Examples include the market for a boatload of fish, as described by Wilson (1980), where the buyer cannot know the value of the fish without unloading the boat, which causes the product to deteriorate; or Akerlof's (1970) seminal model of the used car market, where sellers of used cars know their value but buyers only perceive the vehicle's appearance and immediate driveability. In such situations, the market is in danger of failing because buyers and sellers cannot agree on a fair price. The solution is to develop mechanisms to deal with the risk, either by providing additional information (such as costly mechanical examinations in the case of used cars), or by substituting for impersonal, short-run "spot market" relations the personalized, equilibrating long-term economic relationships studied by anthropologists (cf. Plattner 1985, who also discusses Williamson's classic 1981 theoretical article). The market for crafts and decorative art can have some of these attributes, for instance when salespeople introduce considerations of a piece of art's historical significance for a work designed to be purely decorative. Consumers cannot assess value by visual inspection, but need information about the artist's position in the market.

Table 6.1   Types of Markets

Consumers' Rules of Commodity Value	Producer's (Seller's) Main Return from Production	
	Monetary, Market Supply	*Psychic, Social Identity, Social Supply*
Clear, Uncontested Rules, Adequate Information, Physical Attributes Dominant	Developed market, manufactured commodities (art-craft items, automobiles)	Professions, academics (investment art)
Confused, Contested Rules, Inadequate Information, Social Attributes Dominant	Underdeveloped market, poor infrastructure (used cars, perishables, high-art craft items)	Local art markets

Most readers of this chapter are also familiar with a market where the rules governing economic value are clear yet the goals of producers have more to do with identity than with income—namely, the academic labor market. In principle, academics understand why professors in the business school earn more than those in the college of arts and sciences. Although individuals in the academic marketplace may object to various aspects of the valuation rules (e.g., arguing that applied "gray literature" reports be valued along with formal publications), the rules are nonetheless clear. In anthropology, for example, the academic who publishes a book every four years and receives an average of $50,000 per year in grants clearly deserves a higher-than-average salary in most research institutions. Less-published or less-granted peers laboring in undergraduate courses may grumble about the neglected importance of teaching, but they are objecting to the consequences of the rules, not their explicitness. In this sense, the "product stream of services" supplied by an academic is like a new car, in that the rules governing economic value are clear.

But academics, like artists, do not choose their professions for the money. It would be ludicrous to suggest to an anthropologist that her income would be improved if she spent her time selling real estate rather than teaching and doing anthropological research. Academia, like art, is more a "calling" than an occupation. Practitioners of such "identity" professions typically work far more hours than could be justified by their income alone. (The need for creative expression and significant independence in job performance are probably important in this sort of work, but this chapter is not concerned with the selection factors for each market type.) My point here is that even when the producer's identity is intimately involved with the product, the rules governing value can be unambiguous.

The upper-right quadrant of table 6.1 refers to this sort of market situation, including the market for "investment quality" art. The buyer of a work by a well-known artist like Picasso has a clear idea why the piece is valued as it is. The buyer may lose money when the piece is sold, but that places art investors in the same situation as investors in the stock market, gold, or any other precious object.[6]

In local art markets, the rules governing economic value are obscure and the motives of producers are not predominantly economic (the lower-right quadrant of table 6.1). The identity and self-respect of these producers are defined by their work. They certainly want to make money, but their primary motivation is not monetary. They work because they cannot exist without the activity; they are addicted to their work (some economists use the term "psychic income"). Some ethnographic quotes from St. Louis artists illustrate this point:

> [Making art] is not a job at all, it's what I do, it's what I am. So basically I spend as much time as I can here [the studio]; it comes before anything else. . . . My strongest feeling is that I make my art because I'm driven to, I have to. If I don't make it, you might as well lock me up in the crazy house. If nobody buys it, nobody reviews it, that's OK, I don't need it. On the other hand, it's wonderful to be noticed, wonderful to have people want your work. (thirty-four-year-old single artist, supports herself through freelance media work, interview by author, no. 52)

When I'm doing my artwork, I'm not saying it's like a psychiatrist, but it keeps me sane. (forty-year-old single artist, full-time faculty job, interview by author, no. 131)

A senior artist and senior professor at Washington University, the local elite art school, who could have supported himself from selling paintings, summed it up as follows: "Given a choice between selling everything we do without exhibiting it and being able to show everything with no sales at all, we would go for the second option" (McGarrell 1986).

For consumers, the rules of aesthetic value are unclear for local art that has not entered high levels of the national market. The average upper-middle-class consumer who has enough disposable income to buy original art, and the college education and cultural status to value it, would be unable to explain why one watercolor painting is worth $300, another $3,000, and a third $30,000. The size, shape, quality of materials, and other visual attributes would not vary significantly. None of the pieces would have an auction record to establish their investment quality. And how can prices be compared across genres: how is one to know whether the installation sculpture composed of thirty large cubic-foot blocks of salt, each covered with a different natural granular substance such as sand or bone meal, is better art than the mammoth horizontal tree trunk with what seems to be a negative canoe shape carved and burned in it? This conjunction of identity producers and confused consumers defines a local art market. It is composed of a large number of producers relative to their actual sales, and a small number of consumers representing a potentially enormous cohort of buyers who avoid the market.[7]

THE VAN GOGH EFFECT ON AESTHETIC AUTHORITY

Why are well-educated potential consumers not able to tell "good" from "bad" in contemporary avant-garde art? Since consumers do not have problems perceiving the difference in quality and value of a sofa worth $8,000 from one worth $800, why are they not able to do the same with paintings? I suggest that would-be collectors do not enter the market because of risk, due ultimately to the postmodern state of art theory. The impressionist artist Vincent van Gogh is a critical figure in this analysis; he sold only one painting during his lifetime, although his brother was an art dealer in Paris, the center of the late nineteenth-century art world.[8] Furthermore, his work was despised and dismissed by all but a few faithful friends and supporters. One hundred years after van Gogh's death, his *Portrait of Dr. Gachet* sold at Christie's New York auction house for the staggering price of $82.5 million, the highest price ever paid for a work of art in a public sale. Even if contemporary artists do not know these facts about van Gogh, fine arts culture is constructed upon them.

Van Gogh is a successful representative of the impressionist movement in art, which has been influential in shaping the modern art market. Impressionism developed in Paris during the latter half of the nineteenth century.[9] The impressionists showed their works in a series of exhibitions independent of the official salons, culminating with their last group show of 1886, which finally established their acceptance by key critics and collectors. Their work was originally seen as scandalous, rejected by the art authorities, and reviled by the public. But they were supported by a few key dealers and friendly critics. The dealers' gallery exhibitions labeled the impressionists as a unique art movement and set them apart from the masses of paintings in salons. Although much of the publicity was negative, the artwork was well known and notorious. In a modern marketing sense, the impressionists, their dealers, and critics created their own brand name.

Enormous wealth was being created in the nineteenth-century Western world, and the newly rich of America wanted to buy European art. Prices for contemporary paintings could be extraordinary: Meissonier, the preimpressionist French Academy art star, sold a painting to Vanderbilt in 1887 for the current equivalent of $1.5 million. In 1890, a painting by the Barbizon (preimpressionist) artist, Millet, sold for the current equivalent of $5.2 million (albeit after the artist's death in 1875). By 1912 a painting by the impressionist Degas sold to an American collector for $95,700 (equivalent to $5 million today, a world record at the time for a work by a living artist) (Watson 1992).

The impressionist movement in art demonstrated that dealers and supporters of avant-garde artwork could enjoy significant profits. The dealer Durand-Ruel believed in the importance of the impressionists and bought their paintings in exchange for subsistence stipends. This great dealer lived to see prices reach extraordinary heights. A group of elite young Frenchmen known as the "Bearskin" collecting club collectively bought impressionist art beginning in 1904. Only ten years later, they auctioned the collection off for *four times* what they had paid. A quarter of the auctioned works were bought by members of the Bearskin group themselves, who complained that they would have bought more if not for the high prices (Watson 1992). These fabulous profits from the resale of works of art that were so recently disparaged, and the cultural legitimacy the high prices implied, had a great impact on the modern art world.

The impressionists demonstrated that going against the received wisdom in contemporary art could be profitable for artists, dealers, and collectors alike.[10] Potential taste-makers in society learned that the negative opinions of major critics and gatekeepers, who had dismissed the impressionists' work because of crucial flaws and inadequacies, did not necessarily undermine its eventual aesthetic or market success. Impressionist art went from being so outrageous that coachmen on the street were seen loudly insulting a Monet painting in a gallery window[11] to being valued, respected, and emulated in a relatively short time.

This was a powerful lesson. Work initially rejected by both elite and popular taste could prove to be a good aesthetic choice as well as a profitable investment without a long wait. If the critics of impressionism were so wrong, if their near moral outrage over the apparent incompetence of impressionist artists turned out to be merely the complaints of orthodoxy incapable of accepting change, then the claim of other critics about ineptness or fraud in contemporary work would also be suspect. Decades later, this was the case with the abstract impressionists and the pop artists in the United States. Perhaps the most famous case was the Scull auction of pop art in 1973, where work that was recently disparaged sold for up to ninety times its original purchase price of just a few years before. There were many similar cases of extraordinary price appreciation of avant-garde art in the post–World War II era, until the art market crashed soon after the van Gogh sale in 1990.

THE CRITIC'S EFFECT ON AESTHETIC AUTHORITY

A critic in *Artnews*, a major contemporary American magazine, concluded a 1993 review article on the work of the controversial artist Jeff Koons with these words:

> most of the . . . objects struck me . . . as purposely dumb and perverse, acid, totally aware criticisms of the needs and preferences of the Great Western Unwashed *and of the attitudes of smirking, sophisticated collectors willing to pay huge prices in order to mock the bad taste of their inferiors.* (Littlejohn 1993, 94, emphasis added)

This is serious and negative, but the final words of the critic's essay are surprising:

> But that's not the way they strike [the artist] Jeff Koons . . . or, indeed, the way they strike many of his critics. If these things seem to you either desirable or profound, I know of no way to persuade you that my response is worthier than yours. (Littlejohn 1993, 94)

Of course, it is the critic's job to persuade readers of the salience of his or her taste. The abject admission that a critic had "no way to persuade" means that he had no accepted set of aesthetic values to which he could refer. This lack of values may be part of the impact of the impressionists' success.

After the impressionists, people gradually realized that much art criticism—meaning pronouncements about art quality by elite connoisseurs—had lost its authority. If so many of the "important" critics and curators were so wrong about the impressionists, why should today's commentators be different? This skepticism primarily affected those who were negative about new work; Why should they be any less wrong than their predecessors who rejected the abstract impressionists, pop artists, conceptual artists, or any of the other styles that aggressive artists and dealers pushed on the art-buying public? In each case of modern art styles, work that was initially disparaged by experts came to have very high critical *and economic* success. The underlying lesson was that it is dangerous not to embrace the new. If a respectable authority did not appreciate the new art, and the work later became successful through the efforts of other critics, curators, marketers, and collectors, then the so-called authority risked looking foolish. This fear encouraged an (un)critical rush to be the first to recognize the merit of the newest trend (which then engendered its own backlash of critical complaints that "the emperor had no clothes," meaning that much of contemporary art is, in fact, aesthetically vacuous) (Hughes 1991).

The mistrust of a dominant critical authority leads to a problem: The only available short-run measure of artistic significance, aside from the opinions of critics and curators, is market success. The market defines success in the present, and the lesson of the impressionists was that market failure today does not *necessarily* mean that the work will have no artistic significance in the future. Van Gogh's fall and subsequent rise have been taken to heart by the art world. In contrast, artists such as Meissonier and Alma-Tadema were stars in their lifetimes, and their work sold for the contemporary equivalent of millions, yet their aesthetic significance is trivial today. The lesson that lack of market success in the present does not have to mean future artistic irrelevance permeates the value system of the contemporary art world. Good artists do not *necessarily* sell paintings, and all of the paintings that sell—even for high prices—are not necessarily good. Only history can affirm aesthetic significance. This understanding, which I call the van Gogh effect, encourages artists to persevere in their work and not to be devastated by negative criticism or market rejection.

Curiously, the critics' loss of influence only works in one direction; negative pronouncements are not as authoritative as positive remarks. Key critics can still build the careers (and markets) of favored artists, but they do not seem able to damage them as readily. I believe it is the postmodern condition of contemporary culture that accounts for the weakening of negative critical authority.

POSTMODERNISM

Although I argue that the problem of identifying value in paintings can be traced to the impressionists, this pattern is part of a broader social change that has transformed contemporary high culture. Cultural life is "postmodern," meaning that the aesthetic rules that governed modernist art (including all the arts, from architecture to music to literature) have lost their hegemonic authority (Herwitz 1993). Self-referentialism, pastiches, and other sometimes playful and ironic values govern the high end of contemporary taste. Thus the general cultural environment offers no help to someone looking for clear rules of value in cultural products. Art styles (including pop art, op art, earth art, installation art, performance art, minimalism, pattern-and-decoration, and photo-realism) have whizzed through the art market at apparent lightning speed. A collector may enter a gallery, whose high white walls and impressive spaces connote a sacred place, and find small, brightly colored cubes of wood attached to the walls, or candies strewn on the floor. These works may have price tags of $2,500, $10,000, or more. The dealer says this is brilliant work made by an emerging artist who will soon be an important force in the New York art world, a new Warhol. What is one to do? Serious, committed collectors find themselves in the position of the St. Louis connoisseur who admitted,

> It's always hard to say [about a work of art], "Oh boy, this is rotten," because then you have to eat your words a couple of years later. (seventy-two-year-old retired businessman, interview by author, no. 6)

Thus far I have argued that art is a strange commodity whose commercial value is not apparent from its physical attributes, and I have discussed historical roots of the extreme consumer risk involved in buying contemporary local, noninvestment quality art. The postmodern nature of contemporary culture weakens the negative more than the positive authority of critics because it attacks the legitimacy of orthodoxy and supports the development of heterodoxy. In the next section I focus on artists in order to understand why so many exist with so little economic success.

THE GROWTH OF THE U.S. ART WORLD

How can fine artists maintain such disdain for popular taste when it leads them to a position of market weakness? This section argues that U.S. economic growth after World War II facilitated an overproduction of art; there are now more artists producing far more work than the existing consumer market can absorb. Artists' incomes are usually ensured by other sources, including full-time faculty jobs, part-time freelance work, and support from sympathetic family members. The definition of an avant-garde artist has been stretched by the van Gogh effect to include those with little or no exhibition success, enabling committed persons to maintain an artist's identity with practically no market activity. An artist who produces no art will have a hard time maintaining her identity as a "real" artist; but the hard-working artist who never sells or exhibits her work publicly, stuffing paintings into every available storage space, is nevertheless accepted as a "real" artist. Since the odds of economic success are so heavily against them, and the culture provides a rationale and justification for disdaining popular taste, artists may as well retain their sense of self-direction in their work and repudiate the market.[12]

Changes in American society after World War II created opportunities for artists of all sorts who believed that art might provide enough income to support a middle-class lifestyle. The growing wealth of the postwar U.S. economy increased the number of universities, museums, and cultural organizations that supported the arts. Public support of higher education dramatically expanded the number of institutions of higher learning, including new junior colleges, in addition to universities and colleges. This expansion created opportunities for students to study art, as well as new jobs for professional art teachers.

American art moved from the fringes of "bohemian" life to the center of middle-class values during the post–World War II period. Zukin (1982) analyzed this process in her book on SoHo. She pointed out that high prices for the few successful artists' work, coupled with the regularization of their employment as artists, "enabled them for the first time in history to make a living off a totally self-defined art" (1982, 96). Zukin (1982, 97) cited artist Larry Rivers saying, "one could go into art as a career the same as law, medicine, or government" in the early 1960s. A *Life* magazine article on Jackson Pollock and several experiments in mass marketing contemporary fine art helped to make an art career more familiar, if not fully acceptable, to working- and middle-class families. Zukin argued that the abilities of more artists to earn a living from "self-defined" art (i.e., not from commissions or production work), coupled with the art world's abandonment of the "radical ethos" of the prewar period for a "basic consensus" with the middle classes, made art a part of middle-class life. Artists "saw the same world that the middle class saw: a 'continuous past' made by rapid social and technological change, the passing of industrialism . . . and a mass production of art objects and cultural standards" (Zukin 1982, 97).[13]

According to the 1980 U.S. census, 153,162 adults identified themselves as "painters, sculptors, craft artists, and artist printmakers," an increase of 76 percent over the 1970 census figure, and a striking increase in comparison to the 28 percent growth in the labor force during this same period. By 1990, the labor force for visual artists had increased to 213,000, a 39 percent increase during a period when the total labor force grew only 19 percent. Between 1970 and 1990, artists increased by 145 percent, while professional occupations at large increased by only 89 percent and all jobs increased by just 55 percent (National Endowment for the Arts, 1992).

The increase in artists' educational levels and opportunities[14] was paralleled by museum construction. More than 2,500 new museums opened between 1950 and 1980 (Marquis 1991, 275). Fifty-eight percent of 749 arts organizations (museums, art centers, and corporate collections) studied by Crane in 1987 were founded after 1940, and over one-third were founded after 1960 (Crane 1987, 6).[15] Between 1960 and 1975, the number of dealers and galleries listed in the New York City telephone directory nearly doubled, increasing from 406 to 761. Crane examined the year of establishment of 290 New York galleries that she identified as specializing in avantgarde contemporary American art. She found that 80 percent of them were started after 1965. She also estimates that one-person exhibitions in New York rose from 800 per year in 1950 to almost 1,900 in 1985.

The growth in the postwar U.S. economy allowed many corporations to use some of their wealth for art collections. Since the 1960s, corporations of all sizes began to collect more art (Martorella 1990). Although most of these collections were closed to the public, the IBM corporation opened a public exhibition space in New York and put on important shows.[16] A new niche in the art market was created for "art consultants," who specialized in buying art in bulk, as well as in curating and conserving corporate collections.

State legislative appropriations to state arts agencies went from a total of $2.6 million in 1966 to $214.7 million in 1992 (down from a high of $292.3 million in

1990). By any measure, the growth in public investment in the arts has been impressive. In short, the increased wealth of the U.S. economy was associated with a booming interest in the arts and a significant production of artists trained to create museum-quality art, who could not earn a living from fine art production.

MARKETS FOR STARS

Fine artists are not unique in working very hard for variable, insignificant payments, in a market where few players receive enormous payments for their work. Economists consider this situation to be similar to the model of tournament, or "winner-take-all" employment contracts (Lazear and Rosen 1981).[17] In this model, employees at the highest end of the scale (such as chief executive officers of large companies) are not paid according to the value of their output, or even their input, as traditional economic theory assumes. Instead they are paid an amount corresponding to their status, which they receive because of their rank along an "executive position" scale. If lower-ranking workers are paid according to their productivity or effort, the closer one gets to the top executive positions, the less the large salaries reflect easily measurable qualities. Achieving the top wage is analogous to winning in a contest or tournament, where each worker competes for the prize against others with similar credentials.

This model is relevant to the art market because it describes a situation where workers receive payments that do not seem to reflect their effort. According to the model, it may be economically rational for companies—and by extension for society at large—to pay workers whose productivity is hard to measure, yet important, as if they were engaged in a tournament. The crux of the model is that workers competing for the top level will accept relatively smaller wages in the short run in hopes of someday winning the lottery and getting the wage prize. Fine artists, most of whom fantasize about being discovered and lionized, also maintain dreams of success. The work of serious artists—most of whom are "workaholics"—is not commensurate with their short-run income.

Rosen (1981) discusses a model of the market for superstars, where some people—often sports and entertainment stars and best-selling authors—reap gigantic payments for work that is not proportionally better than that of other slightly less talented producers in that field. The size of the top payments is justified by mass media distribution of the "product" (be it a sports or entertainment performance via television or print media), which rewards small differences in quality with large increases in audience. Since audiences prefer higher quality, the better, or "star," performances (although they seem to be extraordinarily expensive) easily dominate lesser performances in net revenue because of the mass demand and low distribution cost.

This argument was extended by Adler (1985), who pointed out that in situations where knowledge affects the pleasure a consumer receives, such as in the arts, stars can emerge who have *no* perceivable superiority of talent. Adler assumes that a consumer's knowledge is dependent on social learning, such as discussing art appreciation with other like-minded consumers. For those types of art (e.g., performing arts), the greater the availability of potential discussants, the easier it is for a consumer to amass more expertise or "consumption capital," which increases one's enjoyment even more. Adler argues that when an artist rises in popularity, even if for reasons unconnected to superior performance, it makes sense for consumers to patronize the more popular artist; the larger the group of fans, the lower the synergetic cost of searching for knowledgeable discussants. As Adler puts it, "Stardom is a market device to economize on learning costs in activities where the more you know the more you enjoy" (1985, 208).

Towse (1992) provides a corroborative case study of these theories as they apply to the market for classical music singers in Britain:

> People who know very little about opera will buy a record by a singer "they've heard of," in order to avoid disappointment; opera houses can always fill seats by performing "warhorses." . . . As there are many more people with a little knowledge, this explains why superstars have much bigger markets. (1992, 211)

Towse notes that the theory's key element deals with search costs for information, and she discusses the problem faced by opera companies looking for singers. The average company deals with significant search problems, since it must hire approximately 300 to 400 principals a year, and relies on a wide range of informational devices, from auditions and national competitions to agents and promoters. Towse defines talent as a "bundle of services—voice, voice type, stage presence, physical appearance, musicianship, ability to work with others—and a 'talented' singer is one with the right combination at the right time" (1992, 213). If defined this way, she notes, talent is socially determined. Adler's concept of consumer's capital (with synergistic interdependence between consumers) implies that star singers, whose talent is widely known, attract large audiences and demand high fees. In performing art, the size of the fee can correlate with the cost of the ticket; hence, consumers recognize that higher prices denote higher talent. Lowering an established fee for a singer indicates waning talent, since the fee represents demand for the singer's "bundle of services." Towse (1992, 214) observes that, "at the bottom end of the market the result is that struggling singers cannot increase the demand for their services by lowering their fees, since all that indicates is that they are struggling! Instead of a lower fee stimulating demand, it will depress it."

This of course is an economic paradox in a capitalist society, where lower prices are supposed to increase demand. The paradox applies as well to the market for visual art. A St. Louis artist recalled her dealer pricing some work, saying (only half-jokingly), "Let's put it at $1,200. If it doesn't sell we'll raise it to $1,800" (interview by author, no. 138). The underlying assumption that explains such paradoxes is that art consumers mistrust their own judgment and use price as a measure of quality.

In the absence of a well-defined set of rules for judging quality in art, price and how widely the work is distributed are often taken as signals of excellence.[18]

The "superstar" model is also relevant to the visual art market in that it describes a few producers earning most of the money spent on comparable products. It also explains why museums will pay extraordinary sums for artwork, since the cost is amortized over the huge audiences that the "art star" can attract. The model further accounts for why buyers in the private dealer market hesitate to spend significant sums of money for work that is not "museum quality"; namely, they do not feel supported by a wide enough group of co-consumers (the visual art standard is whether the art has "legitimacy"). Towse's argument about the disjunction between the price of a singer's services and the size of the singer's market reminds us that the standard economic relationship between price and demand often fails to apply to art goods. Most artists cannot increase demand by lowering prices; a reduction in price signals a preexisting reduction in demand, except for those with established markets. In short, art differs from other commodities because average consumers cannot discern quality from visual attributes alone, and price works as a marker of quality (Veblen 1934 [1899]; Liebenstein 1950).

THE POWER OF DEALERS

Some artists bypass dealers and sell their work on their own. Energetic artists can earn a respectable income by selling in the large network of U.S. art fairs. But work sold in these venues tends to be decorative and of low aesthetic quality. High art producers depend on professional dealers to legitimize the value of their work and to sell it. The typical gallery carries exclusively the work of about one to two dozen artists, meaning that the dealer has a monopoly right over all art sales in a defined area. There are fewer than 4,000 private galleries, dealers, and consultants in the country to represent the work of the serious fine artists, who number about 70,000.[19] As one dealer put it:

> Because there are so many more artists than there are dealers, they are always going to feel like they are getting the fuzzy end of the lollipop. (fifty-five-year-old single male dealer, interview by author, no. 10)

Dealers in high art usually attempt to monopolize the sales of their artists:

> We require an exclusive for the area that we cover, the entire Midwest. . . . I run a pretty tough organization with respect to that. If an artist takes advantage of me they are out of here. . . . Where an artist will try to do an end run and do a direct sale with a client or try to cut us out.
>
> [SP: So you will insist on getting your full 50 percent even if, what if the person who comes in is a next door neighbor of the artist?]

I don't believe that it matters whether it is or not. You either have a professional relationship and you honor it both ways or you don't have one. . . . It's a business arrangement from that standpoint. It doesn't matter to me if it's a next door neighbor or who it is. If they are discounting work or selling out of their studios they are not meeting their obligations and any artist should do that with any dealer. I'm very, very straight on that. I don't make exceptions on that . . . it simply is a function of whether you have the trust and the relationship, that you are there for the long term. Normally what happens is that when you [the artists] try to get a quick sale, it is a short term game and if it's a short term game that outweighs the long term orientation then that's a decision that they [the artists] have to make. They have to understand that if they make that decision, we're through. (forty-six-year-old dealer married to an artist, interview by author, no. 118)

In a normal market, dealers who follow such monopolistic practices would compete with dealers who do not insist on exclusionary rights. But the consumer risk inherent in buying contemporary local art means that there are many fewer collectors than the economy could support. Even with their monopolistic practices, dealers have a difficult time making ends meet. In St. Louis, the most successful dealers rely on nonart income for long periods of time. The dealer business works best for people who truly love art and do not need to earn a living from their work. Even then, the typical dealer leaves the business after about five years of hard work, lackluster sales, and minimal support from the local community.

CONCLUSION

Prevailing market ethics allow dealers to claim a share of an artist's studio sale to a customer the dealer may never have seen. Dealers argue that an artist's affiliation with their gallery legitimizes the art's price; they claim the gallery's general support of the artist as a reimbursable part of every sale. Similarly, interior designers claim a share of a dealer's sale to a shared client, even though the designer may never have set foot in the gallery and, dealers suspect, may never have seen the artwork before the sale. The designer's aesthetic approval of the work's presence in the client's home, albeit after the sale, is claimed as a reimbursable factor in allowing the sale to become permanent. This argument only works if the actual buyer (the collector) does not have the reputation of making up his or her own mind in aesthetic matters, which justifies a designer's claim to have validated the purchase. Since a client usually has the right to return a work to the gallery, even after payment, the designer's demand for a share of the sale is often grudgingly rewarded.

These sorts of payments are routine and testify to the complex nature of art sales. The subjective value of a work of art can vary with subtle changes in attitudes. The value of every economic transaction is complex and includes subjective as well as objective features, and social as well as physical attributes. Even mass-produced manufactured goods have (appropriately) different prices depending on the specifics of the transaction; for example, consumers routinely pay more for hardware or packaged foods at local stores that provide personalized services or convenient hours.

In this chapter I have argued that art is an extreme case of subjective and social valuation. Consumers' difficulties in recognizing commercial value in local fine art lead other economic actors to claim shares of such transactions because such additional actors have positively affected buyers' attitudes. This chapter has shown that economic behavior in the art market can be understood without reference to aesthetic theory or the transcendent value of art. While these conventional economic theories explain the unconventional behavior of many artists, dealers, and collectors, the entire lived experience in the art world is not understandable without recognizing the real love and passion that art inspires in those who are committed to it.

NOTES

The material in this chapter draws from the monograph *High Art Down Home: An Economic Ethnography of a Local Art Market* (Chicago: University of Chicago Press, 1996), and from "A Most Ingenious Paradox: The Market for Contemporary Fine Art," *American Anthropologist* 100(2): 482–493 (June 1998). This chapter is based on twelve months of ethnographic research in St. Louis, Missouri (August 1992–July 1993) while the author was on leave from the National Science Foundation. I thank the American Anthropological Association and the University of Chicago Press for permission to draw on previously published material.

1. Characterizing sellers and buyers in this way dichotomizes the two dimensions to simplify the exposition. In reality any individual seller or buyer is a complex, multidimensional and contingent blend of these values.

2. The elite art dealer, Arnold Glimcher of Pace Gallery in New York, said a similar thing in salesman's language: "Artworks are worth much more than the prices that are put on them, or they're not worth anything. What is X million dollars next to this tool by which society sees differently, understands itself another way? These are the great mirrors of our time." (*New York Times Magazine,* 3 October 1993, 33).

3. Interview numbers refer to a series of 138 formal interviews conducted by the author in St. Louis during the 1992–1993 academic year. All interviews were conducted in person; most were tape-recorded.

4. The term "museum-quality" is my term. Artists of that type use the phrase "real artist" for themselves, and "commercial artist" to denote artists doing commercial work. They reserve the pejorative "hack artist" or worse for profit-oriented types who produce work speculatively.

5. That does not mean that all buyers are always callously inconsiderate of the conditions of production of every type of good they buy, or that all producers are insensitive to their public image. The consumer political pressures on international companies doing business in South Africa before democratization and the growth of "issue" investment funds and credit cards are examples of consumers acting on their concern about the political or ecological

context of production of the goods they buy. The long-standing Farm Workers' Union political boycott against U.S. table grapes, while not a success, probably has had some impact on the industry. Yet in the aggregate these represent minor counter forces to a massive consumer concern about goods irrespective of their conditions of production.

6. Major academic studies of the investment value of art have been done by Baumol (1986), Frey and Pommerehne (1989), Goetzmann (1993), Pesando (1993), and Singer (1990) and are surveyed in Frey and Eichenberger (1995). Watson also summarizes the experience of the British Rail Pension Fund (1992, 423–432). The main conclusion of these studies is that art investment is risky and tends to give a rate of return not significantly greater than the safest investment possible, government securities, somewhere around 2 percent a year. The shorter the holding period of the artwork, the larger the risk and potential profit or loss.

Pesando (1993) analyzed prices for 27,961 repeat sales of modern prints from 1977 to 1992, coded from annual publications of print auction prices. His study is particularly interesting because he dealt with multiples, which in principle reduces the uncertainty of dealing with unique works such as paintings, and with modern masters such as Picasso, Chagall, and Miro. He also coded prices after the bust of 1990, which corrects for the price and sales inflation leading up to that period in earlier studies. Pesando found that the mean real return on an aggregate print portfolio (1.51 percent) was less than the mean real return for Treasury bills (2.23 percent), long-term bonds (2.54 percent), and far less than stocks (8.14 percent). The standard deviations of the real returns to the print portfolio were almost 20 percent. Thus investors in modern prints suffered more risk for lower returns than they would have in the safest alternative investment.

Pesando separated the most expensive works from others, to test the hypothesis that investment in the best works is safer than investment in average works. A portfolio of Picasso prints (6,010 repeat sales) yielded a 2.10 percent real return with a standard deviation of 23 percent—a higher return with more risk than the entire portfolio, but still a worse investment—lower gain and higher risk—than the safest alternative. Pesando also separated the most expensive 10 percent of all the prints by any artist and examined their price appreciation, which he found to be no better—and sometimes worse—than the average-priced prints.

7. See Halle 1993 for an impressive sociological study of art collecting by a range of people in the New York metropolitan area.

8. While van Gogh is technically classified as a "postimpressionist" painter by art historians, his work functions in the auction market as impressionist work.

9. "The name 'impressionist' was in the great tradition of rebel names. Thrown at them initially as a gibe to . . . insult them, it was adopted by the group in defiance . . . and made into a winning pennant" (White and White 1965, 111).

10. This lesson did not apply to classical or "old-master" art, where the opinions of established experts are crucial.

11. According to the biography of the dealer Daniel-Henri Kahnweiler, by Assouline (1988).

12. For an interesting discussion of literary origins of the high art rejection of popular taste and the market as arbiters of aesthetic significance, see Woodmansee 1994.

13. Rivers and Zukin notwithstanding, art students still joke that no one's father ever sat them down and said, "Your mother and I would be most happy to see you consider a career as a sculptor."

14. By 1989, there were 1,146 institutions in the United States offering bachelor's degrees in visual and performing arts, and 362 institutions offering master's degrees in these areas. (The Master of Fine Arts [MFA] degree is the terminal professional degree for artists. These data are from Table 3-42 of the 1989 *Sourcebook of Arts Statistics* and Tables 3-2 and 3-4 of the 1992 *Addendum to the 1989 Sourcebook,* both published by the National Endowment for the Arts.) From 1970 to 1989, these institutions graduated 733,099 bachelor's degrees and 157,982 master's degrees in the visual and performing arts. Of these, I estimate that 42 percent of the bachelor's and 33 percent of the master's degrees were in the visual arts, for a total of 307,900 bachelor's degrees and 52,134 master's degrees in the visual arts alone. (The estimate is based on averaging two years of data broken down by subfield given in the NEA publication.) This is an annual average of 16,205 bachelor's and 2,744 master's degrees.

For comparison, in 1988–1989, 30,293 bachelor's degrees were awarded in English; that same year, 37,781 bachelor's degrees were awarded in the visual and performing arts, of which 16,172 were in fine arts. In 1988–1989, 4,807 master's and doctor's degrees were awarded in English, and 8,989 master's and doctor's degrees were conferred in the visual and performing arts, of which 2,924 were in fine arts.

15. Crane analyzed only those institutions whose date of origin between 1900 and 1979 she was able to ascertain, excluding museums in New York City.

16. Until it was closed in 1994, a victim of the declining profits of the company.

17. This work has recently been popularized by Frank and Cook (1995). I thank Daniel Newlon for pointing out the relevance of these economic models. He is not responsible for any misunderstanding professional economists may see in this discussion.

18. Goods susceptible to this sort of pricing are sometimes called "Veblen" goods, since the economist Thorstein Veblen's influential work on "conspicuous consumption," where buyers seek to pay more to display their financial strength (see Veblen 1934 [1899]).

19. The figure for private dealers comes from the Art in America *Annual Guide to Museums, Galleries, Artists* (New York: Brant Art Publications Inc., 1992). It is very hard to estimate the number of fine artists. The 1990 census lists 212,762 "painters, sculptors, craft-artists, and artist printmakers." My ethnography in St. Louis found about 800 serious artists out of a census figure of about 2,200. Applying the same ratio to the national figure produces an estimate of over 77,000 serious artists nationwide.

REFERENCES

Adler, Moshe. 1985. Stardom and Talent. *American Economic Review* 75: 208–212.

Akerlof, George. 1970. The Market for "Lemons": Quality Uncertainty and the Market Mechanism. *Quarterly Journal of Economics* 84: 488–500.

Assouline, Pierre. 1988. *An Artful Life: A Biography of D. H. Kahnweiler, 1884–1979.* New York: Grove & Weidenfeld.

Baumol, William. 1986. Unnatural Value of Art Investments as Floating Crap Game. *American Economic Review Papers and Proceedings* 76 (May): 10–16.

Crane, Diana. 1987. *The Transformation of the Avant-Garde.* Chicago: University of Chicago Press.

Frank, Robert, and Philip Cook. 1995. *The Winner-Take-All Society.* New York: Free Press.

Frey, Bruno S., and Reiner Eichenberger. 1995. On the Return of Art Investment Return Analyses. *Journal of Cultural Economics* 19: 207–220.

Frey, Bruno S., and Werner W. Pommerehne. 1989. Art Investment: An Empirical Enquiry. *Southern Economic Journal* 56: 396–409.

Goetzmann, William. 1993. Accounting for Taste: Art and the Financial Markets over Three Centuries. *American Economic Review* 83: 1370–1376.

Halle, David. 1993. *Inside Culture: Art and Class in the American Home.* Chicago: University of Chicago Press.

Herwitz, Daniel A. 1993. *Making Theory/Constructing Art: On the Authority of the Avant Garde.* Chicago: University of Chicago Press.

Hughes, Robert. 1991. *The Shock of the New.* New York: Knopf.

Lazear, Edward, and Sherwin Rosen. 1981. Rank-Order Tournaments as Optimal Labor Contracts. *Journal of Political Economy* 89: 841–864.

Liebenstein, Harvey. 1950. Bandwagon, Snob and Veblen Effects in the Theory of Consumer Demand. *Quarterly Journal of Economics* 65: 183–207.

Littlejohn, David. 1993. Who Is Jeff Koons and Why Are People Saying Such Terrible Things About Him? *Artnews* 92(4): 91–94.

McGarrell, James. 1986. Interview. *New Art Examiner* (June): 12.

Marquis, Alice Goldfarb. 1991. *The Art Biz: The Covert World of Collectors, Dealers, Auction Houses, Museums, and Critics.* Chicago: Contemporary Books.

Martorella, Rosanne. 1990. *Corporate Art.* New Brunswick, N.J.: Rutgers University Press.

Museum Print Mix-up. 1990. *Art & Auction.* (Dec.): 32–33.

National Endowment for the Arts (NEA). 1984. *Visual Artists in Houston, Minneapolis, Washington, and San Francisco.* Research Division Report no. 18. Washington, D.C.: NEA.

———. 1989. *Sourcebook of Arts Statistics.* Washington, D.C.: NEA.

———. 1992. *Addendum to the 1989 Sourcebook of Arts Statistics.* Washington, D.C.: NEA.

Pesando. 1993. Art as an Investment: The Market for Modern Prints. *American Economic Review* 83: 1075–1089.

Plattner, Stuart. 1985. Equilibrating Market Relationships. In Stuart Plattner, ed., *Markets and Marketing.* Monographs in Economic Anthropology, no. 4. Lanham, Md.: University Press of America for the Society for Economic Anthropology.

———, ed. 1996. *High Art Down Home: An Economic Ethnography of a Local Art Market.* Chicago: University of Chicago Press.

———. 1998. A Most Ingenious Paradox. *American Anthropologist.* 100(2): 428–493.

Rosen, Sherwin. 1981. The Economics of Superstars. *American Economic Review* 71(5): 845–858.

Simpson, Charles R. 1981. *SoHo: The Artist in the City.* Chicago: University of Chicago Press.

Singer, Leslie P. 1990. The Utility of Art versus Fair Bets in the Investment Market. *Journal of Cultural Economics* 14(2): 1–13.

Towse, Ruth. 1992. The Earnings of Singers: An Economic Analysis. In Ruth Towse and Abdul Khakee, eds., *Cultural Economics.* Berlin: Springer-Verlag.

Veblen, Thorstein. 1934 [1899]. *The Theory of the Leisure Class.* New York: Random House.

Watson, Peter. 1992. *From Manet to Manhattan: The Rise of the Modern Art Market.* New York: Random House.

White, Harrison, and Cynthia White. 1965. *Canvases and Careers: Institutional Changes in the French Painting World.* New York: Wiley.

Wilson, James. 1980. Adaptation to Uncertainty and Small Numbers Exchange: The New England Fresh Fish Market. *Bell Journal of Economics* 11: 491–504.

Woodmansee, Martha. 1994. *The Author, Art and the Market: Rereading the History of Aesthetics.* New York: Columbia University Press.

Zukin, Sharon. 1982. *Loft Living: Culture and Capital in Urban Change.* Baltimore: Johns Hopkins University Press.

7

The Commodification of Hybrid Corn: What Farmers Know

Randy Ziegenhorn

INTRODUCTION

When buying a jar of jam at the grocery store, one takes the ingredient label for granted. When purchasing a bottle of pain reliever, one may give the label more thought, choosing between generic and brand name versions of a chemical. In Iowa, farmers buy herbicides that bear fanciful names such as Prowl and Stinger, but again chemical constituents are indicated on the label. Livestock are sold with gilt-edged pedigree certificates that specify the animal's forebears for several generations. Truth-in-labeling laws protect consumers from unsafe products and allow us to know what things are made of and whether they are genuine. Such clear identification, and the protection it affords, was not always possible, and consequences ranged from economic loss to shattered lives. One segment of the American agricultural economy, however, has evaded our product identification system.

The hybrid corn seed industry hides from farmers the underlying identities of marketed hybrid seed. Analysis of that marketing disguise is relevant to this volume's commodity focus for a number of reasons. First, it addresses core epistemological issues about artifacts we exchange and value: what is this item, what are its parts, what makes it unique, how is it like other goods, do its characteristics make it more or less valuable? Second, the history of hybrid corn seeds also illustrates how capitalism reshapes the identities of things, bestowing on them a value they may not otherwise possess. Third, this chapter emphasizes the state's role in establishing rules that give a commodity its particular social and economic characteristics. Appadurai describes these complex relationships: "At every level where a smaller system interacts with a larger one, the interplay of knowledge and ignorance serves as a turnstile, facilitating the flow of some things and hindering the movement of others" (1986, 56). This chapter focuses on that interplay of knowledge and ignorance and its consequences for Iowa farmers.

THE DEVELOPMENT OF HYBRID CORN

The industrialization of American agriculture brought a gradual erosion in farmers' ability to produce inputs required to sustain high production levels. Seeds, fertilizers, and tools that were once produced on farms were increasingly obtained in the marketplace. As farmers adopted new technologies, earlier kinds of knowledge were lost. Farming became less a matter of the farmer's own skill and products than of purchasing technologies and knowledge developed by others.

This chapter explores one such agricultural innovation: the transformation of corn seed production from a skilled task carried out by farmers to the product of a scientifically complex and highly profitable industry. The relationship between farmer and seed changed so that seeds were no longer a handicraft or their progeny evidence of skillful husbandry. Instead, seed became an artifact of an industrial system. Farmers viewed this system through a lens of advertising and government-sponsored research aimed at convincing them of the new technology's superiority.

Crucial to the success of the technical innovation known as hybrid corn was a complex social and economic process designed to hide the underlying identities of seeds from farmers. This monopoly on information enabled seed companies to reap profits and establish a successful industry. Hybrid corn's commercial success depended on a complex system of trade secrecy that limited competition. Before hybrids became available, natural and social barriers prevented capital accumulation in seed production. No seed industry developed since plant breeders and seed producers faced a common dilemma: seed-bearing plants are readily copied. The developers or promoters of a new seed-bearing plant can only sell the novel variety a few times before the value of their effort is diluted in the marketplace. Customers and competitors alike reap the benefits of a breeder's efforts merely by growing the crop and saving seeds.

In the early twentieth century, however, geneticist George H. Shull proposed a novel form of plant breeding that involved inbreeding and, subsequently, crossbreeding corn plants (Shull 1909). The new product was called a hybrid. The term itself was not new; any cross of two genetically different members of a species is called a hybrid. The inbred-hybrid method of breeding, however, was new. Shull termed the increased vigor and yield of hybrids "heterosis." Heterosis carried an unusual characteristic: the value of the effect declined in succeeding generations. That is, the vigor and yield of plants produced from hybrid seed declined significantly after the first generation. As hybrid corn moved from an interesting laboratory experiment to a

product with commercial potential, the decline in heterosis assumed significance. A farmer who planted hybrid seed would be unwise to save any of the progeny for his next crop and therefore probably would return to the seed company as a customer in subsequent years.

Although the decline in heterosis is a necessary condition for capital accumulation in the hybrid seed industry, it is not a sufficient explanation for the economic success of either the industry or of particular companies. Success hinged on the ability to keep secret the specific combination of inbreds used in the production of a particular hybrid. Secrecy allowed the developer of new corn hybrids to protect the identity of each. Such protection created a barrier to knowledge between competing firms. Secrecy also allowed more than one company to sell the same hybrid by disguising it with different names, thus creating a knowledge barrier between farmers and seed companies. The combined effect of these two practices insulated the fledgling hybrid seed corn industry from potentially ruinous competition. Secrecy also prevented farmers from making the kinds of informed choices that drive competition.

Land grant universities acted as catalysts in this corn seed industry transformation. State universities in the Midwest played a pivotal role not only in carrying out much of the basic research underlying hybrid corn development but also in identifying specific inbreds and hybrids that had commercial potential. The universities aided the widespread diffusion of hybrid corn by helping to establish the system of trade secrecy known as the "closed pedigree" distribution method. Closed pedigrees drew a curtain across the inner workings of the industry by disguising the common origin of many hybrids. Universities established a network of yield-testing programs that presented each new commercial hybrid as a unique innovation evaluated by objective research. The authority of agricultural research institutions obscured the intricate arrangements that protected the seed industry from competition.

HYBRID CORN: IDENTIFICATION AND DISTRIBUTION

By the late 1920s both technical and social conditions favored the commercial introduction of hybrid corn. Hybrid corn's technical feasibility had been demonstrated by the work of Shull and many others. In Iowa, Henry A. Wallace became the focal point of this activity. Wallace's promotion of hybrid corn in his family's magazine, *Wallace's Farmer,* coupled with his early experimental hybrids' strong showings in the Iowa Corn Yield Test, attracted the attention of a wide variety of individuals interested in corn improvement. Researchers on experiment stations and in universities, college students, merchants, and farmers wrote to Wallace in the late 1920s requesting samples of inbreds and hybrids for research, commercial exploitation, and on-farm use. To popularize hybrid corn, Wallace entered the Iowa Corn Yield Test with individuals who produced hybrids under his direction. In 1926, after three years of

producing and selling limited quantities of hybrid seed corn himself, Wallace, along with several others, formed the Hi-Bred Corn Company (later renamed Pioneer Hi-Bred). Wallace entered into various arrangements to produce and distribute hybrid corn during this period. Even as he was developing Hi-Bred as a recognizable brand name Wallace shared his inbreds and pedigrees not only with university researchers but with other companies interested in commercial development of their hybrid lines. At the same time, Wallace began to establish barriers to information flows both within and outside this rather loosely organized group. By 1930 Wallace's correspondence clearly indicates that he and other private breeders were concerned with protecting the advantage gained from their research by curtailing the spread of pedigree information (Pfister 1928; Wallace 1930a). His documents also reveal that on at least one occasion an individual misappropriated breeding materials that Wallace had sent him to test (Wallace 1931a). Meanwhile, Wallace acquired from a university breeder in Indiana the inbred that he and others regarded as key to the Hi-Bred company's early commercial success (Urban 1976, 50; Baker 1994).

In March 1931, Don Griswold, a county agent from Clarinda, Iowa, wrote to Wallace about a conversation he had had with Ross Salmon, a salesman for a company Wallace supplied with breeding materials. Griswold reported that Salmon told him, "he was not at liberty to give us the pedigree on this commercial stock of inbrid [sic] corn. It seems unfortunate that producers cannot get pedigrees just the same as livestock producers can at this time. Perhaps that is a development that will come later." Griswold adds, "I am writing to you especially to learn about this matter of keeping us in the dark on pedigrees" (Griswold 1931, 1).

In his reply, Wallace (1931b) agreed that "there should be some guarantee of identity." Wallace also acknowledged that it was possible to confuse the performance of one corn with another. He explained that those who had "developed good combinations are not likely to give out information that will enable other people to use those same combinations." Wallace also mentioned plans at Iowa State College to establish a "system of certification" under which "it will then be possible to buy commercial hybrid corn with a certificate as to its genetic composition" (Wallace 1931b, 1).

Wallace's correspondence with Griswold, Salmon, and others points to the second set of problems associated with hybrid corn's introduction. Wallace did not mention to Griswold that he and Salmon had often attempted to skew the results of the Iowa Corn Yield Test in their favor. By entering several low-yielding varieties under the names of Salmon's employees, Wallace hoped to exaggerate the relative performance of certain commercial entries (Wallace 1930b, 1930c). In addition, Wallace frequently entered a particular hybrid under different names in different locations and years (Wallace 1929; Holbert 1929). The visual uniformity of hybrids actually aided this deception since farmers were told to de-emphasize appearance when judging hybrids. Two visually identical hybrids often had marked performance differences. Wallace had actively campaigned against aesthetic criteria of corn selec-

tion that had guided farmers in the past. Wallace also obscured the parentage of his products because he and others had developed a dual system of nomenclature for identifying hybrid corn. With those he trusted Wallace exchanged information about inbreds and hybrids using a form of private nomenclature called the pedigree. This open exchange of information did not extend to farmers and often excluded the staff of the Iowa Agricultural Experiment Association (IAEA), the sponsors of the Iowa Corn Yield Test. By giving hybrids arbitrary public names, Wallace created a barrier to knowledge. The intention was to preserve for breeders the benefits of their private plant selection. The unintended consequence was that farmers really did not know much about the product in the seed bag.

In 1929 the U.S. Department of Agriculture's experiment station in Ames, Iowa, which was staffed mostly by researchers from Iowa State College, distributed single-cross corn for field testing by farmers. In 1931 the station also began to distribute double crosses developed from its research program. Single crosses were distributed in 1932 with specific instructions for making double-cross hybrids. Inbreds were first released in 1934 (Robinson and Knott 1963, 148–152). In 1932 the IAEA instituted a certification program for hybrid corn, which followed a system adopted for other crops and provided farmers with some information about hybrid identity. Seeds produced for certification were grown under the inspection of the association, an organization affiliated with Iowa State College. The association adopted stringent guidelines for certification and awarded the "blue tag" that was affixed to seed bags as proof of quality. A few years after adopting this certification program, commercial double-cross hybrids released by the Ames experiment station and elsewhere were listed in the Iowa Corn Yield Test with their unique names and pedigrees. Privately developed hybrids, sold under a variety of "trade" names, were eligible for certification as well, provided that the company requesting certification met certain guidelines and allowed a thorough inspection of their seed fields by the experiment association staff. These companies also furnished pedigrees to help the staff determine the purity of resulting crosses. In short, the IAEA certified both the "public hybrids" released by the experiment station as well as hybrids produced privately.

The hybrid corn certification program was intended "to confirm the trueness to name of the seed stocks," and "to give purchasers reasonable assurance that the seed is true to designation, and is in satisfactory condition for planting" (Iowa Agricultural Experiment Station 1937, 1). The association, however, did not require the certification of hybrid seeds as a condition of sale, and it did not disclose the pedigrees private companies provided for hybrid certification. To protect the legitimate rights of private plant breeders to protect their trade secrets, the association and the university overlooked farmers' rights to make informed choices. Thus, the university oversaw the creation of public and private arenas of knowledge. In the public arena, farmers and seed producers met as buyers and sellers with common knowledge. In the private domain, only the seed producers fully understood the terms of trade.

THE HYBRID SEED CORN INDUSTRY

The release of certified single-cross hybrids by the universities allowed companies and individuals interested in commercial hybrid production to enter the market without engaging in the difficult work of developing inbreds. Rather than test the thousands of possible inbreds and hybrid combinations as Wallace had done, this second wave of hybrid producers took advantage of university researchers' work. Not only did the universities release inbreds and single crosses eligible for certification, they also tested double-cross hybrids that were released to all producers. New seed companies either produced public hybrids, for which pedigrees were given to farmers, or they created their own brand names and numbers out of the many possible combinations of single crosses available. Information available to farmers revealed nothing about pedigrees of brand name hybrids or the source of a company's breeding stocks. Since certification was optional, companies were free to place hybrids on the market without any independent verification of their identity.

The issue of hybrid identity and closed pedigrees caused tension between the public and private sectors in the seed industry. At the Sixth Corn Improvement Conference of the North Central Region held in St. Louis in November 1941, R. A. Brink, a geneticist from the experiment station at the University of Wisconsin, presented the public plant breeding community's viewpoint. Ken Ford, an executive of the Triangle Advertising Agency of Chicago, presented the industry's point of view. Brink considered and rejected a number of arguments for disclosing hybrid corn pedigrees to farmers. However, he presented one reason that he felt had merit:

> I infer, although from the nature of the case cannot affirm, that a given hybrid is not infrequently sold under different designations by various seed concerns. Out of the vast amount of testing done by public and private agencies, let us suppose that a certain combination emerges that is superior to the others and for which a demand arises from farmers who grow it. Companies operating in the territory for which it is suited desire to add the hybrid to their line. Now if each concern applies to it a number of their own without showing the pedigree, we have a common stock being represented under a variety of designations which only confuse the farmer who wants to buy it. The object of such diversification of nomenclature by seedsmen, I take it, is to gain some competitive advantage. . . . Disclosure of the pedigree would knock down the whole row of aliases at once and—to change the metaphor—restore the hybrid to the path of incorruption upon which it was presumed to have been set at first christening. (Brink 1941, 5)

Following Brink, Ford opened with a cautionary tale based on the experience of an unidentified hybrid seed producer. His description matched much of the recorded experience of Lester Pfister of Illinois and the correspondence was surely not lost on Ford's audience (cf. Fitzgerald 1990, 185–189). The producer had originally acquired breeding stocks in the early 1930s and marketed his hybrids as "Hybrid Corn." When the open pedigree public hybrids were released he followed the required naming schemes. At the same time this producer had developed a valuable inbred that he distributed to public and private breeders alike. Over time the inbred lost any connection to his name and he considered it just as well. After all, if it were used in a poor-yielding cross, any identification with his name might reflect badly on his hybrids. The same producer also vigorously promoted the earliest public hybrids but in later years often found himself confronted with competitors who undersold him. These competitors had not developed the same techniques to guarantee quality that the more experienced producer had. Ford portrayed this as an unfortunate occurrence, with the newcomers to the market "fly[ing] on the tail of the other man's kite" (Ford 1941, 10). The solution was for the producer to place his products under a private brand name and number. Ford gave two crucial reasons for this action: "as a means of protection against price slashing competition, but also as a means of positively identifying his product which he honestly believed to be superior to other peoples' products with similar pedigree, but with different quality safeguards" (1941, 10). After a few years, competitors charged this producer with selling "a widely used open-pedigree number with a code name and a fancy price" (1941, 10). The same individual faced the paradoxical prospect of opening his pedigrees to claim the uniqueness of his own hybrids.

Ford noted the disagreement in the new industry over this issue. Hybrid producers were splitting into two antagonistic camps and their competitive practices were frequently destructive. His view of the future seems, in retrospect, prophetic:

> In a more mature industry competitive hybrid seed corn producers may still look for weaknesses in one another's armor. Each producer will strive to give the public the perfect product it wants and to overcome what the public dislikes. . . . But the formulas of competitors, or whether or not the competitor discloses his formulas, will be of no concern in the merchandising program and will never be mentioned in advertising or selling. (Ford 1941, 12)

In closing, Ford cited a comment from an unnamed industry source suggesting that the pedigree issue was not important: "I believe the average buyer of seed does not give a 'hoop' whether the pedigree is closed or open so long as he gets corn which performs and which he knows he can replace in another year" (1941, 16).

Ford advocated a system that would foster cooperation and limit price competition. He also sidestepped the issue Brink considered crucial—the farmer's ability to choose and to benefit, as a buyer, from open competition. Ford exemplified a second shift that had occurred in the long endeavor to improve agricultural productivity. The first change occurred with the commodification of knowledge, a shift from the mass education of farmers to the knowledge-bearing product, or from selection to seed. The second modification was privatization of that knowledge through commodification of the seed itself. Ford argued that the knowledge contained in the seed product should be reserved for a few (namely, the seed industry) in order to guarantee the economic security of individual firms. Brink argued that knowledge obtained at public expense ought to be publicly available. The final commodification of hybrid seed occurred when seed producers argued successfully that the arbitrary social relations that economically advantaged the industry were irrelevant to farmers. Farmers' attention and universities' research efforts should focus on the commodity itself, rather than on the social relations underlying its distribution. Brink's and Ford's positions reflect the further separation of farmers' interests from those of the seed industry and the universities. Universities helped create the seed industry to enhance farmers' productivity and profit. Within a few years, however, it was industry that dictated who was to benefit.

By the early 1940s, the hybrid seed corn industry had developed a stable structure. Universities funded basic research in genetics and agronomy, as well as practical breeding programs that continued to provide inbreds and single crosses to the industry. Universities also trained new plant breeders, many of whom then worked in the seed corn industry. A few companies increased the supply of university seed lines, maintained their purity in succeeding years, and distributed these lines to the industry. Both universities and these "foundation" seed companies tested the inbreds and single crosses in various combinations, hoping to find successful hybrids for general distribution. Individual seed companies also undertook as much testing as their resources would allow, in order to identify promising combinations. A segmentation began to take place among commercial hybrid seed corn producers. The largest firms, Pioneer in Iowa and Funk and DeKalb in Illinois, increased their market shares and supported their own internal breeding programs. By combining lines that they alone controlled with lines developed by universities, these large firms were able to develop unique products. They sought a national and eventually international market for these commodities and attracted many of the brightest graduates of the land grant universities. In addition, a number of middle-sized companies emerged in regional rather than national markets. These companies had limited research budgets and depended more heavily than the large firms on the results of university breeding programs. Another industry segment consisted of many small, family-owned firms with local markets. These firms relied entirely on the universities for hybrid crosses, and many produced only certified hybrids. Others marketed hybrids that were often, as Ford noted, open-pedigree hybrids with code names and high prices. As one industry veteran described it, "everybody sold U.S.13 but called it something else" (John Spence, telephone interview, 28 October 1994).

The seed industry's emergent structure is illustrated by the case of Roland Holden and his father Carl Holden, of Williamsburg, Iowa. Both had years of experience in breeding open-pollinated corn and in entering state yield contests. Roland Holden began producing and selling foundation seeds in the early 1940s. In 1943, Holden agreed to let John Spence, a Des Moines businessman, handle promotion, sales, and collections for the growing business (Spence 1983, 5). This left Holden free to concentrate on technical aspects of the foundation seed business. Spence later established his own firm, Corn States Hybrid Service, in Des Moines, to market foundation seeds and processing equipment. Spence and Holden maintained testing plots in various locations to evaluate hybrids (Spence 1983, 50). Corn States and Holden maintained a special relationship with the seed producers who were their customers. Both firms knew what combinations made up the closed pedigree hybrids their customers offered for sale to farmers, but they maintained a policy of not disclosing one of their seed producer's pedigrees to another. In addition to protecting pedigree secrecy, Corn States Hybrid Service performed a brokerage function for the seed industry. With knowledge of individual pedigrees, Corn States acted as a middleman between seed producers who needed to acquire or dispose of particular hybrids. Corn States could facilitate transfers from one company to another. For example, it helped firms sell U.S.13 under their own names. In short, Corn States's middleman position allowed cooperation and trade among the seed companies while preserving trade secrecy. In addition to such intercompany trading in the United States, Corn States and other firms facilitated the export of large quantities of U.S.-grown hybrid corn to Europe (Spence, telephone interview, 28 October 1994).

In the late 1960s, when research budgets at public universities suffered large cuts, public development of inbred lines was threatened. Retail seed companies that depended on these lines looked to the foundation seed companies to fill the gap. Roland Holden's son Ronald, who joined the company in the late 1960s, began a research program to develop private inbred lines for his customers (Holden 1985). His efforts were successful and Holden Foundation Seeds emerged by the 1970s as the clear leader in developing inbreds for small- and middle-sized seed corn companies.

PIONEER VS. HOLDEN

In contrast to other companies, Pioneer Hi-Bred International had long maintained a policy of releasing only unique hybrids to farmers; this firm did not sell U.S.13 or other public hybrids. Pioneer did use publicly developed inbreds in its hybrids, but always in combination with its own privately developed lines. The firm prospered with this strategy and by the late 1970s led the industry in market share. In the summer of 1979, however, Pioneer's district sales managers across the corn belt increasingly reported that the company's competitors offered hybrids resembling Pioneer's products. Despite the uniformity of individual hybrids, marked differences in hybrid appearance often occurred, and these distinguished one company's products from those of another. As the fall harvest season opened, reports of striking similarities in yield and moisture increased as well. Pioneer previously had encountered isolated instances of such problems on a smaller scale. Pioneer's most successful hybrid (3780) and one of its successors (3541) now faced nearly identical competitors across the corn belt. Pioneer's district managers and dealers reportedly felt they were competing against themselves when they encountered new offerings from several small seed companies (Bollen 1985).

In December 1979 the American Seed Trade Association held its annual corn and sorghum research conference at a Chicago hotel. In its hospitality room, Holden Foundation Seeds displayed two ears of corn, one labeled Pioneer 3541 and the other LH38xB73. The two ears were nearly identical and drew a great deal of interest from Holden's customers. During the meeting, Pioneer officials heard a rumor that Holden had acquired one of the inbreds for Pioneer's most popular hybrid and had begun marketing this inbred to its customers who would then produce the identical hybrid (Duvick 1985).

The news that a foundation seed company might be distributing Pioneer's proprietary material alarmed that company's senior management. The possibility that numerous small companies had access to one of Pioneer's most successful lines opened Pioneer—one of the highest priced retailers of seed corn—to potentially devastating price competition. It also contradicted informal rules of competition within the industry. Though always competitive, the industry had followed Ken Ford's advice in the 1940s by keeping the discussion of pedigrees and other such secrets in the background. Now cheaper "look-alike" hybrids were apparently being sold as similar or identical to Pioneer hybrids.

This possible misappropriation shattered the image of a close-knit, unified industry. By the late 1970s the number of companies selling hybrid seed corn had leveled off at approximately 250. Thomas Urban, Pioneer's chief executive officer, characterized the seed industry as "a fraternity, a fraternity of seedsmen. Over the years it's been a fraternity of honor." (Urban 1985). During the winter of 1979–1980, Pioneer officials began to investigate the suspected breakdown in that honor. The stakes were high. If the investigation produced convincing evidence, Pioneer would almost certainly be forced to take Holden to court. A case involving a major supplier of foundation seed would in effect implicate a large proportion of the industry.

In the fall of 1980 a farmer from Illinois, Neil Einsele, told a Pioneer sales representative that he had information about the theft of an inbred used in Pioneer's 3780 hybrid. Einsele had been a district sales manager for Wyffels Hybrids, a small family-owned seed company in Henry County, Illinois. He told the Pioneer sales representative and company officials that in November 1977 he had observed his employer, William Wyffels, Jr., obtain a small sample of inbred seed from a farmer who grew seed corn for Pioneer. Einsele later testified that when the farmer asked Wyffels what he was going to do with the seed, Wyffels replied that "he was going to send it to Hawaii, have it expanded, and put into production" (Einsele 1981, 8). Hawaiian Research Ltd., a firm engaged in seed testing, was owned by Roland Holden.

On 5 February 1981, Pioneer Hi-Bred filed suit against Holden Foundation Seeds, Corn States Hybrid Services, and Hawaiian Research. Pioneer charged that the defendants violated the Lanham Act, the premier federal trademark act, and asserted that they wrongfully acquired and distributed seeds in which Pioneer claimed a proprietary interest. Included in the suit were charges of unfair competition, intentional interference with business advantage, and unjust enrichment. In addition, the suit charged that Holden's action would cause "the erosion or destruction of the competitive structure of the industry" and "the loss of the consuming public's ability to choose from among various inbred and hybrid lines" (Pioneer 1981, 6).

News of Pioneer's lawsuit spread quickly throughout the hybrid corn industry. The suit threatened not just Holden but the 200 companies that depended on Holden for inbreds. For forty years the industry had maintained its structure of private and public sources of inbreds. Misappropriation and widespread dissemination of Pioneer's lines threatened to blur the distinction between public and private breeding in the seed industry. It also deprived Pioneer of its claim to be a supplier of unique hybrids to farmers. The lawsuit threatened the rest of the seed industry in another way. Not only was Pioneer suing Holden, but it was threatening to expose the extent of the closed pedigree system that so many small companies depended on to conceal their sale of hybrids of identical pedigree. In recounting the process leading up to the lawsuit, Thomas Urban noted:

> We had a number of meetings. I said we got two choices. We could do nothing and continue our research program as we are doing and try and develop better products as we always do, or we can try to take some action, recognizing that if we take action we take some risks. We take a risk of stirring up the industry in a way that isn't very friendly and we take some legal risks. (Urban 1985, 630)

The case of *Pioneer vs. Holden* was in the courts for the next thirteen years. Judge Donald O'Brien (U.S. District Court–Des Moines) ruled in favor of Pioneer on both liability issues and damages. His verdict was upheld by the Eighth Circuit Court of Appeals in July 1994. Attorneys filed over 600 pleadings, over 9,000 pages of testimony were recorded, and thousands of documents were entered into evidence. The final award for damages to Pioneer exceeded $46 million. It is likely that the decision in the case will set a precedent for future disputes over property rights in plant genetic material.

Apart from its sheer size and legal ramifications, the case had a significant impact on the hybrid seed corn industry. Pioneer's suit threatened the system of trade secrecy that had long protected the industry. Both Pioneer and Holden recognized this and sought protection orders from the court for case testimony and evidence. Both sides were forced to divulge information that might be of value to competitors. In Holden's case, the numerous small seed companies were threatened with exposure of what R. A. Brink forty years earlier had called "the whole string of aliases." The unraveling of the tale threatened to expose breeding strategies as well as commercial relationships that had been kept secret for many years. That exposure could lead to the ruinous competition that the industry had carefully avoided.

Pioneer attempted to prove that Holden had wrongfully acquired its breeding material. The investigation of William Wyffels's alleged misappropriation led to a dead end. Given the date on which Wyffels acquired Pioneer's seed, that incident could not have been the source of Holden's new inbreds. Pioneer tried to demonstrate other incidents where Holden might have acquired Pioneer inbreds, but none proved convincing. Pioneer could only point to discrepancies in Holden's records, discrepancies that left considerable doubt as to Holden's claims to independent development of the disputed inbreds. In the end, compelling evidence of misappropriation came from a series of genetic tests introduced into evidence by Pioneer. With a procedure known as electrophoresis, Pioneer researchers demonstrated the high degree of genetic similarity between Pioneer and Holden inbreds. Holden's attorneys protested that these tests and the claims made from them were based on probability rather than direct proof. Although direct evidence that Holden had misappropriated genetic material was lacking, the scientific evidence, coupled with Holden's inadequate breeding records, proved convincing. Because the case involved charges of trademark infringement rather than theft, Pioneer was able to shift the burden of proof onto Holden (U.S. Court of Appeals for the Eighth Circuit 1994, 26). The court found proof based not on evidence of a particular act of theft but on the similarity of Pioneer's seed to Holden's.

The damages portion of the trial presented the broadest threat to Holden's customers since Pioneer requested sales information from Holden. Holden vigorously resisted supplying Pioneer with the names of its customers. It also denied that it knew the specific combinations of inbreds used by its customers or that it required them to purchase certain combinations of inbreds. In the end, the names of most of Holden's customers were kept secret. Pioneer's accountants, however, were allowed to examine Holden's and Corn States's sales records to determine the extent of sales of the disputed inbreds. Pioneer argued that it had lost sales to Holden's customers. Holden's sales were small in comparison to the magnified sales of the seed companies that produced the seed sold to farmers. From 1980 to 1990, Holden's customers sold over twenty-five million bags of seed corn using the disputed materials. Given its historical market share, Pioneer calculated its gross sales loss at just over $200 million (Pioneer 1991, 1).

In 1988, Dr. Stephen Smith, a researcher with Pioneer, published an article entitled, "Diversity of United States Hybrid Maize Germplasm: Isozymic and Chromatographic Evidence," in the journal *Crop Science*. Smith's article reported on a series of genetic tests of 138 corn hybrids sold in the United States under a variety of brand names. Employing a measure of genetic distance, Smith arranged the hybrids into associated groups. The companies included ranged from large-scale competitors to small family firms. Market share surveys, obtained from Pioneer, reveal that although many of these hybrids held a relatively minor market share, the combined market share of the highly similar hybrids often represented one of the largest segments of the market.

Smith's article was part of a long-running academic debate on genetic diversity in the nation's corn crop. It also sent a clear message to the industry that Pioneer had developed a means to verify any misappropriations of its genetic material. According to Pioneer vice president Richard McConnell, Pioneer intended to enhance the credibility of genetic testing not only in the courtroom but in peer-reviewed scientific journals (telephone interview, 28 July 1994). At the same time the *Crop Science* article appeared, Pioneer released similar information to the popular farm magazine *Successful Farming*. Again, the message to the rest of the hybrid corn industry was clear: we can let your customers know what is behind the aliases. The *Crop Science* article was carefully constructed for a scientific audience and expressed its conclusions in terms of "similarity." The writer of the *Successful Farming* article went further, suggesting that many hybrids were, in fact, identical (Fee 1988, 52).

Since 1988, Pioneer has continued to employ genetic testing techniques, reflecting an explosion of such testing in many other areas. Stephen Smith has published a number of articles dealing with the testing technique known as Restriction Fragment Length Polymorphisms (RFLP). The implicit message is still the same: genetic testing can enforce claims to ownership of plant genetic resources. A parallel development to Smith's research is the appearance of many private genetic testing laboratories in the United States. These laboratories' genetic tests of corn seeds allow individual companies to assess seeds for genetic purity, as well as to compare their seeds to those offered by their competitors. Recent conferences sponsored by the American Seed Trade Association have included discussions of the use of RFLP techniques (Murray et al. 1988).

If the effects of RFLP testing within the seed industry are uncertain, its consequences outside the industry are not. No other popular farm magazine has printed anything similar to the 1988 article that appeared in *Successful Farming*. That is not surprising given the number of pages of advertising purchased by the hybrid seed corn industry in popular farm magazines. The practice of labeling identical hybrids with different names continues. If farmers were given access to RFLP tests, as well as the performance testing now done by the land grant universities, they quite possibly could force many seed companies into greater price competition for those varieties. Seed producers have frequently argued that genetic similarities are less important to farmers than differences in production techniques that affect seed quality. Farmers, they argue, should look for the seed company that maintains the highest standards in its production practices (Muhm 1993, 6W). Yet the thriving wholesale trade, together with genetic identity and purity testing, suggests that seed producers themselves regularly trade products they know to be identical. Genetic testing is too expensive and the knowledge of its existence too far removed from the world of most farmers to pose much threat to the industry.

CONCLUSION

Despite Pioneer's attempt to expose the actions of its competitors, since 1994 little attention has been paid to questions of fair labeling or to threats to the genetic diversity of America's corn crop posed by the closed pedigree system. Holden Foundation Seeds was acquired by chemical giant Monsanto in 1997 for $1 billion. The same year Pioneer sold a 20 percent stake to DuPont. Both of these sales demonstrate the continued high profits in seed production, as well as potential developments in plant biotechnology. If anything, biotechnology enhances the mysterious nature of seeds, pushing knowledge about them even further beyond many farmers' reach.

Hybrid corn as innovation supposedly succeeds because it produces yields superior to those obtainable from open-pollinated breeding methods. Particular hybrids are presumed to succeed because they outyield competitors. Hybrid seed corn companies in turn profit because of their ability to produce these hybrids. This chapter has presented a series of documented objections to these conventional wisdoms. I have suggested why it is misleading to assume that a new commodity succeeds in the market (i.e., supplants what came before) by virtue of intrinsic superiority.

Instead, I propose three key components to the successful penetration of a new commodity in the marketplace: (1) uncertainty about its fundamental identity (Appadurai's [1986] turnstile of knowledge and ignorance); (2) the interests of capitalist actors who introduce a commodity and take action to ensure its success; and (3) the interests of the state, which constructs the rules of the game and the framework in which commodities exist and capitalists pursue their goals. The latter two points are among the more common issues social scientists address as we encounter the spread of capitalist economies throughout the world. Yet it is the first issue—uncertain commodity identity—that makes this example from Iowa compelling and of wider interest. The capacity to manipulate and confuse the very identities of commodities should concern us whether we are buying jam, pain relievers, or hybrid corn seeds.

NOTE

This chapter is based on interviews and archival research carried out by the author in 1994, with funding from the Department of Anthropology at the University of Iowa. I wish to thank Mike Chibnik, Paul Durrenberger, and Donald Duvick for helpful comments on earlier drafts of this chapter.

REFERENCES

Appadurai, Arjun. 1986. Introduction: Commodities and the Politics of Value. In Arjun Appadurai, ed., *The Social Life of Things: Commodities in Cultural Perspective.* New York: Cambridge University Press.

Baker, Raymond F. 1994. Interview with author. Des Moines, Iowa, 26 August. Tape recording.

Bollen, Carrol Dean. 1985. Trial Testimony. *Pioneer Hi-Bred International, Inc. v. Holden Foundation Seeds, Inc. et al.* Civil Action No. 81-60-E. U.S. District Court, Southern District of Iowa, Central Division. Des Moines, Iowa: Johnson Reporting Services, Ltd.

Brink, R. A. 1941. Closed versus Open Pedigrees for Corn Hybrids. In *Report of the Sixth Corn Improvement Conference of the North Central Region*. Washington, D.C.: U.S. Department of Agriculture.

Darrah, L. L. 1986. United States Farm: Maize Germplasm Base and Commercial Breeding Strategies. *Crop Science* 26: 1109–1113.

Duvick, Donald N. 1981. Genetic Diversity in Corn Improvement. In *Report of the 36th Annual Corn and Sorghum Research Conference*, 48–60. Washington, D.C.: American Seed Trade Association.

———. 1985. Trial Testimony. *Pioneer Hi-Bred International, Inc. v. Holden Foundation Seeds, Inc. et al.* Civil Action No. 81-60-E. U.S. District Court, Southern District of Iowa, Central Division. Des Moines, Iowa: Johnson Reporting Services, Ltd.

Einsele, Neil. 1981. Deposition Testimony. *Pioneer Hi-Bred International, Inc. v. Holden Foundation Seeds, Inc. et al.* Exhibit 54. Civil Action No. 81-60-E. U.S. District Court, Southern District of Iowa, Central Division. Des Moines, Iowa: Johnson Reporting Services, Ltd.

Fee, Rich. 1988. Pioneer: "Many Hybrids Closely Associated." *Successful Farming* (February): 52.

Fitzgerald, Deborah. 1990. *The Business of Breeding: Hybrid Corn in Illinois, 1890–1940*. Ithaca, N.Y.: Cornell University Press.

Ford, Ken A. 1941. Closed versus Open Pedigrees for Corn Hybrids: A Hybrid Seed Corn Industry Point of View. In *Report of the Sixth Corn Improvement Conference of the North Central Region*. Washington, D.C.: U.S. Department of Agriculture.

Griswold, Don. 1931. Don Griswold to Henry A. Wallace, March 18. Ia58-511, Henry A. Wallace Papers. University of Iowa Libraries, Iowa City, Iowa.

Holbert, James R. 1929. James R. Holbert to Henry A. Wallace, March 18. Ia57-153, Henry A. Wallace Papers. University of Iowa Libraries, Iowa City, Iowa.

Holden, Ronald. 1985. Trial Testimony. *Pioneer Hi-Bred International, Inc. v. Holden Foundation Seeds, Inc. et al.* Civil Action No. 81-60-E. U.S. District Court, Southern District of Iowa, Central Division. Des Moines, Iowa: Johnson Reporting Services, Ltd.

Iowa Agricultural Experiment Association. 1937. *Rules for Certifying Hybrid Corn Seed*. Ames, Iowa: Iowa Agricultural Experiment Association.

Muhm, Don. 1993. Small Iowa Seed Companies Stand Firm in the Shadow of Giants. *Des Moines Sunday Register*, January 31, p. 6W.

Murray, Michael G., Yu Ma, Jeanne Romero-Severson, David P. West, and Jane H. Cramer. 1988. Restriction Fragment Length Polymorphisms: What Are They and How Can Breeders Use Them? In *Report of the 43rd Annual Corn and Sorghum Research Conference*. Washington, D.C.: American Seed Trade Association.

Pfister, Lester. 1928. Lester Pfister to Henry A. Wallace, December 28. Ia56-918, Henry A. Wallace Papers. University of Iowa Libraries, Iowa City, Iowa.

Pioneer Hi-Bred International, Inc. 1981. Complaint. *Pioneer Hi-Bred International, Inc. v. Holden Foundation Seeds, Inc. et al.* Pleading No. 1. Civil Action No. 81-60-E. U.S. District Court, Southern District of Iowa, Central Division. Des Moines, Iowa: Johnson Reporting Services, Ltd.

———. 1991. Calculation of Pioneer's Lost Profits. *Pioneer Hi-Bred International, Inc. v. Holden Foundation Seeds, Inc. et al.* Exhibit 6512AA. Civil Action No. 81-60-E. U.S. District Court, Southern District of Iowa, Central Division. Des Moines, Iowa: Johnson Reporting Services, Ltd.

Robinson, Joe L., and Oliver A. Knott. 1963. *The Story of the Iowa Crop Improvement Association.* Ames, Iowa: Iowa State University Press.

Shull, George H. 1909. A Pure Line Method of Corn Breeding. *American Breeders' Report* 4: 296–301.

Smith, J. Stephen C. 1988. Diversity of United States Hybrid Maize Germplasm: Isozymic and Chromatographic Evidence. *Crop Science* 28: 63–69.

Spence, John. 1983. Deposition Testimony. *Pioneer Hi-Bred International, Inc. v. Holden Foundation Seeds, Inc. et al.* Defendants' Exhibit 1029. Civil Action No. 81-60-E. U.S. District Court, Southern District of Iowa, Central Division. Des Moines, Iowa: Johnson Reporting Services, Ltd.

Urban, Nelson. 1976. Interview with Chet Randolph. 3/1 Papers, Pioneer Hi-Bred International. Iowa State University Library, Ames, Iowa.

Urban, Thomas. 1985. Trial Testimony. *Pioneer Hi-Bred International, Inc. v. Holden Foundation Seeds, Inc. et al.* Civil Action No. 81-60-E. U.S. District Court, Southern District of Iowa, Central Division. Des Moines, Iowa: Johnson Reporting Services, Ltd.

U.S. Court of Appeals for the Eighth Circuit. 1994. Judgement. *Pioneer Hi-Bred International, Inc. v. Holden Foundation Seed et al.* Civil Action No. 4-81-CU-50060. St. Louis, Missouri: United States Court of Appeals for the Eighth Circuit.

Wallace, Henry A. 1929. Henry A. Wallace to James R. Holbert, March 4. Ia57-111. Henry A. Wallace Papers, University of Iowa Libraries, Iowa City, Iowa.

———. 1930a. Henry A. Wallace to Frederick D. Richey, February 17. Ia57-697. Henry A. Wallace Papers, University of Iowa Libraries, Iowa City, Iowa.

———. 1930b. Henry A. Wallace to Ross Salmon, March 20. Ia57-788. Henry A. Wallace Papers, University of Iowa Libraries, Iowa City, Iowa.

———. 1930c. Henry A. Wallace to Ross Salmon, April 5. Ia57-832. Henry A. Wallace Papers, University of Iowa Libraries, Iowa City, Iowa.

———. 1931a. Henry A. Wallace to H. D. Hughes, February 9. Ia58-398. Henry A. Wallace Papers, University of Iowa Libraries, Iowa City, Iowa.

———. 1931b. Henry A. Wallace to Don Griswold, March 20. Ia58-515. Henry A. Wallace Papers, University of Iowa Libraries, Iowa City, Iowa.

Zuber, M. S. 1975. Corn Germplasm Base in the U.S.—Is It Narrowing, Widening, or Static? In *Report of the 30th Annual Corn and Sorghum Research Conference.* Washington, D.C.: American Seed Trade Association.

8

The Impact of Colonial Contact on the Production and Distribution of Glaze-Paint Decorated Ceramics

Winifred Creamer

The northern Rio Grande valley of New Mexico[1] is distinguished from the rest of North America during the Protohistoric period (A.D. 1450–1680)[2] by the use of lead glaze-paint to decorate ceramics. From its introduction after 1300 until 1700, glaze-decorated ceramics were widely exchanged among indigenous people and with European colonists. This chapter explores the changing place of glaze pottery (as reflected in variations of function and style) in this region's commodity exchange system during this four-hundred-year period. The pottery manufactured after European colonization in 1540 was, I argue, designed to attract Europeans as the primary end users. Once the European market for glaze ceramics disappeared with the Rio Grande valley's political unrest of the 1680s and 1690s, this pottery type was no longer made. Although indigenous ceramic producers had shown great resilience over time and adapted to changing markets, their products were eventually supplanted by Tewa polychrome.[3] By viewing this pottery as a commodity whose producers were responding to changing cultural, political and economic contexts, new insights can be gained into its distribution in the archaeological record through space and time.

THE CHANGING FUNCTION OF GLAZE WARE

True lead-based glaze was discovered in only two places in the New World: the American Southwest and highland Guatemala (Shepard 1942; 1948). In the Southwest, glaze originated in the Zuni area[4], from which its use spread to what is now northern New Mexico during the fourteenth century (Cordell 1984, 340; Habicht-

151

Mauche 1993; Shepard 1942). Petrographic study of the earliest glaze-paint decorated pottery suggests these were initially made at a number of locations (Warren
1969, 36) extending north from Albuquerque, but not as far as Santa Fe (Creamer,
Haas, and Renken 1994).

Assuming decorated ceramics were commodities in the sense that they were produced for the purpose of exchange (see chapter 1), we might expect their distribution to reflect the function of such objects in society. For example, if glaze vessels
were a marker of prestige, their distribution might conform to the model of pres-
tige-chain trade (Renfrew 1975, 51). In this case suitable partners for exchange would
be located at a greater distance from one another than would be the case in exchange
governed by reciprocity (Renfrew 1975, 47). In the northern Rio Grande prior to
the arrival of Europeans, glaze ceramics were widely distributed and have been recovered from virtually all archaeological contexts of the period. Glaze-decorated
ceramics that were exchanged in large quantities with the Salinas pueblos to the south
(Motsinger 1997) are found in only minuscule quantities to the north and east. This
distribution pattern suggests the initial importance of glaze ware in confirming long-
distance relationships.

Marked changes in glaze-decorated ceramics were evident during the Protohistoric
period in the northern Rio Grande. During the initial spread of glaze production
(the late 1300s) eight large, highly aggregated pueblo villages were established in the
Galisteo Basin, a marginal area for cultivation. Decorated ceramics at each of these
sites consist largely of glaze wares, which were probably made at each village (Reed
1990). At one of these sites, Pueblo Blanco, the earliest glaze ware was recovered
from all tested proveniences. Accompanying tree-ring dates of 1388vv[5] and later
suggest that glaze ware was present at the site in the latter half of the fourteenth
century. Exchange of ceramics may have brought needed resources from the surrounding region, buffering the effects of the arid setting. Ceramics are among the
few items that could have been produced in surplus in the Galisteo Basin.

At the time glaze ware was being introduced into the Galisteo Basin,
regionalization of ceramic styles was occurring across the rest of the northern Rio
Grande, resulting in different decorated ceramic types being found in subregions that
previously had produced stylistically similar ceramics. North of modern Santa Fe,
black-on-white ceramics were replaced by Biscuit ware, while in the isolated Jemez
Mountains region, Jemez black-on-white replaced Santa Fe black-on-white. At the
same time, glaze wares have been found in the nonglaze producing subregions in
varying amounts, while the dominant decorated ceramics of the other subregions,
Biscuit ware and Jemez black-on-white, are found beyond their zones of production in only small or trace amounts. This shows that glaze-decorated ceramics were
a commodity used more widely in trade than were other decorated ceramics.

The need for metallic ore to make lead glaze favored the Galisteo Basin as a production area. Sources of lead and other metals can be found in the Ortiz and San
Pedro Mountains, on the edge of the Galisteo Basin (Warren 1979). The frequency
of glaze ware in midden deposits at thirteen Protohistoric sites declined in propor-

tion to the distance from San Marcos pueblo. San Marcos has the highest frequency of glaze-decorated ceramics in midden deposits, as well as the densest middens among the Protohistoric sites tested, up to 2,500 sherds per cubic meter (Creamer, Haas, and Renken 1994). This regional pattern of glaze ware distribution is consistent with face-to-face trade and implies widespread access to decorated ceramics through reciprocal processes, rather than a prestige-oriented exchange system (Renfrew 1975, 41–51).

Over time, fewer sites appear to have made the majority of glaze ware. Warren (1969) has suggested that glaze production was focused around the site of Tonque during the fifteenth and sixteenth centuries, suggesting the possibility of increasingly specialized production. Such specialization would also be in keeping with a continued role for glaze ware as a commodity within a region of aggregated villages. Production of both red and yellow glaze wares continued through the time of European contact in 1540. The use of glaze ceramics as a commodity within the northern Rio Grande and the surrounding regions is complicated by the arrival of Europeans in 1540. With their need for provisioning, administrative demands, and a new battery of trade goods, it is no surprise that Europeans disrupted the regional economic system and introduced new competition between Europeans and pueblo peoples. This competition could have resulted in increased production of ceramics via a shift toward techniques of mass production (Hagstrum 1985; Motsinger 1997), or changes to enhance the desirability of ceramics for one group or the other. Alternative outcomes might include fabrication of ceramics in more locations, or replacement of indigenous ceramics by other materials, such as imported European ceramics or locally made Euro-American ceramics. It appears that initially changes in decoration were made to enhance glaze ceramics for European users. After 1680, glaze was replaced by nonglaze painted ceramics, Tewa polychrome, and during the eighteenth century a local Hispanic ceramic tradition developed (Snow 1984).

After the permanent colonization of the northern Rio Grande region in 1598, and continuing through the seventeenth century, changes in vessel shape, glaze paint, and slip indicate that native potters copied some European tableware forms for exchange with Euro-American settlers. After approximately 1730, we lack evidence of glaze ware being made anywhere in the region. If glaze ware was a commodity, we must also consider why the end of production came relatively abruptly.

GLAZE WARE AND EUROPEAN CONTACT: CHANGE IN STYLE

The first Europeans to reach the northern Rio Grande region were Francisco Vásquez de Coronado and a party of explorers who arrived in 1540. The group spent the winter of 1540–1541 in the Albuquerque area near a large pueblo village and returned to Mexico later in 1541 after further exploration of the Rio Grande and the plains. The European explorers noted and admired the glazed ceramics they observed: "Throughout these provinces one finds pottery glazed with alcohol, and jugs of such elaborate designs and shapes that it was surprising" (Hammond and Rey 1940, 256).

Despite their references to local ceramics, the arrival of Europeans does not appear to have had an immediate impact on production and exchange. Seriation of excavated ceramics from midden deposits at Pecos pueblo by Kidder in the 1920s suggests gradual change through time in vessel form. Kidder's work was carried out before methods of dating archaeological sites had been developed, though we know the Pecos sequence begins in the 1400s and ends after the colonization of the region in 1598. Recent stratigraphic excavations at four glaze-producing Protohistoric pueblo villages has also yielded seriation of deposits spanning the period from the mid-1300s to about 1700 (Creamer et al. 2000; Creamer, Haas, and Renken 1994). Both of these sequences suggest that the shape of ceramic vessels changed slowly. Further, Kidder suggested continuity in decoration, as well as shape, indicating that only four motifs filled the exterior panels drawn on bowls, with minor exceptions (Kidder and Shepard 1936, 172). No abrupt change is recorded in the glaze ware sequence that can be correlated with the arrival of European explorers in the region. It appears that the first contact did not disrupt ceramic production, and perhaps the process of exploration also did not affect what types of ceramics were made.

COLONIAL SETTLEMENT AND SUPPLY

Permanent settlement was established along the Rio Grande in September 1598, when Juan de Oñate settled near present San Juan pueblo with 129 men and their families (Hammond and Rey 1953, 14). These colonists had departed from Mexico laden with supplies, which had dwindled during the long trek north. Though historic reports do not all agree, the Europeans appear to have gone on to exhaust pueblo food supplies as well as their own:

> All these Indians readily and willingly help those who are directing them and give them the supplies they ask for. They supply without failing what is needed in these matters, particularly bringing in fowls, corn, calabashes, and game. (Juan de Oñate, 22 March 1601, quoted in Hammond and Rey 1953, 619)

> The feelings of the natives against supplying it [corn] cannot be exaggerated, for I give your lordship my word that they weep and cry out as if they and all their descendants were being killed. But in the end, necessity also compelled us to do this to keep from starving to death. (Captain Velasco, 22 March 1601, quoted in Hammond and Rey 1953, 610)

> We had consumed all the corn that the Indians had saved during the preceding six years, because there has not been a week since we came here that we have not used up from fifty to sixty *fanegas*[6] of corn, and when the governor and the rest of the people were here we consumed upwards of eighty *fanegas*. As a result of this the Indians have reached the state of famine. (Fray Juan de Escalona to the Viceroy, 1 October 1601, quoted in Hammond and Rey 1953, 692)

These statements suggest two possible effects of European colonization: loss of control over resources by local groups, and threat of famine. Groups who previously participated in exchange to obtain food would have had to expand their networks by exchanging goods with the Europeans, or by contacting additional, and presumably more distant, indigenous groups.

Europeans made unreliable exchange partners because they often appropriated goods rather than participating in exchange relationships. The Europeans did settle in areas where crops could be cultivated, however, and they proceeded to plant both native crops and new European cultigens such as wheat and fruit (Lopinot 1986). To the north and east of the Rio Grande pueblos were nomadic people who did not cultivate corn. To the south, the Albuquerque area was partly abandoned after Coronado overwintered there in 1541 (Hammond and Rey 1940, 227–234). To the west were the Jemez Mountains (over 8,000 feet high in many places); in this area villages were established on high mesa tops. Growing corn on these level mesas would have entailed a number of risks, including damage by wind, rain, or drought, as well as risk of frost in late spring and early fall. Alternative areas for cultivation included patches of land along streams at the foot of the mesas. These plots would have been small, as well as distant from each village. Overall, the Jemez region appears unlikely to have produced surplus corn. The villages have defensive characteristics as well[7] and were used as refuge sites from time to time, which probably limited exchange opportunities.

Archaeologists have hypothesized that foodstuffs such as corn have a practical limit of 50 kilometers for exchange purposes, roughly a two-day walk (Lightfoot 1979; Upham 1982, 117). At a greater distance travel costs are likely to exceed the food value of the load transported. This practical limit to food exchange may have forced the pueblo people to look to Europeans as exchange partners despite possible misgivings. The shift of the European capital from the outskirts of San Juan pueblo to present day Santa Fe in 1511 may indicate an effort by the colonists to take advantage of land at lower altitude, perhaps resulting in more productive fields south of Santa Fe than farther north. Corn was the staple crop of both European and pueblo people during the seventeenth century. As Europeans increasingly took over productive land, they improved their position as trade partners.

During the seventeenth century glaze wares were produced in the Galisteo Basin, the Salinas region, Pecos pueblo, and Zia pueblo (Cordell 1984, 340). By about 1630, all those places had either a resident missionary or a mission chapel and visiting cleric. Distinctive changes in glaze ceramics at this time included new vessel forms and a greenish glaze color. New forms included a low bowl or "soup plate" with a wide rim, and a deep basin, or *vasin*. These forms are believed to have been introduced by the Spanish and are found at mission sites such as San Marcos pueblo. Data from San Marcos pueblo indicate that these late forms were introduced relatively suddenly, as the "San Marcos F" is found in some quantity in archaeological deposits, without the gradual increase noted for other types.

Beginning at about the same time, the vessel exteriors were often less carefully slipped than previously, resulting in rough, gray exteriors bearing the glaze paint decoration. Glaze changed as well, from black and very dark brown, to green and light brown (sometimes called "root beer"). The change in glaze color could have been an independent innovation or the result of changing the source of metallic ore. It could also have been an attempt to accommodate European colonists, who might prefer green glaze similar to those used on European storage vessels, called "olive jars." Together these changes suggest that indigenous potters began to produce items that would be considered desirable by Europeans.

CHANGING VALUES: COLONIZATION TO REVOLT

A distinctive change in decorated glaze wares that became apparent during the seventeenth century was the increasing sloppiness of the designs painted on the vessels themselves (fig. 8.1). This change has been characterized as aesthetic:

It is in the glaze that the most striking contrast with earlier types is seen. Thick and with normally high luster, it runs and spreads to such an extent that designs are often

Figure 8.1   Change in Execution of Glaze Paint Decoration over Time

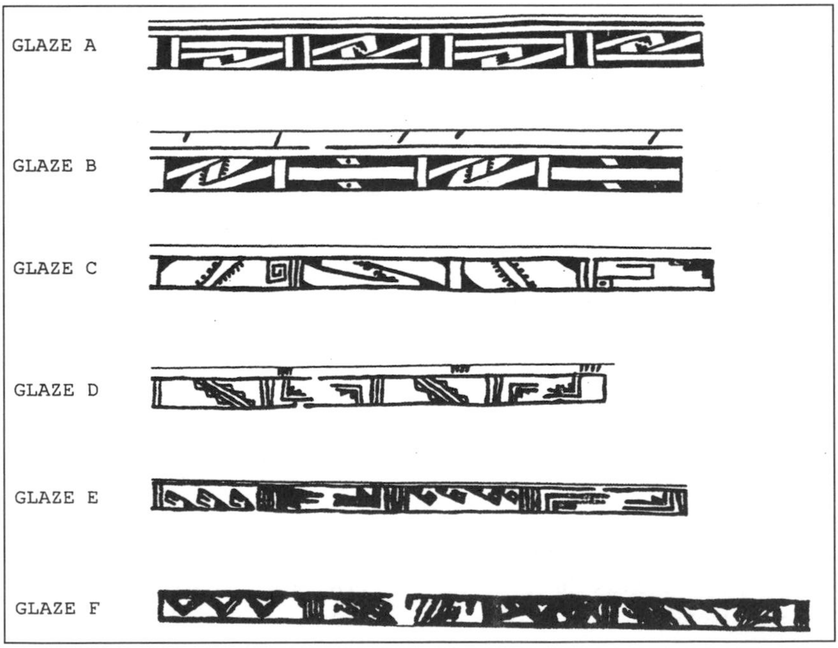

Source: Drawing after Kidder and Shepard 1936.

completely destroyed. . . . The potters obviously took pleasure in the fine effects produced by heavy applications of this glaze; their lines grew broader and broader, nice-
ties of design were abandoned in favor of bold, "blobby" figures, of which the uncon-
trollable runs were of quite as great decorative value as were the original lines. (Kidder
and Shepard 1936, 215, referring to Glaze V (E) ceramics)

While Kidder assumed that dripped glaze effects were intentional, his contemporary Nels Nelson explained the change in glaze as a result of European intervention:

Generally the iridescent glaze substance is of such striking and excellent quality as to
incline one to the opinion that it was compounded after a Spanish formula. The fact
that the artist could not control it at all seems suggestive of the same idea. The designs attempted, though of the very simplest geometric nature, were almost invariably
ruined by the running of the glaze. (Nelson 1916, 176)

Both these perspectives discount the possibility that the "drippy" quality of late glaze
decoration could be the result of ceramics becoming commodities for exchange with
Europeans. Prior to the arrival of European explorers, ceramics were widely exchanged, and the vessels were decorated with motifs that conveyed some generalized message of individual or group identity (Plog 1980; Wobst 1977). Glaze vessels showed great continuity in ceramic motifs over time, as noted by Kidder, yet
increasingly careless execution of decoration. The role of Europeans in exchange may
have been a key to this shift. In initial exchanges, Europeans acquired glaze-decorated bowls because they were available. Eyewitness accounts indicate they recognized glaze decoration and viewed it favorably. It was the medium, lead glaze, that
they recognized, not the message of group identity the design elements were intended
to convey. As exchange with Europeans increased, the glaze decoration itself may
have retained value, but the decorative motifs themselves lost meaning. The generalized message was not interpretable by Europeans, yet colonists utilized an increasing proportion of decorated vessels. As a result, neatness of execution became un-
important. Over time, the designs continued to be made and ceramics traded, though
the execution of decoration became arbitrary.

The value of indigenous ceramics to colonists continued during the seventeenth
century, as there is little evidence for production of ceramics by Hispanic colonists.
Thriving exchange between colonists and pueblo peoples, however, does not imply
peaceful times. Agents of both church and state argued over their authority to uti-
lize indigenous laborers, who were oppressed and punished by both religious and
civil authorities (Scholes 1937; 1942). By 1680 pueblo peoples seem to have tired
of the burden of supporting a European population. Most of the Rio Grande pueblos
united to reject European rule. By killing missionaries and attacking the Palace of
the Governors in Santa Fe, the local people forced the abandonment of the region.
For twelve years, the region was removed from colonial contact, but in the end
European reconquest took place from 1692 to 1696. Most pueblo groups agreed to
accept European rule, while others left the Rio Grande region. After the reconquest,

a rapid decrease of production of glaze-decorated ceramics is noted, with few examples dating as late as 1730. Glaze wares were supplanted by Tewa polychrome ceramics, which developed from earlier Biscuit wares. Tewa polychrome ceramics were decorated with three colors, but not with glaze paint.

Although it is difficult to identify glaze-paint-decorated ceramics that date to the pueblo revolt period (1680–1696), it is possible that some glaze wares were made during this period. The eight Galisteo Basin pueblos, however, were abandoned at the start of the pueblo revolt, and only one, Galisteo pueblo, was occupied after the reconquest. The smaller number of sites occupied in the glaze-making region may have resulted in decreased access to materials for glaze making and may have disrupted the transmission of skills to a new generation of potters.

After the pueblo revolt, with both the Albuquerque and the Galisteo Basin pueblos largely abandoned, the population of the northern Rio Grande was centered on the pueblos north of Santa Fe. This area around San Gabriel, the first European settlement, had never produced glaze wares, but was the zone where Biscuit wares had been made. During the eighteenth century, glaze wares were replaced with Tewa polychrome vessels sharing much in common with Biscuit wares, but differing in their polychrome decoration:

> Some time prior to the Rebellion of 1680, painted pottery of a decidedly modern stamp began to replace the glazed ware at the village of San Marcos, and to a slight extent elsewhere. (Nelson 1916, 176)

> Tewa polychrome was fully developed in 1694 as evidenced by a considerable collection containing only this type and a polished red ware, shards of which were found at house sites erected by the San Ildefonso Indians on Black Mesa, where they were besieged during that year. Again, in the Cochiti village on the Portrero [*sic*] Viejo, occupied only from 1683 to 1694, Glaze VI and Tewa Polychrome may be found in quantity. (Mera 1932, 12)

Previously of limited distribution, Tewa polychrome took the place in the exchange network of the glaze wares, and it is the decorated type ancestral to most "traditional style" pueblo pottery made today.

This pattern can be seen clearly at Tzeguma (Cieneguilla). Midden samples of ceramics include no late Glaze (F) ceramics at all, and two varieties of Tewa polychrome. The site of Tzeguma is located approximately ten miles from San Marcos pueblo, where glaze wares were made, and over forty miles from San Juan pueblo, where Tewa polychrome is likely to have been made. Nelson made a similar observation nearly eighty years ago:

> At Cienega and Cieneguilla the painted pottery occurs in such profusion, and with no admixture of glazed ware, as to lead one to conclude that these settlements were of post-Rebellion times. (Nelson 1916, 176)

CONCLUSION

Archaeological and ethnohistoric data suggest that changes in the production and distribution of glaze-decorated ceramics in the northern Rio Grande region are related to the colonization of New Mexico. The arrival of Europeans in 1540 had no immediately recognizable archaeological impact on ceramic style and production, though we know from documentary sources that European explorers were a drain on regional resources, and that villages nearest the European winter camp were abandoned.

The colonization of the region in 1598 was followed by changes in ceramics in the archaeological record. New vessel forms were made, and glaze paint became lighter in color, in shades of both green and brown. The new forms and design elements were borrowed from European ceramics, and presumably were made for the colonists, while changes in execution of decoration, and even glaze color, were likely to be responses to increasing exchange of ceramics with European settlers and decreasing exchange among pueblo people. Over time there seems to have been a transition from decoration bearing social meaning such as group identity or alliance (on objects traded to other pueblo dwellers), to glaze decoration without such content (on objects traded to Europeans).

The end of production of glaze-decorated ceramics correlates with the aftermath of the pueblo revolt of 1680. Colonists, the target market for glaze ceramics, left the region entirely. Unfortunately for the pueblo people, the departure of Europeans exacerbated the economic problems that political upheaval was intended to solve. Unintended consequences of the pueblo revolt included the termination of production of glaze-painted ceramics and the introduction of technologically simpler decorated ceramics.

What this interpretation suggests is that changes in ceramic production and distribution from approximately 1300 to 1700 in the northern Rio Grande can best be viewed as shifting patterns of commoditization. Ceramics were commodities during the fourteenth century, as shown by the widespread exchange of glaze ware. Subsequent changes in function, style, and value of glaze-decorated ceramics can be correlated with the arrival of Europeans and their appropriation of commodity exchange to supply colonists. The success of this effort is apparent in that indigenous ceramics formed the bulk of all ceramic assemblages in the Rio Grande well into the eighteenth century (Snow 1984).

The eventual supplanting of glaze ware (a desired commodity, according to its distribution patterns) by Tewa polychrome can be viewed as one of the catastrophic results of the pueblo revolt. The revolt chased away consumers of ceramics and disrupted both the flow of raw materials and the teaching and practicing of techniques. The existing exchange system, in which the Galisteo Basin played a central role, collapsed. Glaze-decorated ceramics, a central element in this system, disappeared and were supplanted by the promotion of what had been a minor type, Tewa polychrome, produced at sites in the northern part of the region. Descendant ceramics of many types fill the market for handmade pottery today, testifying to pueblo peoples' adaptability to the resources and the region under constantly changing circumstances.

NOTES

The research on which this chapter is based was conducted between 1988 and 1995 in northern New Mexico. Ethnohistoric research on regional population during the Protohistoric period was carried out in conjunction with archeological research. Field work included mapping and reconnaissance at some sites, text excavations at others (including San Marcos pueblo), and three seasons of excavation at pueblo Blanco. In all, fieldwork was carried out at twelve of the sixty-five Protohistoric sites in the northern Rio Grande region. The research was sponsored by the Harry Frank Guggenheim Foundation; Chicago Field Museum; and Northern Illinois University's Anthropology Department, Center for Latino and Latin American Studies, Graduate School, and Division of External Programs. I am grateful to co-director Jonathan Haas (Field Museum), who has carried out an important share of the project, and to James H. Duncan, Sr., for his long-standing support of our research.

1. The northern Rio Grande valley covers more than 17,000 square kilometers from Taos pueblo on the north to Laguna pueblo on the south. The Jemez Mountains form the western border of this region, and the Sangre de Cristo range forms an eastern boundary with the plains. In the northern Rio Grande there were sixty-five pueblo villages of 400 to 3,000 rooms that were occupied during the Protohistoric period, A.D. 1450–1680.

2. All dates mentioned in the text are A.D.

3. Tewa polychrome refers to vessels made between 1675 and 1720 by pueblo potters working in the area north of Santa Fe. Volcanic pumice was used for temper. The base of a vessel was slipped red, and the upper portion was slipped cream/white and decorated with black carbon paint, instead of glaze paint. Tewa polychrome is considered the ancestral type from which all contemporary painted Rio Grande pueblo pottery developed.

4. The Zuni area refers to the portion of west central New Mexico including the Zuni reservation and the surrounding area, extending to the Arizona border.

5. "Vv" means "sometime after" the date given.

6. A *fanega* is a Spanish unit of dry measure equivalent to approximately one and one-half bushels, but it is variable throughout Latin America.

7. Here I include remote location, difficult access to villages, steep and broken terrain, and choice of settlement in areas not of interest to colonists.

REFERENCES

Cordell, Linda. 1984. *Prehistory of the Southwest*. Orlando, Fla.: Academic Press.
Creamer, Winifred. 1993. A Tale of Two Villages: Protohistoric Pueblo Blanco (LA 40) and

San Marcos Pueblo (LA 98). Paper presented at the fifty-seventh annual meeting of the Society for American Archaeology. St. Louis, April 14–18.

———. 2000. Regional Scale and Regional System in the Northern Rio Grande. In Michelle Hegmon, ed., *Regional Systems in the American Southwest.* Boulder, Colo.: University of Colorado Press.

Creamer, Winifred, Jonathan Haas, and Lisa Renken. 1994. Testing Conventional Wisdom: Protohistoric Ceramics and Chronology in the Northern Rio Grande. Paper presented at the fifty-ninth annual meeting of the Society for American Archaeology. Anaheim, Calif., April 22.

Creamer, Winifred, Jonathan Haas, Lisa Renken, Kit Nelson, and Aaron Wentzel. 2000. The Pecos Classification Doesn't Work at Pecos: Ceramic Analysis in the Northern Rio Grande. Paper presented at the Southwest Symposium. Santa Fe, January 14–15.

Habicht-Mauche, Judith A. 1993. *The Ceramics of Arroyo Hondo Pueblo.* Santa Fe, N.M.: School of American Research Press.

Hagstrum, Melissa. 1985. Measuring Prehistoric Ceramic Craft Specialization: A Test Case in the American Southwest. *Journal of Field Archaeology* 12(1): 65–75.

Hammond, George P., and Agapito Rey. 1940. *Narratives of the Coronado Expedition.* Albuquerque: University of New Mexico Press.

———. 1953. *Don Juan de Oñate, Colonizer of New Mexico.* Albuquerque: University of New Mexico Press.

Kidder, Alfred Vincent, and Anna O. Shepard. 1936. *The Pottery of Pecos.* 2 vols. Papers of the Southwestern Expedition 7. New Haven, Conn.: Yale University Press.

Lightfoot, Kent. 1979. Food Redistribution among Prehistoric Pueblo Groups. *The Kiva* 44: 319–339.

Lopinot, Neal H. 1986. The Spanish Introduction of New Cultigens into the Greater Southwest. *The Missouri Archaeologist* 47: 61–84.

Mera, Henry P. 1932. Wares Ancestral to Tewa Polychrome. *Technical Series Bulletin* 4. Laboratory of Anthropology, Santa Fe, New Mexico.

Motsinger, Thomas N. 1997. Tracking Protohistoric Glazeware Specialization in the Upper Rio Grande Valley, New Mexico. *Kiva* 63: 101–116.

Nelson, Nels. 1916. Chronology of the Tano Ruins, New Mexico. *American Anthropologist* 18(2): 159–180.

Plog, Stephen. 1980. *Stylistic Variation in Prehistoric Ceramics: Design Analysis in the American Southwest.* Cambridge: Cambridge University Press.

Reed, Lori W. 1990. X-Ray Diffraction Analysis of Glaze Painted Ceramics from the Northern Rio Grande Region, New Mexico: Implications of Glazeware Production and Exchange. In Steadman Upham and Barbara D. Staley, eds., *Economy and Polity in Late Rio Grande Prehistory.* Occasional Papers 16. Las Cruces, N.M.: University Museum, New Mexico State University.

Renfrew, Colin. 1975. Trade as Action at a Distance. In Jeremy A. Sabloff and C. C. Lamberg-Karlovsky, eds., *Ancient Civilization and Trade.* Albuquerque: University of New Mexico Press.

Scholes, France V. 1937. *Church and State in New Mexico, 1610–1650.* Historical Society of New Mexico, Publications in History 7, Albuquerque: University of New Mexico Press.

———. 1942. *Troublous Times in New Mexico, 1659–1670.* Historical Society of New Mexico, Publications in History 11, Albuquerque: University of New Mexico Press; reprint, New York: AMS Press, 1977.

Shepard, Anna O. 1942. Rio Grande Glaze Paint Ware: A Study Illustrating the Place of Ceramic Technological Analysis in Archaeological Research. *Contributions to American Anthropology and History* 39. Washington, D.C.: Carnegie Institution of Washington.

———. 1948. *Plumbate: A Mesoamerican Tradeware.* Washington, D.C.: Carnegie Institution of Washington.

Snow, David H. 1984. Spanish American Pottery Manufacture in New Mexico: A Critical Review. *Ethnohistory* 31: 93–113.

Upham, Steadman. 1982. *Polities and Power.* New York: Academic Press.

Warren, A. Helene. 1969. Tonque. *El Palacio* 76: 36–42.

———. 1979. The Glaze Paint Wares of the Upper Middle Rio Grande. In Jan V. Biella and Richard C. Chapman, eds., *Archaeological Investigations in Cochiti Reservoir* 4: 187–216.

Wobst, H. Martin. 1977. Stylistic Behavior and Information Exchange. In Charles E. Cleland, ed., *For the Director: Research Essays in Honor of James B. Griffin.* Anthropological Papers 61. Ann Arbor: University of Michigan Museum of Anthropology.

9

The Commoditization of Goods and the Rise of the State in Ancient Mesopotamia

Mitchell S. Rothman

This chapter explores an early stage in the commoditization of goods. It argues that the process began in the ancient Near East with the rise of primary state societies. I begin by re-examining the term "commodity," and then present the Mesopotamian case, which demonstrates why state origins and the earliest stages of commoditization occur simultaneously.

COMMODITIES AND THE COMPLEXITY OF SOCIETY

The debate about the nature of "commodities" and "commoditization" in economics and anthropology during the past 100 years addresses the very structure and dynamics of human societies.[1] Polanyi (1957) defined the differences between the economies of advanced states and earlier nonstate or noncapitalist societies. His landmark essay, "Marketless Trading in Hammurabi's Time" (1957), concerns the historical nature of societal structures as much as it does mechanisms of trade. Similarly, Marx in *The Grundrisse* (1972) examined the larger political economy—anthropologists would say the different social structures—of capitalist and precapitalist societies. He demonstrated how differing relations of production and control of the means of production ramify throughout a society, from class to governance to family to religion. As Dalton wrote, "modes of transaction are . . . directly related to political organization, social structure, and culture" (1975, 92).

Most economists and anthropologists unnecessarily restrict the definition of commodity, limiting the discussion to capitalist versus noncapitalist, or monetized versus nonmonetized systems. This restricted definition often obscures the origins of commodities and commoditization. Here I use the case of ancient Mesopotamia in the era of state formation to argue that: (1) a broader definition of commodities is necessary; and (2) the process of commoditization began shortly after the rise of the state in Mesopotamia and is directly related to the changes represented by state origins. This sociocultural break between state and less complex forms of social organization is at the heart of the distinctions invoked by the term commodity. The development of the primary state can lead to the modern capitalist state, but the economies of modern states are as different from those of the primary state as the economies of primary states are from those of chiefly or kinship societies.

DEFINING COMMODITIES

Defining commodity therefore becomes a critical task. Unfortunately, there is no commonly accepted definition (Gould and Kolb 1965, 108). Polanyi's specification is as succinct as any: "all commodities—goods produced for sale—are potential objects for sale. . . . All trade is market trade." The value of these goods is set in "price-making markets" (Polanyi 1968, 133). To use the term commodity as Polanyi does is to assume a money-based, or at least quasi-capitalist, market system. Are there no stages, however, between chiefly societies and advanced, monetized states? Did commodities emerge full-blown in the past few hundred years? I argue that the process of commoditization of goods began before true money and before market principles of setting exchange value, although not before the existence of physical marketplaces.

In our attempt to use the term commodity to understand dramatic economic change and its larger organizational corollaries, Polanyi's definition highlights two useful elements. First, it draws a distinction between two kinds of products in a society: those used for exchange—goods having intrinsic or exchange value—and implicitly, those intended for use by the primary producers and their own social groups. Second, it sees commodity exchange and value determination in the context of an institutionalized system of exchange, where impersonal market price-setting principles apply. This conception suggests that commodities exist outside the realm of barter by the primary producer. Appadurai (1986) calls the separate realm of commodities (versus goods) "the commodity situation." His phrase is meant to distinguish commodity exchange from gifts, tournaments of exchange (such as Kwakiutl *potlatch* or Kawelka *moka*), "priceless" ritual items, tax or tribute, and compensation such as bride wealth and pecuniary payment for injury or death.

Polanyi's definition cannot explain the origins of commoditization because his (and other) definitions begin with the mechanism of exchange. These mechanisms depend on the cultural value of things, not the reverse. I argue that the definition of commodity should begin instead with the way cultures at various levels of complexity define cultural and economic values of goods. On this point I agree with Appadurai, who writes: "Value is embodied in the commodities that are exchanged. Focusing on the things that are exchanged, rather than the forms or functions of exchange, makes it possible to argue that what creates the link between exchange and values is *politics*" (1986, 3, Appadurai's italics). That is, the political relations of individuals and groups—the larger organization of society—provide the social context within which economic production and exchange occur. Goods enter the realm of politics in part because of the human characteristic of symboling (White 1949); human beings symbolize (encode) social values in things. More is involved in setting value than the calculus Adam Smith proposes in which goods of equal quality are judged only by their asking price in an impersonal, money-based market (Smith 1904). A cultural calculus of a very different kind is at work. As Kopytoff writes, "From a cultural perspective, the production of commodities is also a cultural and cognitive process: commodities must not only be produced materially as things, but also culturally marked as being a certain kind of thing" (1986, 64). As he notes, goods can move in and out of the commodity situation.

Implicit in the definition of commodities is that cultural marking implies ranking. As Pollock observes, value

> may be understood as a dimension or dimensions along which categories are arranged with a clear implication of ranking among them. In this way the close connection between value and classification becomes apparent, since one cannot refer to value without referring to distinctions and therefore to categories. . . . Like meaning, value is socially constructed and not inherent in actions or in objects. (1983, 11)

Or, as Kopytoff writes, "Out of the total range of things available in a society, only some of them are considered appropriate for marking as commodities" (1986, 64).

To reach a general definition of commodity that permits us to distinguish it from a good and to see the process of commoditization of goods beginning and ramifying, we must be able to see *all* of the following:

1. Classes of goods are culturally marked as commodities, as distinct from noncommodity goods.[2]
2. These classes of goods are created in a system (a commodity situation) outside the usual barter or reciprocal exchange system of primary producers with its emphasis on use-value.
3. This commodity situation is part of an institutionalized system of exchange,[3] though not necessarily based on money and market principles.
4. This institutional system embodies a major shift in individual and group social identities and in overall sociopolitical organization, which reflects the distinction between commodities and noncommodity goods.

Accordingly, a commodity can be defined as:

> any good or service that members of a society can conceive culturally as a separate class of goods having primarily intrinsic or exchange-value, as opposed to use-value, and

which must be exchanged in an institutionalized marketplace or system of trade, often through individuals other than the primary producers of those goods or services.

Again, commodities are not objects of tribal gift giving, tournaments of exchange, "priceless" ritual items, tax and tribute (unless these enter the commodity situation), or compensation.

Having defined commodity, I turn next to the Mesopotamian case, arguing that: (1) the beginning of the commoditization of goods occurs shortly after the development of primary states, and (2) this process correlates with the organizational and ideological nature of state society.

THE INSTITUTIONAL DEVELOPMENT OF STATES IN MESOPOTAMIA

As Wright (1977) and Wright and Johnson (1975) define it, the state is a *society* (it is not merely the organs of the state) with at least three hierarchical levels of full-time, institutionalized administrators, who oversee essential functions. Such functions include production of goods, staple storage, infrastructure maintenance (e.g., irrigation canals), religious ritual, long-distance trade, and warfare. Either because of the technical difficulty or the number of people and diversity of groups, higher-order control, decision-making, and enforcement by the most senior political authorities becomes necessary. That is, political authority of a degree previously unknown is centralized in *administrative* forms of social organization (see Rothman 1987, 1994a). Vertical hierarchy, control, status, and economic realignment are key identifiers of a primary state. Although the analytical focus is on the state's administrative and control centers, in part because they are the best documented, economic and social changes undoubtedly spread throughout the society.

Two elements of state development are essential to describing commoditization. First, the ideology of a socially stratified state society causes a series of goods to become symbols of new statuses, and thus become commoditized. Second, obtaining these goods and necessary exotic materials in a reliable manner and in sufficient quantities, as well as finding a way to distribute them, creates a commodity situation. Such exchange opens the opportunity for nonproducer traders and for production explicitly for exchange. It also sets up the conditions for an institutionalized system of trade.

In Mesopotamia (for map see Roaf 1990, 79) states first appeared in the southern alluvium of modern Iraq and southwest Iran during the middle Uruk period (circa 3500 B.C. uncalibrated). The larger region (which includes the basins of the Tigris and Euphrates Rivers and their tributaries, as well as the foothills of the Taurus and Zagros Mountains) first became integrated economically toward the end of the fourth millennium B.C. (the late Uruk period). This integration apparently emerged from the creation of important exchange networks linking South, North, and East Mesopotamia (Algaze 1993). Development of states continued through the Jemdet Nasr period (3200–2800 B.C.), although regional integration appears to have waned. The primary state was solidified by the early Dynastic period (2800–2350 B.C.), which was associated with the so-called Sumerian culture of the southern alluvium. In 2300 B.C., a coalition of northern Semitic groups under Sargon I forged the first true empire in Mesopotamia, encompassing the South and the northern steppes. This empire collapsed in approximately 2100 B.C. and a southern-based kingdom, the Ur III dynasty, emerged. This kingdom was replaced in the early second millennium B.C. by a second Semitic empire under Hammurabi of Babylon (the Hammurabi referred to in Polanyi 1957).[4]

From the time of its earliest settlement, long-distance exchange was important in Mesopotamia. The alluvium of southern Mesopotamia, the focus of this case, was settled during the sixth millennium B.C.[5] Irrigation agriculturalists moved into the area after the Persian/Arabian Gulf level dropped, and workers in small villages could easily cut short canals from the river beds (perpendicular to the river levees, as discussed by Wright 1981). Grain yields were so high that grain stored in good years was sufficient to keep villagers from suffering frequent shortfalls caused by drought or flooding. Pasture for sheep and goats was also plentiful, although pastoralists often had to take their flocks to the hills in the heat of the summer. To supplement products from the alluvium (grains, vegetables, milk products, pottery, and cloth made from wool or flax), individual groups imported into the South metal ores and products, timber, bitumen (for caulking boats, bowls, and houses), finer chipping stone, and an array of precious and semiprecious materials, such as silver, gold, lapis lazuli, shell, carnelian, steatite, and chlorite. These materials were desired for farming tools, vessels, weapons, jewelry, statuary, seals, and larger buildings (full beams were necessary to span roofs or second stories). By the late fourth millennium B.C., many of these goods appeared over a large area of the alluvium and steppe. Until the fourth millennium (see Renfrew 1977), most were obtained through down-the-line trade, rather than through a formal trading system.

The first 1,500 years of settlement in the southern alluvium appear to have been marked by dynamic political and social changes. Early residents of the region apparently organized themselves into tribal or simple chiefly societies (Adams 1981; Wright 1994). Their dependence on the two rivers, especially the Euphrates, caused the population to aggregate along the two rivers' banks. By the middle of the fifth millennium B.C., signs of marked social complexity appeared, such as different house size, restricted access to certain goods, and some centralization of religious ritual. During the following millennium, site numbers and sizes increased dramatically, indicating a very significant increase in overall population and a restructuring of the physical landscape into central cities, small towns, and villages. In the cities, religious edifices that required substantial labor were built. Mass production of crude bowls began. Interpretations of these bowls' functions vary, but they were likely used as ration bowls by state administrators to compensate workers (Rothman 1987, 85). In addition, images of great storehouses appeared on various artistic media.

This increasing social complexity in Mesopotamia was evidenced by new kinds of formal administrative paraphernalia and new uses of goods to mark status. By the fourth millennium B.C. administrative technology left its remains in the form of clay sealings (von Wickede 1990). Tokens often appear as small models of the goods that were being transported and *administratively* accounted for (Schmandt-Bessarat 1992). Sealings of clay had been used before this, perhaps as amulets, but in the mid- to late fourth millennium B.C. they are associated with a formal system of control in which sealed clay locks limited access to various raw materials and goods (Rothman 1994b, 1994c). The sealing system used accounting procedures. For example, at Arslantepe in the North, remains of a probable auditing technique were found in an abandoned room. Basket-sized groups of sealings were found together, as if they had been retained until they could be audited and then were dumped in the trash (Palmieri 1981; Frangipane 1994). This is reminiscent of the Old Babylonian practice of keeping all the records of one month or one topic in baskets with a clay file tag.

By the middle of the fourth millennium, grave goods had changed from a few pots in simple graves to built tombs with objects made of imported precious stones and metal items (see, for example, Peasnall, forthcoming). The few graves containing these exotic and rare items apparently indicate that their owners were high ranking town and city dwellers.

The self-perception of Mesopotamian rulers is perhaps best represented by a meter-high, carved vase found in an enclosed district of the Uruk/Warka site (Roaf 1990, 61, 71). Three registers are carved on this vase from bottom to top. The lowest register portrays the world of nature and its products, with the staples of Mesopotamia (grains), and, above them, sheep and goats. In the middle register (above nature) are naked men carrying vessels, representing the primary producers of goods. In the top or highest register is the king of Uruk in the presence of the star goddess Inanna. The king and goddess are about the same height, although the goddess is the one receiving goods, both agricultural and craft items (two alabaster vases, apparent metal ingots, and so on). The hierarchy of late Uruk society is clearly visible, as is the use of goods to symbolize that hierarchy. This vase is a form of early propaganda for the primary state, showing the "natural" (that is, culturally defined) order of things (Winter n.d.).

FIRST EVIDENCE OF A SHIFT TOWARD COMMODITIZATION: LATE FOURTH MILLENNIUM

The changes discussed above signal the first steps toward commoditization. Goods were used not just as gifts or tribute to cement social relationships, but rather particular goods took on social value. This intrinsic value marked the good's owner as a person of wealth or status. Thus, the accumulation of goods, unheard of in kinship systems, became common. Competition for status-marking objects increased the demand for a reliable source of these goods, whose raw materials had to be carried over long distances. For example, the only known source of lapis lazuli, one of the key markers of Mesopotamian status, was from Afghanistan.

Although there was a perceptual shift in the value of specific items, does it reflect the creation of a formal or institutionalized system? How were these goods obtained, and to what degree did their acquisition depend on a more complex social and economic order? A key issue in tracing the commoditization of goods is the structure of the ancient Mesopotamian economy. In Mesopotamia (and probably elsewhere)[6] changes in the structure of economic activity accompanied the administrative and other changes noted above. Specialized work[7] became more common, although it represented a small percentage of total work output. In addition, pottery was mass produced, and, as noted, exotic materials, especially metals, were exchanged.

Within the newly founded state institutions of palace and temple a more complex and controlled organization evolved. This new complexity is illustrated by a change in the technology of control. In the last centuries of the fourth millennium B.C., the technology of control represented by sealings was no longer sufficient to handle the information records necessary to administer alluvium city-states. Interactions with those inside and outside the state's centralized institutions had to be managed. In the city of Uruk, a system of writing appeared for the first time (Nissen, Damerow, and Englund 1993). In its earliest form, this system of tablet texts apparently was used exclusively by the palace and the great temples. The tablets recorded movements of the central administration's resources and receipts and disbursements of staples (e.g., grain, beer, and a variety of other goods). For example, a late Uruk-Jemdet Nasr tablet recorded distribution of various types of grain to a temple official for a celebration of the goddess Inanna.

The earliest writings demonstrate a shift away from categorizing goods according to their use-value. An encyclopedic rendering (Nissen and Englund 1993) shows how bureaucrats categorized all the important classes of goods into grains, potables, animal products, metal objects, stone objects, and so on. The symbols used for goods (some of which were already becoming commodities, I argue) are variations on their category signs, which were related to the vessels in which they were stored or transported. That is, scribes did not view the goods as fulfilling direct uses, but as convenient means of storage, transport, purchase of work service (later), or trade. Thus storable, easily transferable goods were more highly valued.

These texts also represent an attempt to create an economic system for the collection and exchange of goods. This is not yet a commodity situation, but it is a necessary precursor, because it represents a more formal exchange system and provides opportunities for agents and traders to modify the economic system into a commodity situation.

To understand the next steps toward commoditization requires attention not just to core institutions but to the wider society. This region did not yet have completely integrated economies, where goods are produced for sale and where the government and nongovernment entities freely trade goods produced for exchange. As evidenced in later texts (Stone 1987), much of the population remained at the margins of state administrators' power and lived in communal or even extended kinship units in which noncommodity production and limited barter were still common. Even within the city centers where the process of commoditization probably began, a dual economy existed. One pole was what later Sumerian, Sargonid, and Old Babylonian scribes called the "city." This consisted of "the community of persons of equal status bound together by a consciousness of belonging [to kinship-based or community organizations], realized by directing their communal affairs by means of an assembly, in which, under a presiding officer, some degree of consensus was reached" (Oppenheim 1977, 95). The other pole consisted of the "great institutions" of palace and major temples. Oppenheim describes these organizations as consisting

> of persons entirely different in structure and temperament from the community just mentioned, whose center and *raison d'être* was either the temple or the palace, either the household of the deity or that of the king. Both were closed-circuit organizations in which goods and services were channeled into a circulation system and where the entire personnel [*sic*] was integrated in a hierarchical order. (Oppenheim 1977, 95)

Both economic poles ostensibly were engaged in production for use-value, although the great institutions and the private sector (especially urban families) used their resources and structured production and exchange quite differently. For a commodity situation to evolve, an interaction between the two poles must emerge in which production for exchange and a shift in the perception of goods occurs. In this case, such a shift is evident and the two poles are not completely separate. The economic estates of palace and temples intersected in a number of circumstances. Because the palace's estate did not provide sufficient income or workers for all of its tasks, private citizens were required to pay tribute or tax to state rulers. In the absence of money (see below), this tribute was converted into useable and storable form. Sometimes these "private" groups were also forced into corvée work gangs to clear canals, build public monuments, or fight wars. Conversely, nondependents of the palace and temples could receive ration payments or temple offices for their work.[8] Temple offices involved fields that were subleased to prominent private citizens in exchange for services. Although palace and temples had dependents who were craftspersons, the insufficient access to resources or expertise within their own organization opened the possibility of exchange outside the palace and temples—that is, a commodity situation.

My proposed definition of the term commodity stipulates (among other criteria) the cultural or ideological creation of a new class of goods or a new way to look at and rank the value of goods. The first evidence of such an ideological shift already existed by the end of the fourth millennium B.C. Again, perceptual evidence of this first step in the commoditization process appears in accounting texts and the use of personal markers of rank in graves. A model of an institutionalized system of exchange had been forged.

A SECOND STEP TOWARD COMMODITIZATION: THE THIRD AND EARLY SECOND MILLENNIA B.C.

As in the fourth millennium B.C., in the early Dynastic period the use of goods was a symbolic representation of the state political structure. In the Sumerian city of Ur,[9] a great royal cemetery contained tombs of the royal house, the rulers of Ur, a series of "death pits," and graves of people whose relatives had sneaked their bodies into the cemetery (Pollock 1983). Unlike any other internment in Mesopotamia, these death pits were huge graves, each containing a single body (male or female) on a central bier. Around the body were the most spectacular objects available, many of them imported or made from imported raw materials. Surrounding this central area were the bodies of servants, musicians, and soldiers with their weapons and ox-drawn chariots, as if these people had been buried alive. Moorey (1977), whose explanation seems consistent with the evidence, suggests that the royal court legitimized its political authority by associating itself with the core fertility ritual of the kingdom. Each year a man and woman reenacted the mating of Inanna and Dumuzi, who were the goddess and god (respectively) associated with soil fertility. As far as we know, the Sumerians believed that these individuals, who were closely associated with the royal house, became the god and goddess. When these reactualizers died, they were buried as if they were the god and goddess. The numerous items placed around the bier were mostly long distance trade goods.

True commodities appeared during the early Dynastic to Old Babylonian periods (2500–1600 B.C.), whose economies were more complex than those of the preceding late Uruk period. As before, the economic base of Mesopotamia was grain agriculture and pastoralism, and it remained a dual economy with palace/temple and private sectors. The private sector was made up of extended families who were connected to larger community or descent groups.[10] Diakanoff (1954) estimates that 40 to 50 percent of the arable land in the Sumerian city of Shuruppak was held by extended family or lineal groups. For example, in one land "sale"[11] document a set of men with the same father benefit (Diakanoff 1954, 25). Meanwhile, the palace/temple agricultural estates had grown to support their administrators and retainers. These estates also remained a source of income for those who were not direct dependents. Both ration workers and sharecroppers received part of their livelihoods by working state land (Rothman 1994d). Craft production was also conducted in private and palace sectors. At the city of Khafaje, the ruler of the city-state had a massive temple district constructed. Immediately surrounding the temple building were small workshops where stonecutters, coppersmiths, bakers, and other specialists worked (Frankfort 1970, 44). Records of metalworking, however, indicate that the palace at Nippur regularly hired private goldsmiths and bronze producers (Zettler 1990). There was an economic interchange in which goods were produced for specific clients or, more generally, for sale. Marketplaces were organized in primary and secondary centers (Röllig 1976).

In addition to local agricultural production, regional trade occurred. Because tool and weapons technology was based on bronze metallurgy and because all metal ores had to be imported, large-scale trading systems must have existed. In the early second millennium Old Assyrian period (parallel to the Old Babylonian period in southern Mesopotamia), texts describe the marketing of Mesopotamian cloth for metals in Anatolia through trading colonies (Larsen 1968). These two categories of goods had certainly become commodities in an international trading system. Trading colonies existed throughout northern Mesopotamia (Edzard 1967, 196), and kings at sites such as Mari on the northern Euphrates became wealthy by taxing southward-flowing barges laden with trade goods (Edzard 1967, 206).

The values of this age were far from the ideals of a kinship society. Kings competed with one another for land and status. Sometimes, as in the case of Larsa and its upstream neighbor Isin, the battle was for access to irrigation water; at other times, it was for the possession of exotic materials. Heads of extended families in the private sector also sought status through possession of land and goods symbolizing their higher rank, as seen archaeologically in differential grave wealth and house size, both of which are related to landholdings or access to arable land.

The quest for individual markers of status and for practical commodities such as cloth or metals through an institutionalized market system fulfills my second criterion for commoditization: an institutionalized system of exchange, often handled by those other than the primary producers and usually not primarily for use-value. In ancient Mesopotamia, the embodiment of that change is the _dam.gàr_'s (in the Sumerian language), meaning business agents and entrepreneurs.[12] _Dam.gàr_'s could be male or female, and some were regularly retained by the palace or temple in other roles. Some rented palace or temple land or received special grants of such land. Others appear to have been completely independent. Each _dam.gàr_ was part of an organization with a common capital account[13] and administrative officers. As Oppenheim writes, "between the opposing modes of integration characterized, on the one hand, by an organization that was tight-knit and bureaucratic (the palace or the temple) and, on the other hand, by an association of individuals of more or less equal status who worked cooperatively as well as individually (the city), an intermediate zone was bound to develop that, as by a law of nature, was attracted to the centers of power and assumed various forms of peripheral co-existence" (1977, 80). In this market system, a palace or temple had its own functionary, the _ga.raš_, who was a buyer for goods that did not come into the state sector through normal taxation or tribute.

The wealth of a _dam.gàr_ came from his or her ability to manipulate exchange-value. Originally, _dam.gàr_ was translated as "merchant" (Leemans 1950). The duties of the _dam.gàr_, however, go beyond shipping and sales. According to records of the Sargonid period (Foster 1977), a _dam.gàr_ took investments in commodities from individuals and groups both in the private sector and from the palace. These exchanges were for long-term gain. For example, an Old Babylonian archive (Stol 1982) indicates that the palace gave to the _dam.gàr_'s a portion of the produce paid to the palace as taxes and rents (sharecrops). In-kind payments to the palace or temples consisted of grain, onions, garlic, fish, and other foodstuffs, most of it coming in the same season. Much of the grain was placed in storehouses by the palace or temples, but the excess, together with perishable goods, were invested with the *dam.gàr*'s on the "docks,"[14] where they were traded to private individuals. The premium received by the palace was less than the going rate (see below), because the palace wanted to receive grain or silver, even at an apparent loss. These two commodities were easily stored and, in the case of silver, easily transported outside the area. Another strategy of a *dam.gàr* was to move commodities from where they were invested to another city-state. One Sargonid period text speaks of 3,500 sheep that were shipped from Umma to Girsu, and then from Girsu to Uruk (Foster 1977, 36), because the exchange rate for sheep was higher in the other city's marketplaces. These goods, by my definition, were commodities in a commodity situation.

A market system driven by an agent or middleman, represented by the *dam.gàr*, was only one way in which subsistence goods circulated in this dual economy. In the private "kinship" or community-based sector (almost undocumented in state records except as taxpayers), barter seems to have existed alongside a new market system to obtain goods not directly produced. This exchange system could include *dam.gàr*'s, who brought resources from the state and sharecroppers. Exchange goods came from primary production or from ration or sharecrop work for the palace or temples, although ration workers apparently did not earn sufficient livelihoods through ration work alone. The palace or temples engaged in trade primarily to convert their receipts into a more useful long-term form, rather than for "profit."

The system I have just discussed is largely a market for subsistence goods, but what about the goods that came from outside the South, such as those needed for tools and those found in the tombs and death pits of high ranking state officials? Foster writes, "There is no evidence in the available records that Sargonid *dam.gàr*'s played any significant role in the acquisition of products foreign to Mesopotamia" (1977, 37). It is true that the records of those *dam.gàr*'s who traded in subsistence commodities do not mention exotic materials. Other records, however, speak of those who traveled north into the Zagros and Taurus Mountains or south into the Gulf to Dilmun, Meluhha, and Makran (Leemans 1950). What distinguishes these long-distance traders is that they did not seem to be independent entrepreneurs, at least not in this first stage of commoditization in the third millennium B.C. Rather, they appear to have been agents for the palace or temples, and perhaps for a very limited number of wealthy city residents. These traders' records mention military escorts (Leemans 1950) and long-distance *dam.gàr*'s silver. The long-distance trading system apparently was designed to bring back those exotic goods that southern Mesopotamian leaders used to signify their higher social position. Pollock proposes that "symbols of prestige will be characterized by the use of (1) different raw materials, (2) different styles, and (3) greater quantity of a type of object or attribute of the object" (1983, 243). Perhaps, like the high chiefs of ancient Panama (Helms 1976), the direct link of earthly rulers with distant gods—as seen in the Uruk/Warka vase and in the death pits of Ur—is mythically affirmed by materials from far away. The state's desire for silver may have been due to the acceptability of silver as a form of exchange for goods outside southern Mesopotamia and because of its easy portability. The leaders of the Mesopotamian city-state clearly sought to obtain and monopolize these exotic goods, which symbolized higher rank.

Contrary to some definitions of commoditization, these early stages of the process in Mesopotamia did not require true money (see Sweet 1958). True money must be a medium of exchange, a means of payment, a unit of account, and a standard of deferred payment (Dalton 1981, 258). Money must be divisible and used daily for common purchases. In ancient Mesopotamia, silver, grain, and sometimes livestock served as standards of exchange value. Many tablets that record an agreement of sale[15] list the value of the things that were exchanged as "x" *minas* of silver or "y" bushels of grain. Tablets that later record the actual transactions almost never mention silver changing hands, unless silver itself was the thing being exchanged. A typical commodity that is purchased with true money is work (labor, as Marx defined it). Ration lists from ancient Mesopotamia, however, never mention silver, only grain, oil, or wool amounts. Nor is there a standard of account in ancient Mesopotamia. The records of *dam.gàr*'s indicate the investment of various commodities, including silver, and there is no mention of silver as a form of payment for any of them. In short, silver did not function as real money.

Price-setting in the institutionalized markets on the docks also did not function according to market principles. Where markets based on money and market principles do exist, the "prices" of commodities fluctuate. According to market principles, an anonymous mechanism sets the exchange value, or the "price" of goods, in part to prevent conflict between buyer and seller over the amount of profit or advantage taken.[16] Perhaps a similar problem arose with the coming of the *dam.gàr*'s as commodities traders, or perhaps it was related to the tribal practice of valuing the relationship between kinsmen over some abstract value in exchange. In any case, a different solution was arrived at in ancient Mesopotamia. The exchange value of goods in Mesopotamian markets was apparently preset by a *ṣimdat ṣarri*, or "a command of the king" (Kraus 1958). Records indicate that over the course of a year, the *ṣimdat ṣarri* did fluctuate (probably according to season), but within a period of months, it was constant. A clever *dam.gàr* played the long odds. Investment contracts (written as loans) were usually open-ended. The *dam.gàr*'s and their clients could either wait for a more favorable *ṣimdat ṣarri* or, as mentioned above, could literally move their flock to another city-state, where the *ṣimdat ṣarri* was better for the commodity they wanted to trade. This was a commodities market, but it functioned very differently from those of modern, monetized market systems.

CONCLUSION

This chapter argues that the process of commoditization is one in which: (1) members of a society see classes of goods culturally marked as commodities, as distinct from noncommodity goods; (2) these classes of goods are created in a commodity situation outside the usual barter or reciprocal exchange system of primary producers with its emphasis on use-value; (3) this commodity situation is in part an institutionalized system of exchange; and (4) this institutional system reflects a major shift in the social identities of individuals and groups and overall sociopolitical organization. For 1,800 years after the emergence of the Mesopotamian state, these conditions were all met. When the palace and temples entered economic life, there emerged classes of goods marked for their exchange-value more than their use-value. Goods that in the fourth millennium were received and distributed by the palace entered a commodity situation, as did goods collected and produced by the state to exchange for work in the third and early second millennia. As a result, a system of exchange was institutionalized, in which a class of traders (*dam.gàr*'s), rather than the primary producers, became agents for circulating subsistence goods, thus commoditizing them. Meanwhile, noncommodity exchange continued in much of the nonstate sector. At the same time, cultural values changed so much that higher rank based on political power or individual wealth was perceived as an appropriate goal, and the desire for status influenced how the value of some goods was set.

This set of circumstances is unlikely to arise in less complex societies or without the kinds of administrative and economic structures created in a state society. The increasing social and political hierarchy of states helps to trigger a revaluing of goods. Complex administrative systems then also become the models for future commodity situations.

This analysis addresses the very case that Polanyi considered. I suggest that Polanyi was correct that the economy of Hammurabi's time was not one of a monetized, almost capitalist economic system in which exchange value was determined by market principles of supply and demand. I believe Polanyi erred in not seeing an entrepreneurial class with a clear profit motive and, of course, the existence of commodities. Given the alternatives that his definition of commodities permits, Polanyi's approach does not capture the subtleties of the Mesopotamian economy or the way it reflected cultural and institutional processes.

NOTES

For many helpful suggestions, I thank Susan Lees, Peter D. Little, Michael Rosenberg, Estelle Smith, Priscilla Stone, and Henry Wright.

1. The term "commodity," as opposed to "good," has permitted assessment of degrees of functional differentiation or cultural complexity. Complexity is defined here as "the degree of functional differentiation among societal units or sub-systems. . . . Complexity has a horizontal axis consisting of the number of units of similar functional type and a vertical axis consisting of the number of hierarchical levels" (Rothman 1994a, 4).

2. Scarcity can enter here, but only for goods already marked as commodities. For example, there are many goods and raw materials scarcer than gold, but gold is first marked as a commodity *before* its scarcity can affect its exchange value. Beyond that the fluctuation

in the exchange rate for gold often has nothing to do with its scarcity, but rather its value against other commodities in good or bad economic times.

3. The existence of an informal economy assumes the presence of a formal system.

4. See Kramer (1963) for a popular description of the Sumerians, and Bottéro, Cassin, and Vercoutter (1965) for a good general economic and political history of the periods discussed.

5. Wright suggests that the earliest settlement occurred in the southern alluvium at 5500 B.C. uncalibrated, 6300 B.C. calibrated (personal communication).

6. A similar case is discussed by Renfrew (1986).

7. By specialized work, I mean work that is aimed at more than production for use-value of the producers and their immediate community (Alchian and Allen 1969).

8. The term for disbursement in the late fourth millennium accounting texts is a combination of ration bowls and a head eating. See Nissen, Damerow, and Englund (1993, figure 12) for the written signs.

9. Ur does not refer to the place from which Abraham supposedly came. That Ur is now known from Ebla texts to be in northern Syria.

10. Since these kinship or community groups were marginal to the state apparatus, they are rarely referred to as such in texts, which in Sumer are produced exclusively by the temple or palace. Such groupings do appear in Old Babylonian nonstate texts, indicating they almost certainly existed before that time (Stone 1987; Rothman 1994d).

11. It is moot whether these sale documents were true transfers of rights or merely temporary usufruct rights (perhaps to other kinsmen).

12. The Semitic Akkadian language equivalent is *tamkarum*. The equivalent term in the Anatolian trading colonies of Assyrian merchants in the Old Assyrian period is *karum* (Edzard 1967, 196).

13. At third millennium Umma, this account was called the "Fund of Balanced Account" (Foster 1977, 34).

14. The term from which this is translated carries the broader connotation of "market."

15. It is not even clear whether productive resources such as land are ever really sold (i.e., that transfers of all rights to use and dispose of the resource are made). Many "sale" documents from Old Babylonian period Larsa are followed by redemption texts in which the "seller" takes back the land for the same silver amount as the original sale (Rothman 1994d).

16. The proof of the potential for conflict (including violence) over profits is frequently apparent in union strikes against management.

REFERENCES

Adams, Robert McCormick. 1981. *Heartland of Cities*. Chicago: University of Chicago Press.
Alchian, Armen, and William Allen. 1969. *Exchange and Production Theory in Use*. Wadsworth, Calif.: Wadsworth.
Algaze, Guillermo. 1993. *The Uruk World System*. Chicago: University of Chicago Press.
Appadurai, Arjun. 1986. Introduction: Commodities and the Politics of Value. In Arjun Appadurai, ed., *The Social Life of Things*. Cambridge: Cambridge University Press.
Bottéro, Jean, Elena Cassin, and Jean Vercoutter, eds. 1965. *The Near East, the Early Civilizations*. New York: Delacorte Press.

Dalton, George. 1975. Karl Polanyi's Analysis of Long Distance Trade and His Wider Paradigm. In Carl C. Lamberg-Karlovsky and Jeremy Sabloff, eds., *Ancient Civilization and Trade.* Albuquerque, N.M.: Schools of American Research.

———. 1981. Primitive Money. In George Dalton, ed., *Tribal and Peasant Economies.* Austin: University of Texas Press.

Diakanoff, Igor M. 1954. Sale of Land in Pre-Sargonid Sumer. Paper prepared for the twenty-third International Congress of Orientalists.

Edzard, Dietz. 1967. The Old Babylonian Period. In Jean Bottéro, Elena Cassin, and Jean Vercoutter, eds., *The Near East, the Early Civilizations.* New York: Delacorte Press.

Foster, Benjamin. 1977. Commercial Activity in the Sargonid Period. *Iraq* 39(1): 31–43.

Frangipane, Marcèlla. 1994. The Record Function of Clay Sealings in Early Administrative Systems as seen from Arslantepe/Malatya. In Piera Ferioli, Enrica Fiandra, Gian Fissore, and Marcèlla Frangipane, eds., *Archives Before Writing.* Rome: Ministry of Culture.

Frankfort, Henri. 1970. *The Art and Architecture of the Ancient Orient.* London: Penguin Books.

Gould, Julius, and William Kolb. 1965. *A Dictionary of the Social Sciences.* New York: Free Press.

Helms, Mary. 1976. *Ancient Panama.* Austin: University of Texas Press.

Kopytoff, Igor. 1986. The Cultural Biography of Things: Commoditization as Process. In Arjun Appadurai, ed., *The Social Life of Things.* Cambridge: Cambridge University Press.

Kramer, Samuel N. 1963. *The Sumerians.* Chicago: University of Chicago Press.

Kraus, Fritz. 1958. *Ein Edikt von des Königs Ammi-saduqa von Babylon.* Leiden: Brill.

Larsen, Mogens Trolle. 1968. *Old Assyrian Caravan Procedures.* Istanbul: Uitg. v.h. Historisch-Archeologisch Instituut te Istanbul.

Leemans, W. F. 1950. *The Old Babylonian Merchant.* Leiden: Brill.

Marx, Karl. 1972. *The Grundrisse,* ed. and trans. David McLellan. New York: Harper and Row.

Moorey, R. 1977. What Do We Know About the People Buried in the Royal Cemetery? *Expedition* 20: 24–40.

Nissen, Hans, Peter Damerow, and Robert Englund. 1993. *Archaic Bookkeeping: Early Writing and Techniques of Economic Administration.* Chicago: University of Chicago Press.

Nissen, Hans, and Robert Englund. 1993. *Die lexicalischen Liste der archaischen Texte aus Uruk.* Berlin: Gebr.Mann.

Oppenheim, A. Leo. 1977. *Ancient Mesopotamia.* Chicago: University of Chicago Press.

Palmieri, Alba. 1981. Excavations at Arslantepe (Malatya). *Anatolian Studies* 31: 101–109.

Peasnall, Brian. Forthcoming. Burials from Tepe Gawra. Appendix A. In Mitchell Rothman, ed., *Fourth Millennium B.C. Tepe Gawra.* Philadelphia: University of Pennsylvania Museum.

Polanyi, Karl. 1957. Marketless Trading in Hammurabi's Time. In Karl Polanyi, Conrad M. Arensberg, and Harry W. Pearson, eds., *Trade and Market in Ancient Empires.* Glencoe, Ill.: Free Press.

———. 1968. The Economy as an Instituted Process. In Edward LeClair and Harold Schneider, eds., *Economic Anthropology: Readings in Theory and Analysis.* New York: Holt Reinhart and Winston.

Pollock, Susan. 1983. The Symbolism of Prestige: An Archaeological Example from the Royal Cemetery of Ur. Ph.D. diss., University of Michigan.

Renfrew, Colin. 1977. Alternative Models for Exchange and Spatial Distribution. In Timothy Earle and Jonathan Ericson, eds., *Exchange Systems in Prehistory*. New York: Academic Press.

————. 1986. Varna and the Emergence of Wealth in Prehistoric Europe. In Arjun Appadurai, ed., *The Social Life of Things*. Cambridge: Cambridge University Press.

Roaf, Michael. 1990. *Cultural Atlas of Mesopotamia and the Ancient Near East*. New York: Facts on File.

Röllig, Wolfgang von. 1976. Der Altmesopotamische Markt. *Die Welt des Orients* 8(2): 286–295.

Rothman, Mitchell. 1987. Graph Theory and the Interpretation of Regional Survey Data. *Paléorient* 13(2): 73–91.

————. 1994a. Introduction, Part I. In Gil Stein and Mitchell Rothman, eds., *Chiefdoms and Early States in the Near East*. Madison, Wisc.: Prehistory Press.

————. 1994b. Sealings as a Control Mechanism in Prehistory. In Gil Stein and Mitchell Rothman, eds., *Chiefdoms and Early States in the Near East*. Madison, Wisc.: Prehistory Press.

————. 1994c. Seal and Sealing Findspot, Design Audience, and Function: Monitoring Changes in Administrative Oversight and Structure at Tepe Gawra During the Fourth Millennium B.C. In Piera Ferioli, Enrica Fiandra, Gian Fissore, and Marcèlla Frangipane, eds., *Archives Before Writing*. Rome: Ministry of Culture.

————. 1994d. Palace and Private Agricultural Decision-making in the Early 2nd Millennium B.C. City-State of Larsa, Iraq. In Elizabeth Brumfiel, ed., *The Economic Anthropology of the State*. Lanham, Md.: University Press of America.

Schmandt-Besserat, Denise. 1992. *Before Writing*. Austin: University of Texas Press.

Smith, Adam. 1904. *Wealth of Nations*. London: Methuen and Co.

Stol, Martin. 1982. State and Private Business in the Land of Larsa. *Journal of Cuneiform Studies* 34 (3–4): 127–230.

Stone, Elizabeth. 1987. *Nippur Neighborhoods*. Chicago: Oriental Institute.

Sweet, Ronald. 1958. On Prices, Moneys, and Money Use in the Old Babylonian Period. Ph.D. diss., University of Chicago.

von Wickede, Alwo. 1990. *Prähistoriche Stempelglyptik in Vorderasien*. Munchen: Profil Verlag.

White, Leslie. 1949. *The Science of Culture*. New York: Farrar, Straus, and Group.

Winter, Irene. n.d. Discussion of Warka Vase. *Classnotes, Mesopotamian Art History*. University of Pennsylvania.

Wright, Henry. 1977. Toward an Explanation of the Origin of the State. In James Hill, ed., *Explanation of Prehistoric Change*. Albuquerque: University of New Mexico Press.

————. 1981. Appendix: The Development of Settlement in the Area of Ur and Eridu. In Robert Adams, *Heartland of Cities*. Chicago: University of Chicago Press.

————. 1994. Prestate Political Formations. In Gil Stein and Mitchell Rothman, eds., *Chiefdoms and Early States in the Near East*. Madison, Wisc.: Prehistory Press.

Wright, Henry, and Gregory Johnson. 1975. Population, Exchange, and Early State Formation in Southwestern Iran. *American Antiquity* 77: 267–291.

Zettler, Richard. 1990. Metalworkers in the Economy of Mesopotamia in the Late Third Millennium B.C. In Naowl Miller, ed., *Economy and Settlement in the Near East*. Supplement to MASCA Research Papers in Science and Archaeology, no. 7. Philadelphia: University of Pennsylvania Museum.

10

Always Cheaply Pleasant: Beer as a Commodity in a Rural Kenyan Society

Bruce D. Roberts

The basis of their diet . . . is . . . appalling. . . . Would it not be better if they spent more money on wholesome things? . . . Yes, it would, but . . . no ordinary human being is ever going to do such a thing. The ordinary being would sooner starve. . . . And the peculiar evil is this, that the less money you have, the less inclined you feel to spend it on wholesome food. When you are unemployed, . . . underfed, harassed, bored, and miserable, you don't want to eat dull, wholesome food. You want something a little bit "tasty." There is always something cheaply pleasant to tempt you. (Orwell 1958 [1937], 95–96)

INTRODUCTION

England's depression-era unemployed poor spent money in ways deemed "imprudent" by observers, as this chapter's Orwellian epigraph implies. Here I explore the place of one commodity, home-brewed beer (*busaa*), among a group of small farmers in Keiyo District, Kenya. What explains the enduring popularity of this beverage, even in the face of official government proscription? For many Keiyo smallholder farmers home-brewed beer is equivalent to tea and other luxury foods, including bottled beer, that Orwell identified for the English poor of the 1930s. Beer, often condemned by outsiders, is of vital importance in Keiyo culture for many reasons. After identifying types of home-brewed beer, as well as the contexts in which they are consumed, I consider the role of beer as a commodity—a product exchanged for other goods. Beer brewing constitutes a potential income source, particularly for women. This function does not supplant others that beer performs, nor do I argue that the effects of brewing and selling beer are entirely positive. Economic benefits can be offset, for example, by the diversion of financial resources away from alternative family uses, such as payment of school fees or purchase of food, medicines, books, and school uniforms. Furthermore, heavy drinking negatively affects health and labor productivity. Home-brewed beer is far from a mere commodity; rather, it is a multifaceted and integral component of Keiyo and many other African socioeconomic systems.

THE ETHNOGRAPHIC SETTING: THE KEIYO OF KENYA

Keiyo are officially categorized as Kalenjin peoples, an ethnic amalgamation of eight groups from western Kenya, including Kipsigis, Nandi, Tugen, Marakwet, Pokot, Sabaot, and Terik. Despite the salience of the Kalenjin label in contemporary Kenyan politics, this identity, like many others in Africa, is a relatively recent invention (cf. Hobsbawm and Ranger 1983). The Kalenjin appellation dates to the 1940s, when these groups sought political strength from the increased numbers such an association generated (Kipkorir 1973, 1978).[1] Despite their diversity, these peoples do share language, religion, and political organizations (Daniels, Clark, and McMillan 1987; Evans-Pritchard 1940; Huntingford 1953; Massam 1927; Sutton 1976).

Keiyo peoples reside in Elgeyo-Marakwet District,[2] an ecologically heterogeneous region. The district includes three major ecological zones: (1) a highland plateau of 2,000 meters and above; (2) the hilly, rocky face of the Elgeyo Escarpment, between 1,200 and 2,000 meters; and (3) the Kerio River Valley floor, with elevations ranging from 800 to 1,200 meters. In the early colonial period (circa 1920s), disparate subsistence economic activities were conducted across these zones. Ledges on the rocky face of the Elgeyo Escarpment (*lagam* or *kurgat*) provided safety from Maasai raids in the highlands. Here people constructed dwelling places and cultivated millet and sorghum, both used in beer brewing. The hot, dry Kerio Valley floor (*soi* or *keu*) was used for grazing goats and sheep, as well as for hunting and collecting wild foods such as honey (used in brewing honey beer). The valley floor was not settled because of numerous human and animal diseases, such as malaria and trypanosomiasis. Finally, the narrow strip of the fertile and well-watered Uasin Gishu highland plateau (*mosop*), just above the escarpment face, was used for grazing cattle.[3]

The *korotinwek*, the smallest indigenous political and territorial units, reflected this vertical orientation, since they included land in all three ecozones. *Korotinwek* boundaries were vertical rather than horizontal and were marked by stones or natural objects such as trees or streams. Vertical orientation enabled each community to gain access to three different types of land, an advantageous practice here.

Although livestock are ideologically important (compare Herskovits 1926 with Kettel 1986), Keiyo and most other Kalenjin peoples probably have long depended on both farming and animal husbandry (Sutton 1976, 29). Most Keiyo today are small-scale farmers, and land is, depending upon location, either already registered or in the process of becoming so.[4]

Political units (administrative sublocations and locations) are now usually horizontal rather than vertical. Nonetheless, people continue to use multiple plots in different ecological zones in the time-tested manner of peasant cultivators elsewhere (Bentley 1987; Netting 1993). The crops grown and the mix of cultivation and animal husbandry, as well as other subsidiary activities (both on- and off-farm), vary across ecological zones and socioeconomic strata. Maize and beans are the staple food crops of the highlands and escarpment, but their cultivation lower in the valley is riskier due to lower precipitation and scarce surface water there. Finger millet, sorghum, and cowpeas are better adapted to the drier conditions of these lower elevations. Maize and beans also double as cash crops (Little and Horowitz 1987) in the highlands and on the escarpment. Additionally, the highlands offer production conditions suitable for a wide range of cash crops such as pyrethrum, tomatoes, Irish potatoes, cabbage, kale, and tree crops such as oranges and coffee. Wheat is grown on some larger highland farms in Elgeyo-Marakwet, though not to the same extent as it is on the mechanized wheat farms of neighboring Uasin Gishu District. The escarpment offers more limited possibilities for the same crops, with the exclusion of pyrethrum and wheat, and the addition of bananas. Vegetables do not grow as well on the escarpment as they do in the highlands. The fertile soils close to the face of the upper escarpment itself are a striking exception, and farmers who have plots there tend to plant cabbages and kale.[5]

In the northern part of Marakwet District, several rivers flow from the highlands to the valley, allowing an indigenous irrigation system to flourish (Ssenyonga 1981; Huxley 1959; Hennings 1941; Soper 1981). The same is not true for the central portion of the valley and, as a result, crop production is limited by water scarcity. In those few areas where surface water is available in the form of small but permanent rivers (such as in Kabito sublocation near Biretwo), fruits, including bananas and papayas, can be grown. Cotton and groundnuts do well in the alluvial soils of the valley floor. Cotton has more potential as a cash crop, yet its large-scale production depends on mechanization and chemical pesticides. Such limitations put this option beyond the reach of most Keiyo farmers. In much of the valley proper, there is no permanent surface water other than the Kerio River itself; animal husbandry of East African goats, Red Maasai sheep, and indigenous *Bos taurus* cattle thus prevails.

In all three of these ecological zones (highlands, escarpment, and valley), Keiyo depend primarily on household labor, which is organized by gender (Kipkorir and Ssenyonga 1985). In agricultural activities, men are usually responsible for clearing plots and burning slashed vegetation while women are expected to plant and weed. Harvest is a joint effort that also often requires extra-household assistance. As discussed below, beer performs a critical role in mobilizing such supplementary, extra-household, agricultural labor. Today, divisions between men's and women's work are blurring. Animal husbandry, for example, has often been a male domain, though my research suggests that women perform important—though undervalued and unrecognized—functions in these types of activities, and that these patterns are most pronounced where males migrate to other locations for wage labor (Roberts 1996).

TYPES OF HOME-BREWED BEER

Keiyo peoples, like many other Africans, brew beer from grains.[6] Early accounts, such as that of Massam, note that Keiyo utilized the indigenous staple cereals millet and sorghum in the preparation of their beer (1927, 43–44; see also Kipkorir and Ssenyonga 1985, 43–44 for basic preparation steps). As elsewhere in Africa, maize now has largely displaced indigenous grains as the dietary staple (Miracle 1966)[7] and has become the principal ingredient in home-brewed beer (McAllister 1993). (Small quantities of millet are still grown to add to the brew for better flavor.)

Called *busaa* in other parts of Kenya and *mayek* among Keiyo and other Kalenjin peoples, this beer also can be distilled into a more potent and sometimes dangerous drink, called *chang'aa*, or *wirgi* in Kalenjin (Kipkorir and Ssenyonga 1985, 44). *Busaa*, with an alcohol content of approximately 4 percent, is relatively nontoxic and may even possess some positive nutritional qualities (Krige 1932; McAllister 1993). Platt (1955, 121) claims that:

> Ascorbic acid, several B vitamins, and proteins (microbial) are the main nutrients derived from the fermentation and at least some of these, especially at certain times of year, are likely to be of considerable value in maintaining the health of the consumer.

Chang'aa, on the other hand, is entirely different. Often referred to facetiously as "kill-me-quick," the common symbol for *chang'aa* in Elgeyo-Marakwet is a slashing motion performed on the neck with one's index finger. Kenya's daily newspapers often carry stories of people (usually men) dying after consuming *chang'aa* at a drinking party. The following reports are illustrative:

CHANG'AA KILLS 20 IN MURANG'A

> The illegal alcoholic brew, Chang'aa, has killed twenty people in four villages in Murang'a district. Sources say the brew was laced with poison. Many other people are said to be in critical condition. . . . The brew, popularly known as Gasohol in the area, was reportedly bought in Nairobi's Eastleigh suburb. Victims died within hours of drinking the highly toxic concoction in which a variety of chemicals are added to make it more potent. (*Kenya News*, http://news.AfricaOnline.nu, 17 September 1996)

FOUR PEOPLE BLINDED BY KILLER BREW

Four people have been made permanently blind by the illegal alcoholic brew (chang'aa) which killed twenty people in four villages in Murang'a district over the week-end. The four blinded men were recovering at Murang'a District Hospital. Police have arrested the man suspected to have sold the killer brew . . . at his home after a siege that lasted the whole night by police. [The man], who does not drink, is said to have had 15 other related court cases. . . . Outraged people in Murang'a have called for government action against the continued brewing and selling of illicit alcoholic brews in the country. (*Kenya News*, http://news.AfricaOnline.nu, 18 September 1996)

This health hazard is the ostensible rationale behind President Daniel arap Moi's decision in the late 1970s to ban home production of alcoholic beverages. Haugerud (1995) observes that this move may have been motivated as well by Moi's desire to develop a populist political agenda and his own discernible civil image in the tentative, early stages of the post-Kenyatta era. The ban on home brew became one of the issues Moi used to create his own political identity. Full enforcement of the ban, however, has been almost impossible, given the widespread brewing of beer in rural areas.

Finally, Keiyo also brew a honey-based beer called *muratina* throughout Kenya, *kipketin* in Kalenjin (Kipkorir and Ssenyonga 1985, 43), or *tej* in Ethiopia, where it is most famous. In Kenya's Kerio Valley, honey beer tends to be available seasonally, in accordance with the availability of its main ingredient. It is usually reserved for special occasions.

USES OF HOME-BREWED BEER

The highly diverse uses of beer by Keiyo are comparable to those identified by anthropologists for other African societies. Since ancestral spirits (*oyik*) could intervene in affairs of the living, it was often necessary to make sacrifices (*koros*) of meat or beer to propitiate them. The same was true for deities, such as Asis, the supreme god manifested in the form of the sun (Huntingford 1953). Beer also remains an important feature of wedding, circumcision, and naming ceremonies (Massam 1927; Moore 1986). Beer was offered in bride wealth payments; Keiyo men presented beer to their future fathers-in-law in lieu of the more substantial bride wealth required elsewhere:

Unlike other Kalenjin-speaking peoples, traditionally neither the Tugen nor the Keiyo paid a brideprice for the acquisition of a wife. Even though they regarded themselves as pastoral peoples marriage was contracted through the presentation of gourds of beer to the father of the bride. The husband also provided livestock to his bride for her use. This is a tradition that has disappeared especially if a young woman has received a secondary education. Some fathers now insist on cash payments rather than the customary gourd of beer. (Thom 1978, 96–97)

Beer has long been consumed by participants in communal work parties. Keiyo farmers, like other Africans, use such groups to overcome labor bottlenecks at critical periods in the agricultural cycle, such as planting and harvesting (Karp 1980; Krige 1932; Netting 1968; Saul 1981; Schmidt 1992; Stone, Netting, and Stone 1990). Neighbors cooperate in tasks such as breaking land, planting, weeding, and harvesting, in return for beer and sometimes reciprocal assistance at a later date.

Such arrangements alter as rural economic differentiation occurs. For example, Watson (1958, 107–108) noted that among Mambwe peoples:

> Beer is not considered repayment for work done, but rather is essential refreshment for work done. The basis of Mambwe cooperative work is reciprocity. A man who attends another's work party obliges the other to work his own fields in return. Beer is not pay: it is the work which is reciprocated. . . . A man cannot get his gardens dug simply by providing beer for others to come and work for him; if he does not work in return, no one will again accept his invitation.

More recently, however, Pottier (1985) documents socioeconomic processes in Mambwe that have contributed to a decline in reciprocal labor and an emergent tendency to view beer as payment for services rendered. He links this to affluent farmers' capacities to avoid reciprocating altogether, so that the beer pot has changed from a symbol of guaranteed reciprocity to a means of final payment.

In Elgeyo-Marakwet District, some people now perform casual agricultural labor in return for cash, a practice known as *kibarua*. In 1991, the going rate in these areas for a half-day of *kibarua* was approximately twenty shillings (slightly less than $1), or five liters of *busaa*, whichever the laborer chose. In the three study villages, the percentages of households that claimed to need outside help at some period during the year were uniformly high: 78 percent in the highlands, 87 percent on the escarpment, and 72 percent in the valley. Most households either reciprocate or provide food or beer or both for their outside workers. Some provide cash in addition to the food or beer.[8]

Keiyo beer drinking remains intimately associated with sociality, as it is elsewhere in Africa (Karp 1980; Mandelbaum 1965; Rekdal 1996). British colonial administrators had difficulty viewing the practice this way. Their 1946 Annual Report from Elgeyo-Marakwet District suggests that "tribal life consists in the main of convivial beer drinks among men who leave nearly all work to be done by women. The distinct problem is mainly that of 'the ignorant wife with a hoe' and her lazy beer drinking husband" (Kenya, Elgeyo-Marakwet District, DC/ELGM/1/6). The Elgeyo-Marakwet District Commissioner's 1956 Annual Report states the same concerns ten years later[9]:

The problem of drink commented on at length by Mr. Tate last year remains in as virulent a form as ever. It is least a problem as might be expected if the people are busy and reasonably prosperous, e.g., in Chepkorio, but in the more backward areas the pattern is all too often the same. Sufficient work to pay taxes and if possible a junior member of the family will do it, then a lotus eating life interspersed with periodic bouts of drunkenness and indolence with the minimum requirements for life being discharged with little effort.

In the past, Keiyo beer drinking was the nearly exclusive privilege of adult males, as was the case among other groups such as the Kofyar of Nigeria and Tiriki of Kenya (Netting 1964; Sangree 1962). Although most earlier uses of beer remain, despite its commodification and official proscription, drinking it is no longer the sole prerogative of adult elder males (Kipkorir and Ssenyonga 1985, 43). Anyone can drink *busaa* now, provided that he or she has the few shillings necessary to buy it.

COMMODIFICATION OF BEER

In addition to its other usages, Keiyo beer is a commodity, as it is in other African societies (Colson and Scudder 1988; Saul 1981). I define commodity here as a socially desirable thing intended for exchange.[10] Home-brewed beer is commonly bought, sold, and consumed by individuals, a status that has evolved during decades of incorporation into the colonial and postcolonial market economy. Archival documents from Elgeyo-Marakwet District suggest that beer has probably been bought and sold on a small scale since the introduction of cash, or at the very least since the 1940s.[11] During the colonial era, Africans were forced to find ways to pay the taxes imposed upon them by the British administration. Since beer brewing was already important in indigenous culture, it would have been a small step to begin selling it in order to earn cash for the required taxes.[12] In Elgeyo-Marakwet District during the 1920s and 1930s, other (sometimes more profitable) avenues to acquire currency included working for wages on nearby white settlers' farms, working on the Uganda railway, and selling animals or hides and skins to local government purchasers.

Ambler (1991) argues that in central Kenya British colonial policy toward alcohol shifted over time, partly in order to draw people into the market economy:

> Beginning about 1930 a series of ordinances restricted legal brewing to relatively few officially designated marketplaces. . . . Confining consumption to specified sites also reduced the possibility that social drinking could provide the context for resistance or opposition. Ultimately, the policy of licensing alcohol outlets discouraged the informal beer trade in the countryside, subordinating previously autonomous economic activities to the spatial model of the colonial political economy. In the long run this process . . . made the cultural definitions of drink and drinking more compatible with

the structures and ideology of that [colonial] system. *Beer was increasingly viewed as a commodity.* The growing use of imported machinery and raw materials in beer production was an early stage in a gradual separation or alienation of producer and product, marked especially by the *steady loss of ritual significance of beer.* The migration of the locus of alcohol production and consumption from the homestead to the marketplace was accompanied not only by the commoditization of local beer but also by an association (in terms of both time and place) between drinking and a specifically defined period of leisure—in opposition to work. Thus, as colonial society matured, the control of drinking became less a means of social control and more the instrument of economic "development." (Ambler 1991, 178; emphasis added)

Similar changes occurred in Keiyo, most notably the gradual commoditization of beer. Unlike central Kenya, Keiyo did not use imported machinery in beer production, and production and consumption did not shift to the marketplace. In Elgeyo-Marakwet, the relatively uncomplicated technology used to brew *busaa* is available to nearly everyone, and the loci of both production and consumption remain village homesteads. The ritual status of beer in Keiyo has changed; its consumption is no longer restricted to elder males, ceremonial contexts, or after-work parties but can include drinking as a leisure pursuit. Nonetheless, beer continues to be important in local rituals such as *barbariso,* a ceremony designed to ensure good relations between in-laws, as well as at more recent adoptions such as the receptions that follow Christian wedding ceremonies.

In spite of its illicit status today, home-brewed beer is ubiquitous in villages in all three ecological zones of Elgeyo-Marakwet. Brewed primarily by women and sold to anyone who has the cash to buy it, beer has become an important source of income, especially for females.[13] Beer sales are not a rapid means to affluence, but rather many women who sell beer have few alternative means to earn cash, especially if they are heads of households. Beer brewing and sale is just one of a number of ways many households supplement their incomes from the sales of crops or animals and animal products (e.g., milk, skins, hides). Although most Keiyo are small farmers and earn their livelihoods mainly from their farms, nearly all households rely on multiple strategies for income augmentation. The two most secure options are salaried employment and entrepreneurial activities (such as running shops, bars, transportation), but for a variety of reasons (e.g., lack of education or unavailability of start-up capital), these opportunities are only open to a minority of households (Roberts 1993; see also Kettel and Kettel 1976). For most households, the only viable alternatives are casual agricultural labor (*kibarua*) and a variety of small-scale income-generating activities such as beer brewing and sale, charcoal manufacture and sale, and craftwork—such as decorating calabashes and making ropes (Roberts 1993).

The social aspects of beer parties alleviate boredom, especially during slack periods in the agricultural cycle. Similarly, Audrey Richards writes that, in addition to the Durkheimian function of enhancing solidarity (see also Rehfisch 1987; Rekdal 1996), one of the reasons Bemba drank socially was for entertainment, or perhaps more precisely, distraction. She claimed that beer drinking is "the peoples' only kind of entertainment, the chief break in the monotony of village life" (Richards 1939, 76). In Keiyo, *busaa* is no longer drunk from communal pots with long straws, as it was in the past. Today empty tin cans from cooking fat (brands such as Cowboy, Kimbo, Kasuku) are the drinking vessels. In 1991, a two-liter tin of *busaa*, referred to in the local vernacular as the "town clerk," supposedly because of its large size,[14] sold for five or six shillings in these areas, while a one-liter tin cost two or three shillings.

As a commodity, *busaa* is brewed specifically with the intent of making money. Given the government ban on home brewing, data on beer preparation and sales were extremely difficult to acquire. Particularly in the early stages of research, people were understandably reluctant to admit to brewing and selling *busaa*, much less provide estimates on how much income they earned from these activities. When people were unwilling to provide my assistants and me with approximations of how much they earned from beer sales, I relied on my research assistants' local knowledge of individuals and their economic situations. Of the three villages studied, we estimated the percentages of households whose members brew and sell beer to generate income as follows: 45 percent in the highlands, 61 percent in the escarpment, 74 percent in the valley.

Elsewhere I have argued that the economic opportunity structure in Elgeyo-Marakwet District is highly uneven, that this inequality is based upon both ecological and historical variables, and that it strongly influences the life chances of individuals and families (Roberts 1993). People in the highlands are in the most advantageous position, due both to the more favorable agricultural climate and to prior British investment in this area (e.g., roads, schools, and farm infrastructure such as cattle dips). People living in the valley, on the other hand, are the least well off because of the hot and dry climate as well as the low level of infrastructural investment there.[15] The situation on the Elgeyo Escarpment is intermediate between the highlands and valley extremes. Most relevant to this discussion of beer is the high percentage of valley households reliant on beer brewing and other small-scale income-generating strategies; this pattern accords with other indicators of an imbalance across zones (Roberts 1993). Because there are fewer opportunities for salaried employment and small businesses in the valley, people there are forced to rely more heavily on alternative small-scale income sources.

NEGATIVE ASPECTS OF BEER CONSUMPTION

The discussion thus far has concentrated on the importance of beer brewing and sale in people's daily attempts to make a living. The persistence and commodification of home-brewed beer, however, is not without detriment. Anthropologists have been slow to recognize the negative aspects of alcohol use in the societies they study. Heath

(1987a, 1987b) and Room (1984) have both noted (cf. Douglas 1987) that this tendency probably arises from the functionalist bias of earlier anthropological literature on alcohol consumption (Horton 1943; Washburne 1961), as well as from the discipline's strong emphasis on cultural relativism. Nonetheless, as Colson and Scudder's (1988) work on Gwembe clearly illustrates, such considerations cannot be ignored.

In Keiyo, although beer does provide needed income to those who brew it, heavy monetary expenditure on home-brewed beer also diverts cash that could be spent on foodstuffs (e.g., cooking oil, sugar, salt), medicine, schoolbooks, and uniforms. Although the illicit nature of the practice precluded collection of actual figures, I am confident that it is primarily men who make most beer expenditures. The different spending priorities of men and women are well established in the literature on African household economics (Moock 1986). Women are much more likely than men to spend money on items such as food and medicines. Since money spent on *busaa* is money diverted from the purchase of such necessities, this pattern is the opportunity cost of beer drinking (Plattner 1989; Schneider 1974). Keiyo themselves clearly articulate such anxieties over everyday expenses (Roberts 1993).

British colonial administrators expressed apprehension about the effects of excessive drinking on health. The Elgeyo-Marakwet District Commissioner's 1955 Annual Report notes[16]:

> Provision of further means for getting drunk in the shape of European type bottled beer is, in the writer's opinion, a disaster. It would be interesting to know what percentage of all Elgeyo and Marakwet Government ADC employees' wages go on drink, either honey mead, European beer or Nubian gin. Fortunately there is comparatively little Nubian gin distilling. The local mead is sufficiently potent. It is worthy of note to quote Dr. Calcott, an eye specialist with the Royal Empire Society for the Blind who immediately on looking at the Elgeyo in Tambach said a peculiar feature of Tambach, however, is the amount of drinking. This seemed to be producing a certain amount of avitaminosis and some cases of optic atrophy. It is little wonder that night blindness was a common complaint. Some sort of wise control of this habit would be more advisable.

Beer in Keiyo is now often consumed early in the day, sometimes even before dawn. On numerous occasions my research assistants and I encountered people who were so incapacitated that, by nine o'clock in the morning, they were unable to answer even the simplest question. The rationale for such early drinking, I was consistently informed, is that it supposedly lessens the risk of raids by Administration Police. When beer is consumed so early in the day, it must sharply reduce the energy levels of those who drink it (cf. Huby 1994; Robbins 1979).

Rekdal (1996, 382) notes the panoply of negative consequences that may accrue from alcohol abuse:

> Excessive drinking is a major source of human suffering worldwide . . . and the Iraqw are certainly no exception. Homicide, suicide, violence, and particularly domestic vio-

lence, neglect of children, and criminal offenses like theft and corruption, are all phenomena which are frequently connected with excessive drinking.

Lee (1993, 145–146) describes the effects of drinking on the Ju/'hoansi of Dobe:

The new Ju culture is based on selling and drinking beer and listening to hit tunes from Radio Botswana. . . . Drinking is confined to the hottest hours of the day, beginning at ten in the morning and continuing to late in the afternoon. The hot sun overhead must speed the alcohol's effect, because most people are thoroughly drunk by two in the afternoon.

I cannot offer a simple explanation of excessive drinking in Keiyo, other than to suggest that those individuals who consume much beer seem to be in the least secure economic positions. Overall Keiyo people have done quite well since President Moi took office in 1978. Indeed some outsiders say that Kalenjin areas of the Rift Valley Province have benefited from a disproportionate level of infrastructure investment during the past twenty years.

Colson and Scudder (1988) link increased drinking in Gwembe to sheer abundance as well as to stress:

Stress aside . . . Gwembe men, and increasingly women, drink more because drink is much more readily available than it was in the 1950s . . . and those who never had to learn to stop drinking, because supplies quickly ran out, now face an abundance. (1988, 5)

They also make the important point that "apparent functional integration at any one moment does not predict how the members of a society will cope with alcohol or any other drug in the future" (1988, 19).[17]

CONCLUSION

Monetisation of sorghum beer and milk has not . . . caused a breakdown in established practices, nor in the structures of meaning in which such practices are embedded. . . . The study of thought and practice surrounding sorghum beer and milk among the Iraqw illustrates a simple point that seems to shed light on the apparent paradox, i.e., that *there is not necessarily a contradiction between profound social change and a high degree of cultural continuity.* (Rekdal 1996, 367, 381–382; emphasis added)

Rekdal's remarks reaffirm Bascom and Herskovits's (1959) notion, illustrated in this chapter, that social dynamics in Africa include elements of both continuity and change. Beer has long occupied a pivotal place in Keiyo and other African cultures, and it has been far more than simply an alcoholic beverage. Beer is crucial to sociality and critical for many ritual performances. Although home-brewed beer has become a commodity, it is not a unidimensional economic good.[18] Instead, beer is a multi-faceted cultural component that has both positive and negative daily consequences for young and old, men and women. On the one hand, beer retains some of its past "singularity" (Kopytoff 1986) because of its continued association with ritual and social contexts; on the other hand, the outright sale of beer provides a means for individuals, especially women, to gain needed cash. A drawback is that the money earned by beer brewers is not necessarily spent on essentials such as food, medicine, and school fees. In spite of long-standing official proscriptions, beer continues to be brewed, sold, and consumed daily. The multiple roles of Keiyo home-brewed beer, as both commodity and noncommodity, preclude any simple appraisal by social scientists or policymakers.

NOTES

The research on which this chapter is based was conducted in the Central Division of Elgeyo-Marakwet District, Republic of Kenya, from February 1991 to February 1992 with research clearance from the Office of the President, Republic of Kenya, Permit No. OP 13/001/196/12512. It was assisted by a grant from the Joint Committee on African Studies of the Social Science Research Council and the American Council of Learned Societies with funds provided by the Rockefeller Foundation. Institutional affiliation in Kenya was arranged with the School of Social, Cultural, and Development Studies of Moi University, Eldoret. I wish to acknowledge the generous help of Dr. Joshua Akong'a in this process. I would also like to thank my research assistants Emmanuel Cherop, Jonathan Chesesio, Philip Barsamber, and Albert Ayabei. I am grateful to editors Angelique Haugerud and Priscilla Stone for their comments on an earlier draft of this chapter and to my colleagues Amy Chasteen and Marie Danforth for their editorial assistance. Any liabilities, however, are entirely my own.

1. Beginning in the 1940s, individuals from these groups who went off to fight in World War II used the term "*kale*" or "*kole*" (the process of scarring the breast or arm of a warrior who had killed an enemy in battle) to refer to themselves. During wartime radio broadcasts, an announcer, John arap Chemallan, used the phrase "*kalenjok*" ("I tell you"). Individuals from these groups who were attending Alliance High School formed a "Kalenjin" club. Fourteen in number, they constituted a distinct minority in this prestigious school in a Kikuyu area. This minority status affected their desire for some outward manifestation of identity and solidarity, as the Kikuyu are not only much more numerous but also culturally and linguistically very different from the Kalenjin. These young high school students would form the future Kalenjin elite. The next step in consolidating Kalenjin identity was the founding of a Kalenjin Union in Eldoret in 1948 and the publication of a monthly magazine called *Kalenjin* in the 1950s.

Throughout this process, however, the growing sense of pan-Kalenjin identity did not emerge in a vacuum; instead, it should be seen as a reaction to both colonialism and anti-

Kikuyu feelings. The British colonial government sponsored the *Kalenjin* monthly magazine out of a desire to foster anti-Kikuyu sentiments during the Mau Mau Emergency, a mostly Kikuyu-led anticolonial insurgency that provoked an official state of emergency lasting from October 1952 to January 1960. Clouded in emotional arguments (e.g., Ruark 1955), the causes of this movement have been reanalyzed in recent years (e.g., Throup 1989; Kanogo 1987). One of the most striking elements is the tension that existed between the numerically dominant Bantu Kikuyu and the less numerous Nilotic and Nilo-Hamitic Maasai and Kalenjin. Given this tension, together with the desire of the colonial government to suppress the Mau Mau movement, it made sense to encourage a pan-Kalenjin identity, which was still local in character, as opposed to a nationalistic movement. Kipkorir states that "the term 'Kalenjin' and the concept of ethnic solidarity which later came to be associated with it . . . had its roots in the Mau Mau emergency. It may thus be said to have been a by-product of Mau Mau" (1973, 74).

2. During 1994–1995 Elgeyo-Marakwet District, like a number of others in the country, was subdivided, in this case into Keiyo and Marakwet Districts. In this chapter, however, I refer to the area as Elgeyo-Marakwet.

3. See Ssenyonga 1979 for a similar description among the neighboring Marakwet to the north.

4. In June 1995 I returned to Elgeyo-Marakwet to conduct research on the process of land registration in the Kerio Valley. Shortly after arriving, my research assistants informed me of the volatility of this subject. A small number of well-placed individuals were appropriating large tracts of land in the valley by "purchasing" them from smallholders. As described to me, the circumstances surrounding these transactions sounded highly dubious. For the safety of my research assistants, I chose to abandon the topic.

My research in three contiguous villages in Central Division of Elgeyo-Marakwet suggests that mean landholdings are five acres in the highlands, four acres on the escarpment, and six acres in the valley. All highland holdings are registered, as are 80 percent of those on the escarpment, and 64 percent of those in the valley.

5. This situation on the escarpment is created by the erosion of the ferromagnesian-rich gneisses (Republic of Kenya 1985, 16) which constitute the primary component of the rock formations at places such as Tambach.

6. In this chapter I do not deal with industrially brewed and bottled beer. Although available in rural areas, these brews (e.g., Tusker, White Cap, and Pilsner) are much more expensive—up to three to four times the cost of an equivalent amount of *busaa*. Their cost is prohibitive for most people in my research zone.

7. There are multiple reasons for this displacement: maize is much easier to weed, it is less likely to suffer pest depredations than sorghum or millet, it is easier to process once harvested, and it has become an acquired taste associated with modernity (Roberts 1999).

8. Highland households surveyed spent an average of 1,267 shillings per year on hired labor, escarpment households spent 945 shillings, and valley households 528 shillings.

9. Elgeyo-Marakwet District Annual Report, 28 January 1957, filed by G. M. Bebb, District Commissioner.

10. This hybrid definition employs elements from those of both Gregory (1982, 10) and Appadurai (1986, 9).

11. See Netting (1968) for a description of this process among the Kofyar.

12. Schmidt (1992, 59–60) notes that, in Goromonzi District, Zimbabwe,

it was customary for women to brew millet beer which was provided to neighbors in exchange for critical points in the growing season. It was but a small step to think of selling beer . . . to the mine laborers who had been imported to the area from Nyasaland, Mozambique, and Northern Rhodesia.

13. Others have noted similar circumstances in other parts of Kenya (e.g., Oboler 1985; Little 1992) and in other African countries, such as Zambia (Hedlund and Lundhahl 1984; Schmidt 1992).

14. A one-half liter bottle of soda was referred to as "Tyson," in comparison with the normal 300 milliliter bottle.

15. On British perceptions of why Keiyo refused to settle in the Kerio Valley proper, see my review of the Kerio Valley Settlement Scheme (Roberts 1993, 77–81).

16. Report filed by P. E. Tate, District Commissioner, 9 January 1956.

17. Colson and Scudder write that:

> the upsurge of drinking in Gwembe provides substantiation for theories that associate the heavy use of alcohol or other drugs with rising anxiety . . . or with rapid shifts in status and perceived threats to identity and power. . . . It gives little support to those who argue that societies that have long used alcohol and integrated it into the overall fabric of social life are thereby protected from excessive and problem drinking when alcohol becomes more abundant or people have new reasons for drinking and "acting out." Ethnographic accounts of some African societies report drinking as non-problematic and contributing to overall social integration [see, e.g., Netting 1979 on the Kofyar of Nigeria; and Sangree 1962 on the Tiriki of Kenya]. If we had written at length on Gwembe drinking on the basis of our 1956–57 experience, we probably would have written in the same terms. . . . Three decades later we see drinking as frequently destructive. (Colson and Scudder 1988,18–19)

The work of Colson and Scudder reinforces the importance of a longitudinal perspective in our analysis of African sociocultural phenomena (Moore 1994). Perhaps even more important, their assertions shake deeply rooted convictions of the functionalist and relativist paradigms in anthropology (Hatch 1983; Edgerton 1992).

18. See Shipton's (1989) treatment of the Luo concept of "bitter money" and processes of commodification.

REFERENCES

Ambler, Charles H. 1991. Drunks, Brewers, and Chiefs: Alcohol Regulation in Colonial Kenya, 1900–1939. In Susanna Barrows and Robin Room, eds., *Drinking: Behavior and Belief in Modern History*. Berkeley: University of California Press.

Appadurai, Arjun, ed. 1986. *The Social Life of Things: Commodities in Cultural Perspective*. New York: Cambridge University Press.

Bascom, William R., and Melville J. Herskovits, eds. 1959. *Continuity and Change in African Cultures*. Chicago: Phoenix Books.

Bentley, Jeffrey W. 1987. Economic and Ecological Approaches to Land Fragmentation: In Defense of a Much Maligned Phenomenon. *Annual Review of Anthropology* 16: 31–67.

Colson, Elizabeth, and Thayer Scudder. 1988. *For Prayer and Profit: The Ritual, Economic, and Social Importance of Beer in Gwembe District, Zambia, 1950–1982*. Stanford, Calif.: Stanford University Press.

Daniels, Robert E., Mari H. Clark, and Timothy J. McMillan. 1987. *A Bibliography of the Kalenjin Peoples of East Africa*. Madison: African Studies Program, University of Wisconsin.

Douglas, Mary, ed. 1987. *Constructive Drinking: Perspectives on Drink from Anthropology*. New York: Cambridge University Press.

Edgerton, Robert B. 1992. *Sick Societies: Challenging the Myth of Primitive Harmony*. New York: Free Press.

Evans-Pritchard, Edward. 1940. The Political Structure of the Nandi-Speaking Peoples of Kenya. *Africa* 13: 250–267.

Gregory, Chris A. 1982. *Gifts and Commodities*. New York: Academic Press.

Hatch, Elvin. 1983. *Culture and Morality: The Relativity of Values in Anthropology*. New York: Columbia University Press.

Haugerud, Angelique. 1995. *The Culture of Politics in Modern Kenya*. New York: Cambridge University Press.

Heath, Dwight B. 1987a. A Decade of Development in the Anthropological Study of Alcohol Use: 1970–1980. In Mary Douglas, ed., *Constructive Drinking: Perspectives on Drink from Anthropology*. New York: Cambridge University Press.

———. 1987b. Anthropology and Alcohol Studies: Current Issues. *Annual Review of Anthropology* 16. 99–120.

———. 1976. Anthropological Perspectives on Alcohol: An Historical Review. In Michael W. Everett, Jack O. Waddell, and Dwight B. Heath, eds., *Cross Cultural Approaches to the Study of Alcohol*. The Hague: Mouton.

Hedlund, Hans, and Mats Lundhahl. 1984. The Economic Role of Beer in Zambia. *Human Organization* 43(1): 61–65.

Hennings, Richard O. 1941. The Furrow Makers of Kenya. *Geographic Magazine* 12: 268–279.

Herskovits, Melville. 1926. The Cattle Complex in East Africa. *American Anthropologist* 28: 230–272, 361–388, 494–528, 633–664.

Hobsbawm, Eric, and Terence Ranger, eds. 1983. *The Invention of Tradition*. Cambridge: Cambridge University Press.

Horton, Donald. 1943. The Functions of Alcohol in Primitive Societies: A Cross-Cultural Study. *Quarterly Journal of Studies on Alcohol* 4: 199–320.

Huby, Garo. 1994. Drinking and the Management of Problem Drinking Among the Bari, Southern Sudan. In Maryon McDonald, ed., *Gender, Drink and Drugs*. Providence, R.I.: Berg.

Huntingford, George W. B. 1953. *The Southern Nilo-Hamites: Ethnographic Survey of Africa, East Central Africa*, Part 8. London: International African Institute.

Huxley, Elspeth. 1959. African Water Engineers. *Geographic Magazine* 32: 170–175.

Kanogo, Tabitha. 1987. *Squatters and the Roots of Mau Mau*. Athens: Ohio University Press.

Karp, Ivan. 1980. Beer Drinking and Social Experience in an African Society: An Essay in Formal Sociology. In Ivan Karp and Charles S. Bird, eds., *Explorations in African Systems of Thought*. Bloomington: Indiana University Press.

Kenya, Elgeyo-Marakwet District (DC/ELGM). 1911–1958. *Political Record Books*. Nairobi: Kenya National Archives. DC/ELGM/3/1-4.

———. 1912–1962. *District Annual Reports*. Nairobi: Kenya National Archives. DC/ELGM/1/1-7.

———. 1918–1929. *Miscellaneous Correspondence*. Nairobi: Kenya National Archives. DC/ELGM/4/1.

———. 1926–1954. *Handing Over Reports*. Nairobi: Kenya National Archives. DC/ELGM/2/1.

———. n.d. *Notes on Land Tenure*. Nairobi: Kenya National Archives. DC/ELGM/5/1.

Kettel, Bonnie. 1986. The Commoditization of Women in Tugen (Kenya) Social Organization. In Claire Robertson and Iris Berger, eds., *Women and Class in Africa*. New York: Holmes and Meier.

Kettel, Bonnie, and David Kettel. 1976. Going Ahead: The Businessmen of Seretunin. In William Arens, ed., *A Century of Change in Eastern Africa*. The Hague: Mouton.

Kipkorir, Benjamin E. 1973. *The Marakwet of Kenya: A Preliminary Study*. Nairobi: Kenya Literature Bureau.

———. 1978. *Peoples of the Rift Valley: Kalenjin*. Nairobi: Evans Brothers Limited.

Kipkorir, Benjamin E., and Joseph W. Ssenyonga. 1985. *Sociocultural Profile of Elgeyo-Marakwet District*. Nairobi: Institute of African Studies, University of Nairobi.

Kopytoff, Igor. 1986. The Cultural Biography of Things: Commoditization as Process. In Arjun Appadurai, ed., *The Social Life of Things: Commodities in Cultural Perspective*. New York: Cambridge University Press.

Krige, Eileen Jensen. 1932. The Social Significance of Beer Among the baLobedu. *Bantu Studies* 6: 343–357.

Lee, Richard B. 1993. *The Dobe Ju/'hoansi*. New York: Harcourt Brace.

Little, Peter D. 1992. *The Elusive Granary: Herder, Farmer, and State in Northern Kenya*. New York: Cambridge University Press.

Little, Peter D., and Michael M. Horowitz. 1987. Subsistence Crops Are Cash Crops: Some Comments with Reference to Eastern Africa. *Human Organization* 46(2): 254–258.

Mandelbaum, David G. 1965. Alcohol and Culture. *Current Anthropology* 6(3): 281–293.

Massam, J. A. 1927. *The Cliff Dwellers of Kenya*. London: Frank Cass.

McAllister, P. A. 1993. Indigenous Beer in Southern Africa: Functions and Fluctuations. *African Studies* 52(1): 71–88.

Miracle, Marvin P. 1966. *Maize in Tropical Africa*. Madison: University of Wisconsin Press.

Moock, Joyce, ed. 1986. *Understanding Africa's Rural Households and Farming Systems*. Boulder, Colo.: Westview Press.

Moore, Henrietta. 1986. *Space, Text, and Gender: An Anthropological Study of the Marakwet of Kenya*. New York: Cambridge University Press.

Moore, Sally Falk. 1994. *Anthropology and Africa: Changing Perspectives on a Changing Scene*. Charlottesville: University of Virginia Press.

Netting, Robert. 1964. Beer as a Locus of Value Among the West African Kofyar. *American Anthropologist* 66(1): 375–384.

———. 1968. *Hill Farmers of Nigeria: Cultural Ecology of the Kofyar of the Jos Plateau*. Seattle: University of Washington Press.

———. 1979. Beer as a Locus of Value among West African Kofyar. In Mac Marshall, ed., *Beliefs, Behaviors and Alcoholic Beverages*. Ann Arbor: University of Michigan Press.

————. 1993. *Smallholders, Householders: Farm Families and the Ecology of Intensive, Sustainable Agriculture.* Stanford, Calif.: Stanford University Press.

Oboler, Regina Smith. 1985. *Women, Power, and Economic Change: The Nandi of Kenya.* Stanford, Calif.: Stanford University Press.

Orwell, George. 1958 [1937]. *The Road to Wigan Pier.* New York: Harcourt Brace.

Platt, B. S. 1955. Some Traditional Alcoholic Beverages and Their Importance in Indigenous African Communities. *Proceedings of the Nutrition Society* 14: 115–124.

Plattner, Stuart, ed. 1989. *Economic Anthropology.* Stanford, Calif.: Stanford University Press.

Pottier, Johan P. 1985. Reciprocity and the Beer Pot: The Changing Pattern of Mambwe Food Production. In *Food Systems in Central and Southern Africa.* London: School of Oriental and African Studies.

Rehfisch, Farnham. 1987. Competitive Beer Drinking Among the Mambila. In Mary Douglas, ed., *Constructive Drinking: Perspectives on Drink from Anthropology.* New York: Cambridge University Press.

Rekdal, Ole Bjorn. 1996. Money, Milk and Sorghum Beer: Change and Continuity Among the Iraqw of Tanzania. *Africa* 66(3): 367–385.

Republic of Kenya. Ministry of Planning and National Development. 1985. *District Atlas Elgeyo-Marakwet.* Iten, Kenya: Arid and Semi-arid Lands Development Programme.

Richards, Audrey. 1939. *Land, Labour and Diet in Northern Rhodesia.* London: Oxford University Press.

Robbins, Michael C. 1979. Problem Drinking and the Integration of Alcohol in Rural Buganda. In Mac Marshall, ed., *Beliefs, Behaviors and Alcoholic Beverages: A Cross-Cultural Survey.* Ann Arbor: University of Michigan Press.

Roberts, Bruce D. 1993. The Historical and Ecological Determinants of Economic Opportunity and Inequality in Elgeyo-Marakwet District, Kenya. Ph.D. diss., University of Pittsburgh.

————. 1996. Livestock Production, Age, and Gender among the Keiyo of Kenya. *Human Ecology* 24(2): 215–230.

————. 1999. The Incorporation of Maize in Africa. In Leonard Plotnicov and Richard Scaglion, eds., *Consequences of Cultivar Diffusion.* Ethnology Monograph Series no. 17, Department of Anthropology, University of Pittsburgh.

Room, Robin. 1984. Alcohol and Ethnography: A Case of Problem Deflation? *Current Anthropology* 25(2): 169–191.

Ruark, Robert. 1955. *Something of Value.* Garden City, N.Y.: Doubleday.

Sangree, Walter H. 1962. The Social Functions of Beer Drinking in Bantu Tiriki. In David J. Pittman and Charles R. Snyder, eds., *Society, Culture, and Drinking Patterns.* Carbondale: Southern Illinois University Press.

Saul, Mahir. 1981. Beer, Sorghum, and Women: Production for the Market in Rural Upper Volta. *Africa* 51(3): 746–764.

Schmidt, Elizabeth. 1992. *Peasants, Traders, and Wives: Shona Women in the History of Zimbabwe, 1870–1939.* Portsmouth, N.H.: Heinemann.

Schneider, Harold K. 1974. *Economic Man: The Anthropology of Economics.* New York: Free Press.

Shipton, Parker M. 1989. *Bitter Money: Cultural Economy and Some African Meanings of Forbidden Commodities.* American Ethnological Society Monograph Series no. 1. Washington, D.C.: American Anthropological Association.

Soper, Robert. 1981. A Survey of the Irrigation Systems of the Marakwet. Paper presented at the seminar, Kerio Valley—Past, Present, and Future. May 21–22, at the Institute of African Studies, University of Nairobi.

Ssenyonga, Joseph W. 1979. *Kerio Valley Ecology at the Threshold of Radical Transformations: A Research Proposal.* Nairobi: Institute of African Studies, University of Nairobi.

———. 1981. The Marakwet Irrigation System as a Model of a Systems-Approach to Water Management. Paper presented at the Seminar, Kerio Valley—Past, Present, and Future. May 21–22, at the Institute of African Studies, University of Nairobi.

Stone, Glenn Davis, Robert Netting, and M. Priscilla Stone. 1990. Seasonality, Labor Scheduling, and Agricultural Intensification in the Nigerian Savanna. *American Anthropologist* 92(1): 7–23.

Sutton, John E. G. 1976. The Kalenjin. In Bethwell A. Ogot, ed., *Kenya Before 1900.* Nairobi: East African Publishing House.

Thom, Derrick J. 1978. *Kenya Marginal/Semi Arid Lands Pre-Investment Inventory.* Human Resources and Social Characteristics, no. 6. Machakos/Kitui/Embu-Baringo/Kerio Valley. Part II: The Human and Social Characteristics of Baringo-Kerio Valley. Prepared for the Government of Kenya by the Consortium for International Development (a USAID Contractor), U.S. Soil Conservation Service (USDA), Staff of Ministries of Agriculture, Water Development and Natural Resources.

Throup, David. 1989. *Economic and Social Origins of Mau Mau, 1945–53.* Athens: Ohio University Press.

Washburne, Chandler. 1961. *Primitive Drinking: A Study of the Uses and Functions of Alcohol in Preliterate Societies.* New Haven, Conn.: College and University Press Publishers.

Watson, W. 1958. *Tribal Cohesion in a Money Economy: A Study of the Mambwe People of Zambia.* Manchester: Manchester University Press.

11

Commoditization, Cash, and Kinship in Postcolonial Papua New Guinea

Nicole Polier

For Faiwolmin people of the Fly River interior of Papua New Guinea's (PNG) Western Province, the arrival of Ok Tedi Mining Limited (OTML), a multinational mining operation in the nearby Star Mountains, created a massive new center of power and wealth during the 1980s. Since political independence in 1975, this hinterland of colonial and capitalist expansion has experienced large-scale, capital- and technology-intensive mining, which has brought the state directly into the global economy (Ogan and Wesley-Smith 1992, 56).[1] OTML offers a labor market, foreign capital, and technology, and an imposing infrastructure in the region that surrounds the rich, white enclave at Tabubil where the mine is located.

As recently as the early 1960s Faiwolmin and other Min peoples represented a new "last frontier" for Australian subordination to colonial rule and an economic backwater for regional development. Social relations within small, generally endogamous Min groups of shifting subsistence root crop cultivators were organized around kinship, reciprocity, and exchange. These classifications, however, are no longer adequate, if they ever were. More important, what becomes of kin and kinship when placed in a certain kind of history? When a rural meal comes from a can or a carton unloaded from a charter airplane, and marriage payments are at least partly monetized, how are kinship distance and the moral foundations of exchange socially reconstituted? What does a first generation wage worker do with his paycheck, and what are the effects on the subsistence sector back home? These questions are the focus of this chapter. My concern is not with the *center* of production in Tabubil, but with how global commodity production is experienced on the margins, where cash has flowed into networks once organized outside a cash nexus.

In the central mountain range of PNG, to the west of the Highlands, live a variety of Min groups traditionally organized into endogamous hamlets and villages around the headwaters of the Fly River. Speaking a common family of languages, these Min live in small settlements historically connected by trade, warfare, and sometimes intermarriage. The general territory of Min groups is sometimes referred to as Faiwolmin (Barth 1971)[2], but in this analysis I concentrate on a more restricted ethnic group of Faiwolmin who live in rural villages of scattered hamlets a two-day walk (or roughly thirty minutes northeast by small aircraft) from the mine. Located at the headwaters of the Fly River, Golgobip (the largest of these villages) has several hundred censused residents, including a high percentage of outmigrants. Although the present discussion concerns Faiwolmin from the Golgobip region, the mountain interior of the Western Province, from the Min region west to the Indonesian border, shares a similar history of colonial and capitalist transformations (cf. Hyndman 1994).

When Australian colonial power was consolidated in the mid-1960s, Faiwolmin moved readily and rapidly over a rugged landscape where they hunted and cultivated gardens. Due to the demands of taro cultivation in a setting with constant rain and poor soil, Faiwolmin and their neighbors were highly mobile gardeners. The region was sparsely populated, and throughout much of the *taim kiap* (colonial period) Faiwolmin moved between upper and lower mountain gardens that had varied and staggered harvests. They spent much time cultivating gardens away from rural villages, and household and hamlet residence was fairly fluid. In the postcolonial period, the Min zone of the Western Province remains sparsely populated and without vehicular roads, bridges, electricity, or plumbing. Neglected as an economic backwater during the colonial period, the region now comprises a surplus labor reserve for the mine, which controls a small market for labor and locally cultivated crops.

Min groups throughout the area have historically participated in a variety of local and long-distance exchange relationships and trade networks (e.g., Barth 1971; Craig and Swadling 1983; Cranstone 1990; Jones 1980; Jorgensen 1981, 1991; Morren 1991). Stone ax blades, tobacco, shells, salt, arrows, feathered string bags, and pork, among other items, circulated between groups and trading partners (Barth 1971; Craig and Swadling 1983). For instance, trade included salt that moved from the Oksapmin to the east, tobacco and other goods from frequent partners in the Telefolmin region to the north, and (during the 1960s) steel from the region around Kiunga (Barth 1971, 178). As elders recall, when Faiwolmin first invited Catholic missionaries from the port town of Kiunga to establish a mission parish in the Enkiyakmin village of Bolivip, they hoped the missionaries would be a conduit for steel implements.[3] Faiwolmin also traded to the northeast for bows, blades, and dog teeth (Jones 1980, 16–17). Trading partnerships were long-term and based on direct, delayed exchange between men (Barth 1971; Jones 1980).

Marriages among the Min usually are formalized with the payment of brideprice from the clan and kin of the groom to those of the bride. The kin group of the bride considers this the completion of transactions initiated with the nuptials of her parents; conversely, it is the start of a new cycle of debts for the groom, who is indebted to those who helped with the marriage payment. Over time, these contributions are repaid with counter-gifts from the marriage partners. With an eventual daughter or daughters, nuptial gifts enter into circuits of exchange.

Precolonial and colonial exchange relations among Faiwolmin, and between Faiwolmin and other groups, resembled the structural situation described by Sahlins in his comparative ethnographic analysis of exchange in "primitive" societies (1972, 185–275). Kinship was an organizing feature of exchange, and social distance was often characterized by distance between kin groups. According to Sahlins's "sectoral plan," reciprocity is organized in a system of concentric circles, within which relations are more solidary the closer they are to the household core (1972, 198–199). Thus core relations are characterized by generalized reciprocity; while relations at a greater "tribal" distance are characterized by balanced exchange and those in the most remote sectors by negative reciprocity. Reciprocity and its moral implications are structured by kinship and the tribe (Sahlins 1972, 200). Shared food, for example, moves in circles of generalized reciprocity, insulated from balanced exchange for other items. For a variety of small-scale groups, the exchange or sale of food would create a rupture in "solidary bonds" (Sahlins 1972, 218).

Sahlins's sectoral plan is useful for understanding Faiwolmin reciprocity and exchange until the recent postcolonial period. Global interventions, however, create new conditions under which the bonds of kin, clan, and community have been reorganized, and with them their moral and ethical bedrock.

COPPER AND COMMODITIZATION

Construction of the mine at Tabubil took place between 1981 and 1988. At the height of construction, approximately 3,000 people were employed on a short-term basis.[4] By the end of the decade, one out of three Golgobip men were selling their labor for a relatively steady wage in the township. Some work was associated directly with the mine, but most involved contractor companies and low-level service sector jobs.[5] The other two-thirds of the male workforce were variously engaged in seeking employment, visiting the Faiwolmin residential "corner" in Tabubil, or occupying themselves back in rural hamlets.

Despite a relatively small market for labor in the production phase of the mine, OTML created new circuits of exchange on a scale unprecedented for indigenous groups. These commodity circuits have reorganized the social relations of local men and women more than any other intervention, including colonization or the steady stream of Catholic missionaries and born-again preachers who have infiltrated the mountainside where Min groups live.[6] Over generational time and across space between montane hamlets and the company township where rural migrants live and work, modern state subjects must locate themselves vis-à-vis the mine and the world of wages, labor power, food imports, and supermarket merchandise introduced by foreign capital.

The consequences of OTML for exchange networks and social relations can be thought of in terms of several specific circuits of commoditization. (I use "circuits" heuristically to describe different social and spatial contexts.) Commodity circuits engendered by the mine are discernible, but not discrete; the boundaries between them are permeable, and the circuits are historically contingent and changing.

The first such circuit is that of global commodity trade, in which gold and copper ore are extracted from the mountainside for export and sale on the world market. The global trade of these minerals is related to the importation of heavy equipment and technology for extraction and transport, but also to the infrastructure that was built and is maintained by OTML. Modern mining is capital-intensive but not labor-intensive, and on capitalist frontiers like PNG, mineral extraction is heavily capitalized.

A second, segmented circuit is associated with the commoditization of labor power. The overwhelmingly male-dominated workforce in Tabubil is a technocracy that is highly stratified along national, racial, ethnic, and regional lines. Expatriate labor is imported, generally on two- to three-year contracts with attractive salaries sufficient to support families from Australia and North America. Within this segment, Asian employees are also hired on contracts, sometimes on family status. In addition to expatriate labor, a second primary segment in the circuit of commoditized labor is that of the national labor force. This echelon can also be divided into subsegments according to indigenous ethnic and linguistic differences. Among such local groups, Faiwolmin are located at the bottom of a skills hierarchy and are paid especially low wages.[7]

A third commodity circuit concerns the reproduction of the township labor force, in households run by women who send workers off to the mine. Since the 1980s, the mine has introduced commoditized goods and services such as food, liquor, clothing, entertainment, postal services, banking, and travel. This circuit is also segmented, in that most of these goods and services, from Bailey's Irish Cream and biscuits to banking and small businesses, are imported and would not exist without OTML. International workers, some of whose salaries are deposited in Australian dollars directly into Australian bank accounts, spend much of their income abroad during semiannual leaves. Expenditures range from investments in Australian real estate and boarding schools abroad, to Asian sexual services and shopping sprees.

A small portion of this third circuit consists of European food crops produced by village women in places such as Golgobip and sold by a regional cooperative to customers such as the Company Mess and the Tabubil Supermarket (see appendix). Although a minute fraction of corporate purchasing power goes toward consumption of locally grown garden fare, the modest income earned by rural women in this way finances the purchase of such food commodities as white rice, sugar, and canned fish (locally called "tinfish" or *tinpis*) in local trade stores at high markup.

A fourth circuit concerns the commoditization of social relations, including relations of exchange in villages such as Golgobip. In the context of capitalist encroachments, labor power has been commoditized and the wage relation has been introduced to village migrants. Although only a fraction of adult Faiwolmin receive wages for their work, the consumption, accumulation, and reinvestment of these wages have had profound effects on their kin, clan, spouses, and households in rural hamlets. Given that the labor is almost entirely male, I concentrate on the commoditization of male labor and its local effects. Elsewhere I have analyzed the role of rural women in relation to these transformations (Polier 1992). The role of the "other 50 percent" in the social reproduction of a migrant diaspora cannot be overemphasized. Here, however, I focus primarily on particular Faiwolmin men who direct the traffic in wages that has transformed social relations in rural villages.

My ethnographic focus is commodities and the incorporation of social practices into commoditized channels. Practices such as brideprice, I demonstrate, bring together the numerous short- and long-term strategies of resource management and accumulation of workers and managers.[8]

The rest of this discussion is organized as follows: the next section concerns workers, the following section managers, and the final section brideprice and bank accounts.

WORKERS

A Golgobip man who works for OTML or a contracting company (such as the bakery, the "mess," or a tire repair service) confronts a web of financial obligations and commitments when he is paid every fortnight. Face-to-face encounters with Golgobip village friends (*wantoks*),[9] unemployed brothers and clan cousins, impecunious affines, and hungry teenage boys all impress on him the limits of a low wage. Workers agree it is poor manners to refuse a request from a relative or *wantok* who looks one in the eye.[10] Keeping one's income from being "eaten," they say, creates a challenge to conceal one's resources without flagrantly defying social norms of generosity and caregiving. An estimated accounting of the wages of a relatively prosperous Golgobip worker for OTML would look something like that indicated in table 11.1.[11]

These estimates can vary considerably. Workers agree, for instance, that it is easier to save money if one's wife and children remain in the village, but most women whose husbands held steady positions in the 1980s spent part of the year with their children at Tabubil. From the women's perspective, circular migration is necessary to keep a separated family together economically and emotionally. In addition to financial savings, the advantages to the working husband of a village woman include the short- and long-term benefits of having gardens cultivated in the village. The rural household and hamlet are insurance against food shortages, crowded living conditions, and the fragmented family ties of township life.

Table 11.1   Estimated Distribution of Wages by a Relatively Prosperous Golgobip OTML Worker (K = kina)

Fortnightly Income	**K370**
Expenses	
Deductions (Income tax and misc.)	K38.35
Accommodations	K10
To wife for food	K100
Clothing	K10
To *wantoks* and relatives, spent on rice, tinned fish, sugar, cofee, and air freight to the village	K110
Savings	
Passbook deposit	K110
Annual Income	**K9,620**
Expenses	
Deductions	K997
Accommodations	K60
To wife for food	K2,600
Clothing	K300
To *wantoks* and kin for food, freight, and gifts of cash	K2,860
School fees for male relatives in high school	K500[a]
Savings and investments	
Passbook	K811
Semipermanent house (*haus kapa*)	K1,120[b]
Tradestore	K200
His or a relative's bride-price	K350

[a]Annual school fees for Kiunga High School in the late 1980's were K250. Often when a working-man pays for a boy's school fees, he will also give him pocket money for food, school supplies, and an annual visit to Golgobip.

[b]Building such a house is a project of several years' duration that includes the high cost of commercial air freight for timber, corrugated iron scheets, and the like (a total of K2,000–K3,000 would not be a high figure). Sometimes brothers will collaborate on a house, in which case expenses may be shared. The construction is still time-consuming and costly, even if materials are scavenged from company dumpsites.

A workingman often gives his wife more than she is likely to spend and she gives him allowance money for the following two weeks as needed for incidentals. Other routine claims include remittances and small commodities sent by plane to relatives in the village. A worker is sometimes asked to pay a relative's boarding school fees, and he may also be responsible for the student's spending money. In addition, a worker may contribute to a village brideprice from time to time, or save for his own marriage payment, a process that takes several years.

These demands explain why workingmen from Golgobip often express a desire to find employment at a mine outside the area and beyond the claims of friends, family, and affines. Such a job would make it possible to "live like a white man," who, Faiwolmin sometimes say, shares only with a small, nuclear family. But this desire is muted by needy kinsmen whose claims are met and mediated through strategies of accumulation, some of which are private and personal. Two among a variety of ways for a Golgobip workingman to remove portions of his fortnightly wage from circulation are the passbook and "Sunday-ing."

The Passbook

An employee in town usually has at least one passbook savings account into which he or his employer deposits his fortnightly pay. Many men also have accounts for their wives into which smaller sums are deposited. On average, men deposit one-quarter to one-third of their wages; the amount depends on the other claims they confront. The passbook keeps cash out of the laborer's hands and available for more occasional expenses. These include the *haus kapa*, a semipermanent house constructed of commercial materials (corrugated metal roof, glass, and timber) that are flown to the village at considerable expense. The *haus kapa* is an object of prestige that became a common feature of the rural landscape throughout the Faiwolmin region during the 1980s. It removes one's resources from circulation and cements a social place for the migrant in absentia, in the event he should return to live among his kinsmen. Financial commitments routinely faced by workers also include brideprice or a trip back to the village during annual leave.

Sunday-ing

In addition to using passbooks, workers can participate in an informal revolving credit association known by wageworkers as "Sunday-ing." This is a practice in which two, three, or more working acquaintances pool a sum of cash fortnightly—in principle, on a Sunday—so that each partner to the transaction receives relatively large sums of money less frequently than at payday. This enables them to say they gave their money to so-and-so and as a result are without disposable income. Approximately every fourth to sixth week (depending on the number of people Sunday-ing together), a donor receives a lump sum that can be used for a planned purchase, such as a cassette player, work boots, luggage, corrugated iron sheets for building a *haus kapa*, trade store inventory, and the like.

These savings strategies are meant to conceal one's cash from the claims of relatives and *wantoks*. Other means for allocating one's limited resources, however, are more complex and considerably more public. What may appear to be a one-way flow of resources generally has a future return. Such benefits cannot necessarily be predicted, as in the case of brideprice, whose return is intergenerational. In the short term, a man who sends things back to selected relatives in Golgobip receives occasional counter-shipments of garden fare—such as the prized pandanus nuts or sugarcane—and has gardens maintained for him in his absence. Unless his wife lives in Tabubil continuously, she cultivates gardens with relatives and affines. A worker's children can live in Golgobip and attend primary school even if his wife chooses to remain in town, since the students can be watched by relatives. Through the labor of women, primarily a wife or mother, a workingman will be remembered.

Let us examine the channels of a worker's wage from the town to Golgobip village, where portions of the paycheck are allocated for such long-term returns as a small trade store, *haus kapa*, or brideprice. Max[12] has been an ore processor for several years and lived in Tabubil with his wife, Dani, and their young children in 1989. Dani receives a sum to buy foodstuffs at the supermarket and perhaps cash to deposit in her personal passbook. Most of Max's money goes to Dani, who will share with her own relatives and Max's kin. Alice, Max's younger sister, and Dixie, a "fictive" younger brother, both work for low wages at the supermarket with Max's brother Lucas, who left Golgobip in 1989. Max helps all three, who live with him in Tabubil. If Anita, a teenage cousin whom Max sometimes calls sister, is in town, he may help her as well. To the foregoing relatives Max may give K(kina)20 to K80 each in addition to tinned fish and other food commodities.

Max has five unmarried brothers who will eventually marry and pay a brideprice. Some of them may first attend school and will thus need help with annual fees. For these future expenses, Max gives money to his father several times a year for safekeeping in the village. He also sends his parents supermarket food, small merchandise, and sometimes cash for discretionary spending, including occasional amounts for his grade-school sister. When Dusty (a married villager whom Max considers a brother) visits the township, Max gives him cash and merchandise. Dusty, Max's younger, unmarried brother ("Lost Guy"), and Max's father, Raymond, "look after things" for the clan and Max's *haus kapa,* where each of the three men have private rooms under lock and key. (As a hedge against the high cost of financing five eventual brideprices, note that Max is the classificatory brother of Alice and sometimes Anita, relationships with a calculated return when the young women marry.)

The disbursements mentioned above are spread over time and space with different effects. Some are for the immediate expenses of kinfolk and affines who "eat" the wage through routine purchases of tinned fish and white rice. Others are longer-term "investments" in these relations, such as contributions to school fees, brideprice, or support of a classificatory sister.

MANAGERS

Building a *haus kapa,* maintaining a small shop where food is sold, and contributing to a brideprice cannot be managed at a distance from the township without creating and consolidating kin ties. In this regard, three related points should be stressed. First, the self-described "manager" in Golgobip village is hierarchically subordinate to the worker whose limited resources he helps to protect and maintain. Second, the men in Golgobip and Tabubil are connected in important ways by a flow of cash, kin, and commodities. Third, the manager is careful to distinguish himself from village women, whose contributions to an increasingly feminized subsistence sector are regarded by men as necessary but menial.

Men, who identify their function in the village as supervisory, mediate between wage earners in town and the mothers, sisters, and wives who make up the core of the subsistence workforce (Polier 1996). They help with the construction of bush material huts (*haus kisins*) and *haus kapas,* sometimes perform heavy work in the garden, help to make the occasional pig fence, and perform other tasks for which men have traditionally been responsible. Virtually all village men in this position depend on the worker's wage. He is the "node" from which money and goods are sent to the countryside where they are managed and mobilized.

At any one time, roughly one-third of village men (until they reach their mid-forties) move readily between village and town, where they greet male relatives and scout for either semiskilled or temporary positions such as short-term contract work.[13] Some of these men oversee and manage trade stores; others have small outdoor greenhouses where they produce small quantities of European crops for sale. When they are on the move, management of a trade store or small greenhouse is delegated to a male counterpart or relative. Many men have worked sporadically outside the village at some time (Polier 1992, 225–306); of this group, some younger men speak of returning to work and describe their stay in the village as temporary, while others are more circumspect.

Returning to the example of Max, this workingman has three managers looking out for his interests in Golgobip. Dusty, Lost Guy, and Raymond are beneficiaries who oversee Max's assets. As noted, Max deposits with Raymond cash for eventual brideprices. Dusty has helped to construct and maintain Max's *haus kapa,* and together with Lost Guy runs a small trade-store from a room in the house. Both brothers and the father can count on funding when they visit Max in town. Small grants for immediate consumption are spread lineally and laterally to kin and affines, as mentioned, and longer-term financing goes to Max's trusted appointees back home.

Different types of managers in the village pursue varying strategies of resource management and accumulation. Most ubiquitous is the man who articulates his position in the village as "looking after things" or "looking after the place" (*lukautim ples*).[14] He helps to burn trees in the garden, identifies himself as "boss" over horticulture and village affairs, and receives occasional remittances from sympathetic relatives and *wantoks* in town. Men with histories of sporadic employment maintain that their presence in the village is necessary to its smooth functioning. "Somebody has to look after the gardens, burn the trees, plant the taro, build the houses, help look after the pigs," said one man who worked briefly during the construction phase of the company, "so I am the one in charge." As another Golgobip man who once worked in the OTML mess expressed it, "I am here now looking after things in the village. Who is going to burn the trees and help in the garden? I do that." An older working-age village man of modest ambition put it this way:

My sister Gogaten is married to Moses Salok [who works in town], and she helps me sometimes. When Edward [my brother] worked in Tabubil he used to help, but not now. Sometimes my sister sends food. And once in a while Max will help. If I go to Tabubil and they see my face, they will feel sorry for me and give me some money— maybe K40 or K50. When Edward was working he would give me K100.

The centrality of women's labor to the reproduction of village life is a clear consequence of a cash economy. But as village organizers and managers left behind by the labor market adjust to a reduced male presence in the countryside, they are left to reinvent social prominence, power, and posterity for themselves and their clans, often expressed by managing the work of women.

Trade Stores

One means by which workers can invest disposable cash and take it out of general circulation is by opening a small trade store.[15] Anyone who has a small amount of start-up money may open such an establishment with a bit of inventory and a spare room; in the late 1980s, Golgobip village featured six such shops. A worker who invests in cartons of rice, tinned fish, and Nestle's products is generally confident that he will get at least an equal return on his investment in the future, unless the business is mismanaged.

These stores are entrepreneurial and semiprivate; they are maintained and managed by individuals on their own or on behalf of themselves and a male relative. Generally financed with start-up money from town, stores enlarge a growing gender gap in activity within the village and between it and the town. A trade store "eats" money from a brideprice, a Sunday-ing, or a wage; it keeps money out of circulation and in private control; it reinforces a separation between subsistence labor and *bisnis* (business); and it constitutes a division of labor in which women primarily furnish garden fare (among other services), while men have direct and regular access to cash and commodities.

Trade stores capture the imagination if not the attention of village men who wish to become self-employed small businessmen. From their perspective, such entrepreneurial activity has the advantage of being a self-managed, flexible enterprise one can leave to the supervision of a relative when necessary, while enabling the proprietor to "look after things" in the village while women work in gardens.

In short, the trade store is an enterprise in which financial resources are invested and concealed by workers in collaboration with managers, and by former workers who have become managers. Its existence is not justified by a marginal revenue on rice and tinned fish, nor by items with bigger mark-ups that sell less frequently. The trade store also conceals another resource, namely, the labor of village men who work in, hang out at, or oversee the management of the small store. It is a male economic activity and prerogative that can fill as much or as little time as the manager sees fit.

Haus Kapas

Another means of private accumulation, the semipermanent house with corrugated metal roof (*haus kapa*), takes the worker's income out of circulation and consolidates ties in the village with those relatives who oversee and occupy the house. Some men in the labor force who do not have the modern *haus kapas* (which are managed and maintained by male relatives in the village), speak of having a house built for themselves or jointly with a brother. Such a project requires several years' time, beginning with the gradual accumulation of petty cash, the purchase of supplies—roofing, nails, louvered glass, timber, and so on—the outlay of a large fee for air freight, and finally, the slow construction of the building itself by clansmen and villagers.

When the house is complete, its male custodian is entrusted with a key to one or more of its private rooms where personal and private goods are kept. The custodian legislates who may enter, sleep, and eat in the house; or who may have access to its numerous rooms. A monument to the commoditization of labor, the *haus kapa* may be mostly vacant throughout the year or it may be occupied by the owner and related workers who are at home on leave from Tabubil. Perhaps a room will be used as a trade store, and it is likely that one or more rooms will be occupied by a teenage brother or cousin of the owner. These men also serve a proprietary function.

Haus kapas are central to the contemporary organization of social space in the village along new lines of gender and labor. A masculine space, they are associated with petty accumulation, money, and a labor market, even—and perhaps especially—when the house is empty. Through the appointed managers of their *haus kapas*, Golgobip workers stake a claim to a future in the village for themselves and their immediate kin. This includes a claim to land and, through marriage and kinship, to gardens and their products.

In contrast, *haus kisins,* huts built around central fireplaces of stone and ashes where food is prepared, are woman's places and are associated with the rigors of horticulture, child care, pig husbandry, petty cash crop production, and competing commitments to the mission and village community. This house is a center through and around which labor is conceived, discussed, debated, organized, and executed. Though the two types of houses are interrelated and connected, they also articulate a growing division of labor between women and men, workers and managers, across both time and space.

BRIDEPRICE AND BANK ACCOUNTS

Commoditization of male labor has also engendered the widespread commoditization of brideprice and the local marriage market.[16] During the 1980s, brideprice, traditionally consisting of shell wealth supplemented with knives, axes, bows, arrows, and *bilums* (string bags) woven by village women, has been increasingly augmented with prestations of K20 (now typically totaling over K1,000 in cash per nuptial). The worker's wage has qualitatively transformed the character of marriage transactions in a cash economy.

Faiwolmin marriage itself generally passes without ceremony when a woman moves in with a man and commences her conjugal obligations to fetch water, break firewood, and provide him and his parents with food from the garden. If they are incompatible, the match may dissolve informally; if the match continues and she bears a child, the marriage is recognized with the payment of brideprice from the groom and his relatives to the relatives of the bride.[17] Ropes of shell[18] were kept, traded, and offered in marriage by men as the currency of value during the colonial period. The *faiwol* (shell rope) is still offered in marriage, and it remains the social currency without which the bridal bargain is not truly made. Shell ropes are saved and circulated through male social circuits, along with items of lesser value also used in brideprice. These goods are generally contributed by men, and sometimes women— especially in the case of *bilums*—as the time for the brideprice approaches.

In contrast to shell wealth, cash follows circuits into and within the village whose origins are the wage labor force in Tabubil. The consumption and investment of K20 are more private. Men with steady work are attractive to younger women, often school graduates, who find a life outside the village more alluring than daily residence among new in-laws, to whom a bride is expected to show deference.[19] Men with passbooks and paychecks are expected to offer big prices, often replete with cartons of beer flown into the village for kinsmen (and men only) to consume after the price has been paid and the goods divided.[20] Presenting a brideprice is also an important opportunity for absentee village men to exhibit largesse, wealth, and prestige to a cadre of assembled kinsmen in the village before returning to roles of infinitely less prominence in the wage economy.

Most Golgobip men are not workingmen and, since they have less prestige (*namba*) and fewer resources, they confront the traffic in spouses with less confidence.[21] These men also offer brideprice cash contributed by male relatives and *wantoks*, but with less fanfare and more debts. Meanwhile, sisters are eyed by village and Tabubil brothers alike, who hope to parlay kinship for cash on the marriage market.

Monetization of brideprice during the postcolonial period has been an uneven and contradictory process. Ties continue to be created and reproduced through contributions to the bridal bounty and through reciprocation, sometimes over a long period, with counter-prestations of pork and other gifts to those individuals who helped the groom and his relatives finance the marriage. Yet there is wide consensus in Golgobip that the items offered in brideprice have a set cash value that reflects their regional purchase price. Recently married men from Golgobip insist that some—and often much—of the wealth they gave was purchased with cash from their own bank accounts.[22] To purchase some of these brideprice provisions, workers would send cash to male relatives and managers in the village. "I am pleased with the price," one man said of his recent payment in 1989:

The total cost was somewhere around K5,000 and most of that came from me. I got K500 from my cousin-brother Hebrew—I have no true brothers. My mother helped out by making some of the stringbags but most of them I paid for. Everything there was paid for. . . . I paid around K500 in stringbags—there were at least fifty there, and they cost around K10 each. I paid another K900 in *rop tambus* [shell ropes]. Axes are K15 each, and there were several of those. It cost me around K3,500.

To satisfy old debts, wealth flows in lineal channels to those members of the bride's parent's generation who financed her mother's marriage, and through her, the daughter's marriage. Wealth also flows laterally, however, to men in the bride's generation, such as classificatory brothers. Most cash now tends to flow fastest in lateral channels, and my data are inconclusive on the extent to which claimants from the older generation expect, request, or receive returns of cash on their payments of shell wealth. In an analysis of a similar process of brideprice commoditization among Telefolmin during the early 1980s, however, Jorgensen (1988) points out a critical difference between cash and traditional shell wealth that is apposite to the situation among Faiwolmin. In Telefolmin, shell ropes are neither convertible nor transferable to cash within that region (Jorgensen 1988, 12). Cash, on the other hand, can buy anything, including shell ropes *outside* the Telefolmin region, and it dissolves, in a sense, into trade stores or other circuits of private investment. Shell ropes were once saved to be exchanged in the next generation for a marriage partner; they "kept" better than the kina, whose value is universal. Among Faiwolmin, the process seems to be in a transitional phase, with old wealth being "converted" into a commodity future.

It might appear that brideprice is inflated in retrospect by the groom and his clansmen to enhance their prestige. A cash equivalent is routinely assigned to "noncommoditized" items of value, which is reflected in the estimation of the total payment, even if items of wealth came from a circuit of exchange in which they were not purchased with cash.[23] The monetization of shell wealth, however, follows a much less simple commodity logic. Twenty kina seems a rather high figure for a single rope of shells; Faiwolmin generally agree that *bonang* does not have the purchasing power of a *hetpik* (twenty-kina note) and does not often sell for K20 (within the Min zone). But it is this figure that explains the apparent "inflation" of brideprice: forty ropes, given for the bride described above, are calculated at the cash equivalent of K800; one can quickly run up a contribution valued at K1,000, described by the foregoing informant, if one counts ropes as cash. As one middle-aged man put it:

Yes, a cash value is given to everything. *Rop tambus* are K20 each and they can be bought for that around the Telefolmin side. . . . Bows are K5 or K10—those from around here are K5, but those from the Star Mountains are worth K10. Knives are K5. Stringbags are from K5 to K10, but the bags with the black feathers are worth a lot more, around, say, K25. Around here, *rop tambus* are really *namba* to the old people. You cannot have a brideprice without *rop tambus*. They're good; but they are not like cash in the sense that they can't buy things. But each one is K20, yes. Old people save ropes; it is the old money. You would save them for a brideprice. You would save some and give some to people.

How, then, is a rope of shells reckoned at K20, and why? The outlay of shell wealth may be converted to credit for kina in the current market with the expectation of a cash return for shells and other items of wealth; men whose shells are offered at the feet of village brides are staking a claim *not* on the return of an equivalent number of shells, but for the return of a cash equivalent in the next generation. The high value put on the ropes reflects their exchange value to the elder generation of men who control the "old money," and this valuation keeps ropes from circulating in a monetized sphere of exchange. Shells are still shared and hoarded for the next brideprice; as the villager cited above suggests, they are considered dear, especially by elders. But their value is assessed differently by elders and those of the working-age generation for whom the "old money" stands in relation to a pecuniary return and has little noncommoditized value.

In short, brideprice is a source of cash, credit, and petty finance capital for men in the village and town alike. In the late 1980s, the kinsman of the bride who stood by with a ledger noting each contribution to the brideprice transaction was contemplating its eventual convertibility to cash. Money is "eaten," spent on a house, or invested in a trade store with the hope that investment in a store will reap a private return (Polier 1992, 351–405; Jorgensen 1988). Lines of obligation and reciprocity appear to have been lateralized and attenuated by more private circuits of cash in the sense suggested by Jorgensen in which the bridal bounty is "liquid" and leaves quickly (1988, 32), and in the sense that cash debts are lateralized among a first generation of steady wageworkers. These men contribute cash and finance "noncash" payments in marriage deals, create cash debts, and stake claims to eventual financial returns. At the same time, new ties of obligation are forged between financiers of brideprice and more impecunious grooms.

The practical dimensions of kinship and marriage are not the recent by-product of capitalist expansion and commodification. Bourdieu's point that genealogical relationships, as a form of practical activity, are "continuously practiced, kept up, and cultivated" (1977, 37) could be said of Faiwolmin kinship and exchange relations historically. It is an old game; the watchful kinsman of the bride, writing frantically in a ledger as wealth is showered on the newlywed and her kin group, contemplates the size of the bounty, its investment potential, the repayment of short-term loans taken out against the brideprice, and so on (Jorgensen 1988). The game is heightened and complicated, however, by commodity relations, which have introduced new means for calculation and strategy, with unpredictable outcomes.

One might still argue that cash is being converted into a currency of generalized exchange and that money and commodities are reconstituted as gifts (e.g., Gregory 1982). As Jorgensen (1988) argues for Telefolmin, however, the commoditization of labor has engendered the reorganization and commoditization of marriage transactions themselves.[24] Changes in marriage practices and, I would argue, commoditization in general, have had a dissolving effect on networks of exchange at various levels of kinship distance. Cash is quickly appropriated by male kinsmen for commercial investment or consumption; the challenge is how to conceal it to prevent circulation among a rather wide circle of potential claimants, rather than to redistribute it as widely as possible.

CONCLUSION

The capitalist workspace of the Australian township has reconstituted social and kinship distance in other ways as well. OTML seeks to confine the nonworking population of locals to a minimum, and has introduced new ethics and values, including worker loyalty, the sixty-hour workweek, individual savings and accumulation, punctuality, prudence, and camaraderie among company men. Cheaper reproductive costs for the company workforce (family housing is a privilege reserved for the upper echelons of employees) have meant the attenuation of extended kin ties for workers. Within company circles, the dominant discourse about economic pooling among PNG employees is that the *wantok* at the door is a self-interested wolf. In the commodity logic of accumulation, a floor on material need is also a ceiling on savings; it is hardly surprising that mistrust has been driven into the core of kin relations.

The relatively widespread and recent commoditization of male labor among Faiwolmin has built upon and been organized by indigenous relations of kinship and has been managed by men in various ways. One might argue that money and merchandise have been used to maintain durable ties of kin, clan, and community through local agency and ingenuity, and that indigenous experiences of modernity are culturally constituted. Kin relations continue to organize relations of production in rural hamlets as they have in the past; an exchange ethic puts a floor on poverty, and a young woman's unwaged labor is still purchased wholesale for strings of shell. It might still be said that economic relations of sharing are inflected with moral significance (Firth 1951, cited in Sahlins 1972, 198) and that generosity is considered by Min to be the moral high ground taken by good relatives. An emphasis on selective sharing continues to exert powerful pressures toward exchange at the level of households and clans, now spread out over time and space. It is poor form to refuse a hungry-looking kinsman, especially when one is a wage earner with boots on his feet. Everything else being equal, a working migrant has a greater obligation to a clan brother than to, say, an Enkiyakmin from Bolivip village, with whom he traces descent to a common ancestress. The brother is a *wantok*, while the Enkiyakmin is a potential rival and traditional enemy; yet a Faiwolmin would sooner share with an Enkiyakmin than a Highlands Enga or Chimbu, who are social "others" in a menacing sense.

Whereas the terrain for transformation is local, the local itself has also been transformed. Men like Max are increasingly nodal figures in networks of exchange driven by a cash economy in which a bride's bounty is calculated in monetary terms with a hoped-for windfall. Accumulation in small stores and private houses protects a mining man's assets from distribution and broadcasts a gap between haves and have-nots.

Placing the "primitive" exchange relations of Sahlins's model within the kind of history analyzed in this chapter, we see that the apparent fit between a continuum of kin and social distance and a continuum from generalized to negative reciprocity no longer holds. Commodity relations erode apparent boundaries between inside and outside, and both goods and close kin are revalued. On one hand, commoditization and cash value simplify accounting for postcolonial subjects with an eye to the bottom line. On the other, although the value of modern money and its commoditized equivalents is straightforward, it is also strategically problematic. Reciprocal relations may be a matter of maintenance and negotiation (Bourdieu 1977, 33–43; see also Weber 1981, 355–356), but the bottom line has blurred the boundary between kindred and "others," and there is an increasing incidence of commodity exchange within families and community groups like Golgobip.

Global commodity production, and with it the commoditization of labor power among the Faiwolmin, have reconstituted formerly noncommoditized relations. The exchange value of tinned fish has destabilized the social relations of food sharing; items once traded between regional partners are now purchased at the supermarket or with a worker's wage. From the local supply side, generosity and geniality are increasingly expensive and risky. Within the village of Golgobip food *is* a commodity with an exchange value; inside households and hamlets the pressure on a single paycheck to provide tinned fish and rice raises questions about an eventual return for the miner in Tabubil. The limits of commoditized labor have led to allegations of greed from the unemployed, and undercurrents of resentment and fantasies of flight for migrant men. There has been a rupture in "solidary relations," such as they once were, which is experienced economically and affectively across new lines of social differentiation. Financially impecunious wives, elders without work boots, and children of absentee fathers assail the evident indifference of working men to the needs of their village relatives. And workers privately wish that kin would act more like strangers.

APPENDIX

Consider the contrasting profiles of two men who operated two of some six trade stores in Golgobip in 1989. Edward, a former cook in the Company Mess, works part time—under two days a week—for the Golgobip Vegetable Market for K15 or K20, a part-time position held by three and sometimes four men. In addition, he started a small trade store in 1989 with a modest inventory purchased from the Vegetable Market Wholesale, which sold trade store goods "frontloaded" on the Vegetable Charter to local operators. The rice, tinned fish, and Nestle's powdered beverages were sold from a room in Raymond's *haus kapa* at a small markup, which

Edward hoped would enable him to expand his inventory slowly. His profit was "eaten," however, by himself and kinspeople who happily supplemented their daily menu of root crops with white rice and canned mackerel (tinned fish). Edward confronted a tension between small-scale petty accumulation and social claims on his stockpile of tinned fish, which caused him to contemplate employment in town.

Ningalin Trading, by contrast, is the largest and most prosperous trade store in Golgobip. Named after a local clan, this enterprise has been in existence for nearly ten years under the same proprietorship. Identified as a "cooperative" by its manager who has sold shares to Ningalin for sums ranging from K30 to K150 over the years, the concept behind the cooperative is that shareholders will shop there and at some unspecified time in the future receive a dividend on the profit. A bush material building with iron roof located by the station, Ningalin Trading is well supplied with food commodities, batteries, and the like and does a relatively brisk business with schoolteachers and nurses. The latter are public servants with small gardens (if any), who are paid through the mission and may purchase at the store on credit. It was the first trade store in Golgobip, and its proprietor was also the first catechist who maintains close and friendly relations with the mission. He sometimes advances him credit on the purchase of inventory flown from Kiunga. The manager meets his overhead with the biggest markup in the village, and compensates himself for his unwaged managerial position with supplies of food for his large, extended household. Like Edward, he too maintains a village greenhouse for cash crop cultivation and sale to the Golgobip Vegetable Market. Both men are petty entrepreneurs who manage themselves and mobilize labor within and occasionally beyond their own households, as needed, for horticulture and trade store work.

NOTES

Earlier versions of this chapter were presented at the 1995 annual meeting of the Society for Economic Anthropology, and the session "Rethinking Commodities: Anthropological Views of the Global Marketplace" at the 1995 annual meetings of the American Anthropological Association. Thanks to all the participants, discussants, and organizers. I am especially grateful to Angelique Haugerud, Peter Little, David Nugent, Sutti Ortiz, William Roseberry, Priscilla Stone, and Nicholas Taintor for their insightful comments, good humor, and suggestions.

1. With advice from the World Bank, PNG sought foreign investment in mining as a source of revenue that might enable national development and reduce economic dependency on Australia (Pintz 1984; see also Tanzer 1980).

2. Faiwol is an indigenous name for a language group whose dialects are similar and mutually intelligible and whose speakers live on the Papuan Highlands fringe south of the Hindenburg Wall. "Min," Faiwol for "people," comprise a much broader group stretching north of the Hindenburg to the Telefolmin region in the neighboring West Sepik Province, east to the Strickland River, west beyond the Ok Tedi region and over the border into Irian

Jaya. Faiwolmin, who live up against the Hindenburg Wall, constitute a census division established in the colonial period, now a political constituency with representation in provincial government.

3. For those familiar with comparative material from Highlands groups to the east, Min are not large-scale pig producers for extended and protracted networks of exchange. Exchange is an important facet of social relations, however, as the present discussion indicates.

4. BHP was the managing interest in OTML, a consortium formed in 1976 with Amoco USA, each with a 30 percent interest in the venture; three West German companies, with a combined interest of 20 percent; and the government of PNG with an additional 20 percent.

The Bechtel Group, one of the world's leading contractors, was employed for the construction project, during a period of their own global expansion following a sluggish economic period in the United States during the early 1970s (Rimmer and Black 1983, 117).

5. There remain many more men who would prefer paid positions, for which they are not qualified, and who work sporadically at casual and unskilled labor. Others in this group visit the township frequently but reside in Golgobip. Job prospects are few for them, and the desire for profitable self-employment at home is as alluring as it is unlikely.

6. I have considered the various ways in which Faiwolmin women have confronted these social transformations in some detail elsewhere (Polier 1992, 307–462; Polier 1995). Here, however, my focus is primarily on how Faiwolmin men have negotiated global commodity circuits at the local level. This is saturated with relations of gender, and the shock of state formation and labor migration have been of profound consequence for women (Polier 1992, 1996). There is not space to discuss these transformations in any detail here.

7. An agreement signed between OTML and PNG provided that "nonlandowning" local people would be given hiring preference, other factors being equal, and that the company would lend assistance to local businesses. The Fly River provincial government receives a small royalty payment from the national government to be spent on rural development projects at the discretion and under the authority of provincial politicians. Also in the agreement, OTML consented to the purchase of locally produced goods and services when these were considered competitive with imported goods and services (Jackson 1982, 26; Marty Bos, Office of Community Relations, personal communication).

8. The category or term "worker" was created by the development of Ok Tedi Mining Limited and is both a sociological category and a term of self-description. The category or term "manager" describes a complex set of practices and relationships among village men, who see their activities and responsibilities in the countryside as managerial in character.

9. Unless otherwise indicated, all foreign language words are in neo-Melanesian pidgin.

10. This practice is widely referred to by European expatriates, and indeed many Papua New Guineans, as "the *wantok* system," a term that often emphasizes the inability of the individual to accumulate resources due to a tenacity of cultural belief. However, one does not meet these claims by simply "giving it all away," as the European stereotype suggests.

11. These estimates are based on wage allocation surveys carried out in 1989 with a sample of workers.

12. All names are pseudonyms.

13. Given the mobility of this group, the number of men aged eighteen through forty-five outside the village for short or extended periods in town is difficult to estimate precisely, but approximately one-third of that population were in the village at any one time, and a core of some thirty-two made up the population of youthful village men.

14. More rare and more ambitious is the village man who defines himself as "the organizer" and whose time is spent soliciting funds from *wantoks*, relatives, and associates in town on a regular basis. This entrepreneurial type is likely to have a trade store, a passbook, or sums secured in a private patrol box in his *haus kapa*, and a fair amount of *namba*. Unlike other managers in Golgobip village, he is not in a hierarchical and subordinate relation to the "cash cow" in town.

15. Stores tend to be open for business on an unpredictable and occasional basis, so the return may be slow, but one's money is tied up and unavailable for giving to kin and *wantoks* if it is put into a store.

16. Jones reports that cash was used by younger men in brideprice transactions at the time of her field research in 1975 (Jones 1980, 53). Informants from Golgobip recalled cash given in brideprice from as early as the mid-1970s, a time when most purchases were made without cash. Today it is virtually ubiquitous.

17. Usually, but not always, brideprice is paid after the early infancy of the first child.

18. These strings are called *honang*, Faiwol for shell ropes most people call *rop tambu* in neo-Melanesian pidgin; they are woven together with locally obtained bark fiber, known in Faiwol as *sok*. The shell (*nassa*) is small, white, and shaped like a flat seed roughly one-half centimeter in length, with two small holes on its face through which the shells are woven together with *sok*; a single rope is then sewn horizontally to others, in bands of some four to eight or more ropes in width. *Rop tambu* can be sewn or resewn by men using *sok*; in an age of plastic, the ropes are now sometimes sutured rope-to-rope with commercially available plastic colored string generally used for weaving plastic *bilums*.

19. It is these men whose payment is highest, although a price is seldom set unless the parents of the bride are opposed to the marriage, such as in cases where the groom is from outside the area (*longwe man*).

20. Brideprices are often given on Independence Day or Christmas when workers are on annual leave.

21. For a discussion of the monetization of brideprice and the bachelorization of the unemployed among neighboring Telefolmin, see Jorgensen 1988.

22. Jones (1980) reports that cash was used to buy items for brideprice such as axes in Imigabip as well. It is axes and bush knives that are the most commoditized items of non-cash wealth today.

23. Steel axes and bush knives contributed to brideprice are commodities whose monetary value of K5 is somewhat less than what one would pay for such merchandise in the supermarket. The price of a bow of black palm wood is generally agreed to be K5; an especially elegant bow with feather adornment might be valued at K10, which is what one would pay in Tabubil at an outdoor market, where bows are seen and sold occasionally, often to Europeans. K10 for a large, new *bilum* of bush material, the agreed upon cash equivalent in 1989, reflects a considerable undervaluation of women's labor over the months it generally takes to make one. This price is established, village men say, in Telefolmin where *bilums* are bought and sold on a commercial market for K10 per large bag.

This figure reflects a wider consensus on the cash "value" of locally made *bilums* from this area of the Western Province. In 1988–1989 the Montfort Catholic Mission was also selling bush material *bilums* made by West Irian refugees in the Kiunga area for equally low prices. There is no comparison between the local price for a *bilum* in this region and, say, the price for *bilums* sold in the Mount Hagen market, where large, colored bags may sell for K100 or more.

24. For the neighboring and culturally related Telefolmin people, Jorgensen (1988) has argued that marriage practices must be understood within a colonial history in which sister-exchange and endogamy were fundamentally reorganized.

REFERENCES

Barth, Fredrik. 1971. Tribe and Intertribal Relations in the Fly Headwaters. *Oceania* 41(3): 171–191.

———. 1975. *Ritual and Knowledge among the Baktaman.* New Haven, Conn.: Yale University Press.

Bourdieu, Pierre. 1977. *Outline of a Theory of Practice.* Cambridge: Cambridge University Press.

Craig, Barry, and Pamela Swadling. 1983. Trading Spheres in the Ok Tedi Impact Region. In Pamela Swadling, ed., *How Long Have People Been in the Ok Tedi Impact Region?* Port Moresby: Papua New Guinea National Museum.

Cranstone, Bryan. 1990. The Tifalmin and Their Environment: Material Culture of a Mountain-Ok People. In Barry Craig and David Hyndman, eds., *Children of Afek: Tradition and Change Among the Mountain-Ok of Central New Guinea.* Sydney: University of Sydney.

Gregory, Christopher. 1982. *Gifts and Commodities.* London: Academic Press.

Jackson, Richard. 1982. *Ok Tedi: The Pot of Gold.* Port Moresby: University of Papua New Guinea.

Jones, Barbara. 1980. Consuming Society: Food and Illness among the Faiwol. Ph.D. diss., University of Virginia.

Jorgensen, Dan. 1981. Taro and Arrows: Order, Entropy and Religion among the Telefolmin. Ph.D. diss., University of British Columbia.

———. 1988. From Sister Exchange to "Daughter-as-Tradestore": Money and Marriage in Telefolmin. *Catalyst* 18: 255–279.

———. 1991. Telefolmin. In Terence Hayes, ed., *Encyclopedia of World Cultures.* Vol. 2, *Human Relations Area Files.* Boston: G. K. Hall and Company.

Hyndman, David. 1994. A Sacred Mountain of Gold: The Creation of a Mining Resource Frontier in Papua New Guinea. *The Journal of Pacific History* 29: 203–221.

Morren, George E. B. 1991. Miyanmin. In Terence E. Hayes, ed., *Encyclopedia of World Cultures.* Vol. 2, *Human Relations Area Files.* Boston: G. K. Hall and Company.

Ogan, Eugene, and Terence Wesley-Smith. 1992. Papua New Guinea: Changing Relations of Production. In Albert B. Robillard, ed., *Social Change in the Pacific Islands.* London: Kegan Paul International.

Pintz, William S. 1984. *Ok Tedi: Evolution of a Third World Mining Project.* London: Mining Journal Books.

Polier, Nicole. 1992. The Mines of Min: History, Gender, and Social Transformation among the Faiwolmin of Papua New Guinea. Ph.D. diss., New York School for Social Research.

———. 1994. A View from the "Cyanide Room": Politics and Culture in a Mining Township in Papua New Guinea. *Identities* 1(1): 63–84.

———. 1996. Of Mines and Min: Modernity and Its Malcontents in Papua New Guinea. *Ethnology* 35(1): 1–16.

Rimmer, Peter, and John Black. 1983. Global Financiers, Consultants and Contractors in the Southwest Pacific since 1970. *Pacific Viewpoint* 24(2): 112–139.

Sahlins, Marshall. 1972. *Stone Age Economics*. Chicago: Aldine.

Tanzer, Michael. 1980. *The Race for Resources*. New York: Monthly Review Press.

Weber, Max. 1981. *General Economic History*. New Brunswick, N.J.: Transaction Books.

12

From Handicraft to Monocrop: The Production of Pecorino Cheese in Highland Sardinia

Gabriela Vargas-Cetina

INTRODUCTION

At the beginning of the twenty-first century we live in a world where clean air from forests in Chiapas, information bytes packaged by companies operating on the World Wide Web, commercial franchise rights, future agricultural commodities, present and future national debt certificates, as well as other nonmaterial commodities, can be bought and sold in international stock markets.[1] Such exchanges are the result of our growing dependence on new information technologies. In this chapter I explore the changing commodity status of Pecorino cheese, which was already a delicacy in Europe during the Middle Ages, and became popular in the United States, Canada, and South America in the mid-1800s (when thousands of Italians emigrated to the Americas). Changes in the macroeconomic context of the Pecorino cheese trade helped to transform social relations, gender roles, exchange patterns, and even festive sociability in the Sardinian Central Highlands. In that region, sheepherding expanded with the opening of an export market for Pecorino cheese, a local handicraft. Here I use the case of Telemula,[2] a Highland village in the Ogliastra region of Nuoro Province, to examine local impacts of the shift to pastoralist specialization.

Pecorino cheese is one among many historically specific commodities that became commonplace in the eighteenth and nineteenth centuries and have remained so. Such export crops are produced mainly for the market, and their worldwide prices are established by commodity futures markets that are usually distant from the lands where they are grown and harvested. Export crops are only one historically specific form of capitalist commodities, but they have been part of the regional histories of many areas, including large sections of Asia (Attwood 1992; Behal and Mohapatra 1992; Murray 1992; Wolf 1982), Africa (Hart 1982), Oceania (MacWilliam 1996), the Americas (Nolasco 1985; Roseberry 1995; Wells 1985; Worsley 1984), and Mediterranean Europe (Wolf 1982).

From the middle to the end of the nineteenth century, industrial development enabled the transformation of highly perishable agricultural products into raw materials for export, during what Brass and Bernstein (1992) have called "the second industrial revolution." Agricultural products began to be used in new ways in regions geographically distant from their origins. Some were included as delicacies, others as staples in European and North American diets (Friedmann 1995; Thompson and Cowan 1995; Wolf 1982; Worsley 1984). Pecorino cheese was one of the agro-pastoral products that benefited from new industrial processing, including cheese-making methods, pasteurization, and packing technologies that facilitated the long-distance export of large quantities of the product (Thompson and Cowan 1995, 37). Local earnings from Sardinian exports of Pecorino cheese, however, dwindled so that by the 1950s the shepherds who had supplied the international markets with this specialty faced social and economic problems.

Today's economic crisis in Sardinia's Central Highlands was neither unpredictable nor the result of Central Sardinians' attachment to tradition; rather, it was a logical outcome of the region's excessive dependence on a single export commodity that is now entering the last stages of a recurrent cycle of change from handicraft to monocrop production. This chapter focuses on how people in Sardinia's Highlands have experienced the transformation of pastoralism into the dominant agricultural activity in their municipalities.

My characterization of the passage of Sardinian Pecorino cheese from handicraft status to monocrop production may appear awkward. Although cheese is not usually referred to as a handicraft in everyday language, it shares many of the characteristics of handicrafts when it is not industrially processed. Cheese is made manually from raw materials (milk and whey); its geometrical forms vary with the containers in which it is made; its consistency depends on the proportion of milk and whey; and it consists of varying quantities of rennet, salt, and (sometimes) spices. Cheese was only one of the items certain families produced as a specialty good to exchange with other households.

In addition, the term monocrop usually refers to an agricultural rather than a pastoral product. Industrialized cheese for export results from the transformation of milk and whey by machines operated by a few technicians. Cheese, in any case, is derived from the milk of livestock, which in turn feed on grass and other agricultural products such as cereals. Marx (1967 [1867]) and Luxemburg (1967 [1912]) noted that fertile agricultural lands were being converted to livestock pastures in many areas of Europe before and during the time of their writings. Because they focused on how this change affected land appropriation by large capitalists, they apparently did not note that negative economic consequences also affected small-scale pastoralists, such as the Highland shepherds in Sardinia.

The ecological damage and land infertility resulting from the historical specialization in livestock grazing helped to perpetuate pastoralism. Extensive livestock grazing became the most viable use of lands that had been overgrazed and ravaged through intentional fires. Unless the state, or a metastate government such as the European Union, invests in the regeneration of soil fertility, it is almost impossible for small-scale pastoralists to restore their lands with the necessary water and soil nutrients.[3]

In sum, the displacement of crops by sheep and goats has been a characteristic of capitalist development in many areas, and my choice of terminology highlights the similarities between pastoral specialization and agricultural specialization. Thus, I use the terms "handicraft" and "monocrop" to emphasize similarities between cheese production in the Sardinian Highlands and forms of economic specialization elsewhere (Brass and Bernstein 1992; Hart 1982; Roseberry 1995; Wells 1985; Worsley 1984).

Monocrop-dependent local economies and associated landscape transformations have been analyzed by scholars such as Brass and Bernstein (1992), Friedmann (1995), Braudel (1973 [1967]), McMichael (1995), Roseberry (1995), Wolf (1982), and Worsley (1984). Students of such societies often stress deleterious effects of monocrop agriculture on local economies, while other scholars such as Attwood (1988) and Valdez (1991) tend to view the resulting rural economic changes as steps toward social and economic development.

This chapter demonstrates that the transformation of the countryside has different effects through time, some beneficial, some damaging. Why a society chooses the monocrop path, while others diversify their income-generating products, is not explored here, although this is an important issue that has puzzled historians and anthropologists alike (Annis 1987; Attwood 1992; Melville 1994; Nolasco 1985; Page 1975; Roseberry 1995). Here I examine the social impacts of dependency on a single agricultural commodity. My conclusions contribute to current debates about global agricultural commoditization and change.

THE EMERGENCE AND DECLINE OF EXPORT-ORIENTED MONOCROP ECONOMIES: A GENERAL MODEL

Drawing on my research on henequen fiber production in the Yucatán peninsula of Mexico (Vargas-Cetina 1986), and Pecorino cheese production in Sardinia (Vargas-Cetina 1993a, 1993b, 1994), as well as on anthropological and historical studies of monocrop rural production (Melville 1994; Nolasco 1985; Page 1975; Roseberry 1995; Wells 1985), I propose a general model of the developmental cycle of monocrop economies. I posit the following five phases, from handicraft to monocrop production:[4]

1. Expansion of the international market for a particular local handicraft;
2. Industrialization of the local handicraft;
3. Monocrop production aimed at export of a local product in a booming market;
4. Monocrop production to enable export of a local product in a saturated international market;
5. Postmonocrop economic underdevelopment, sometimes followed by government-directed adjustments.[5]

Associated with these five macroeconomic phases I have also identified five stages in the affected communities and regions:

1. *Handicraft production within a subsistence economy.* Increased international demand for a local handicraft causes a rise in its price, even at the local level. Land becomes a coveted commodity to the extent that it allows production of the handicraft now experiencing growing demand. Patterns of social stratification begin to change as some people benefit from opportunities opened by the emerging market. Within local traditional exchange circuits, the transactions involving this newly translocal commodity begin to be monetized but are still of many types: gifts, barter, and other highly personal forms of exchange.
2. *Mechanized processing of agricultural products.* One crop begins to expand at the expense of other subsistence crops and new industrial manufacturing emerges in association with the local handicraft produced for export. The division of agricultural and mechanized production mirrors social stratification, which favors the owners of industrial machinery. Independent agricultural producers retain some bargaining power because of the industrialists' high demand for their produce. A dual economy develops in which some people remain tied to agriculture and hold wealth in the form of land, other agricultural resources, and limited cash, while another sector of the population specializes in industrial manufacturing and accumulates wealth in money.
3. *Golden age of monocrop and export products.* Diversified production is eliminated or severely reduced in favor of a dominant crop. A sellers' market emerges and the export product brings economic prosperity to the region, whose fortunes now depend on the world market. This prosperity, however, does not necessarily reach everyone in the region, and rigid economic and social hierarchies can appear. International competition or the emergence of substitute synthetic products (or both) begins to undermine any future expansion of the market for the local export product. Most transactions become monetized (at least nominally, through credit). This phase ends with international oversupply of the export product.
4. *Crisis and, in some cases, state intervention.* One crop continues to expand relative to others, even if it now brings reduced returns. It is a buyers' market, and the local manufacturers seek to organize a united front. The regional eco-

nomic crisis leads local people to seek outside help, often in the form of government intervention. If the national (or regional, or metanational) government responds, it tries to redress the extreme social inequality that prevails under the monocrop and export craft system of production. Typically, under government patronage agricultural producers are given ownership and control over some manufacturing plants related to the export craft, but the international market has no more use for their production, and these enterprises fail. A wide region that had become dependent on the export market experiences underdevelopment because of the low returns monocrop production now provides. Agriculturists begin to diversify their crop production, but the land base is now degraded.

5. *The search for alternatives.* People look for alternatives, including temporary migration of rural family members—or even entire families—to other rural areas, the cities, or other countries in search of jobs. At this stage, the price of rural lands decreases because much of the countryside has been abandoned. If the state tries to guide the regional economy in a new direction, it fosters other production alternatives and promotes the diversification of agriculture as well as nonagricultural economic alternatives. The factories that processed the export product either close or are redesigned to produce other goods.

These changes often take place over two or more generations. Their main effect where a monocrop takes hold is to drive relatively self-sufficient subsistence economies into an extreme dependence on the international market. How these changes affect each community's life and cultural values varies across localities and regions. Monetization of most exchanges, however, opens an area to national and international markets and contributes to the emergence of great disparities in wealth.[6] In the rest of this chapter, I explore the later stages of the cycle of monocrop production of Pecorino cheese and its effects on people in a Sardinian village.

TELEMULA: A VILLAGE IN HIGHLAND SARDINIA

Telemula, a mountain village on the Gennargentu ridge of Central Sardinia, is a community that has long depended on the production and sale of Pecorino Romano cheese. When Telemula joined fully in the production of Pecorino cheese for export, the international market was nearly saturated. This village's belated incorporation into export monocrop production did not shelter it from the full impact of the Pecorino cheese market crisis. Its isolation from Sardinia's centers of commercial activity has made it difficult for its inhabitants to return to diversified agricultural production, or to other options.

Telemula has a population of about one thousand inhabitants, and its communal territory covers 11,500 hectares. The territory's steep topography makes it more suitable for herding goats rather than sheep. There are fifty-five registered shepherds in Telemula; in 1990 they owned in all 2,500 sheep and 6,430 goats.[7] Most of Telemula's territory is held in communal tenure (9,000 hectares) and is used as pasture range for the shepherds' flocks. The village itself is on a slope, at 600 meters above sea level, and the lands used for agro-pastoral activities are on Supramonte, a mountain plateau in the Arbatax valley, by the Thyrrenian Sea.

Telemula is predominantly pastoral. Although registered shepherds represent less than 20 percent of the economically active male population, they constitute the total number of villagers employed full time in agriculture (Istituto Nazionale di Statistica, 1994). Employment outside of sheepherding is mostly seasonal, with the exception of a small number of skilled positions. Many young men are undeclared shepherds who tend flocks seasonally or who do so full time without registering the animals in their own or someone else's name. If their official status is "unemployed," they have a better chance to be chosen to work in government-sponsored jobs, such as road maintenance, land reforestation, or industrial jobs. The rest of Telemula's population finds employment as masons or bricklayers, as clerks in coastal villages or towns, or in jobs related to summer tourism.[8]

TELEMULA AND THE PECORINO CHEESE EXPORT MARKET IN SARDINIA

The island of Sardinia, off the coast of Italy, has long been considered one of the most "marginal" or "underdeveloped" areas of Europe (Braga 1990; Vinci 1992). Sardinia—or parts of it—has been ruled and colonized by several Mediterranean empires, including the Carthaginian, Roman, Ottoman, Catalan, Castilian, and House of Savoy (Casula 1982; Meloni 1982; Sotgiu 1982; Tore 1982). Today Sardinia is an autonomous region of Italy. It has its own regional Consiglio (congress) and ministries. It is divided into four provinces: Cagliari, Sassari, Nuoro, and Oristano. Authorities view Nuoro Province as the most underdeveloped and violent region. Nuoresi, the inhabitants of Nuoro Province (which includes Telemula), have a history of violence and kidnapping (Marongiu 1981; Pigliaru 1975; Pilonca 1986). The yearly death tolls resulting from family feuds (known as *faide* in Sardinia), the high incidence of livestock rustling, and incidents of kidnapping contribute to this reputation. Pastoralism, considered a "backward" occupation, is seen as the root of all social problems in the province.[9]

Nuoro's economy is still predominantly agro-pastoral. According to the 1990 economic census, 60 percent of the economically active population is engaged full time in agro-pastoral activities; 40 percent of these agro-pastoral producers are dedicated to animal husbandry (Istituto Nazionale di Statistica 1994), which in Highland Sardinia centers on sheep- and goat herding.[10] Goat and sheepherding are the basis for the manufacture of Pecorino cheese, which once was the main export commodity of Sardinia.

Since 1799, when the royal family established itself in the city of Cagliari, Savoy rulers[11] tried to modernize the island's economy. Between 1820 and 1847, the House of Savoy abolished feudalism, passed the Legge delle chiudende (Laws of Enclosure)—which allowed for the enclosure of ecclesiastic and communal lands—and introduced a money standard to replace the many local currencies then in use. The Savoy monarchs also promoted, through an agricultural extension program, cultivation of vines and vegetables, as well as breeding of improved sheep. In the cities, the Savoy monarchs tried to create favorable conditions for manufacturing and small enterprises (Birocchi 1990; Del Piano 1991).

When the land enclosure laws were enacted in 1820, many Highland communities, including Telemula, refused to convert their communal territory to private ownership. In the mid-1800s, under pressure from the island authorities, Telemula's municipal councilors decided to divide some of the most fertile lands (those in the Arbatax valley) among the families of the village (Bodeman 1979). Today these lands are used for kitchen gardens and vineyards, as well as a winter home for animals.

Part of the Savoys' reform was to impose a system of double taxation whereby the entire municipality was taxed by the government and the families were in turn taxed by each municipality. Savoy legislation did favor the emergence of manufacture in the cities, but their tax scheme created a state of extreme poverty in the countryside. All food items were taxed, including acorn flower, which was not considered very suitable for human consumption and had never been the subject of tribute in the past (Del Piano 1991). The taxes, however, could be paid in kind. Central Sardinia villages became relatively autarchic because, through the *biddazzone* (a system for the annual rotation of communal lands) and their terraced gardens, villagers could make a living with little dependence on the rapidly internationalizing outside economy.

A system of regional exchange developed, whereby each Highland community specialized in one or several trade items. Telemula specialized in *bisaccie* (saddlebags) made from sheep's wool and goat's hair, while other villages specialized in wooden items, basket weaving, or special pastries. Through bartering at *feste* (festivals) and itinerant peddling of their *bisaccie* during nonfestive times of the year, Telemulesi acquired other regional products. Money was scarce and most people did not make use of it in the Highlands.

THE EXPANSION OF THE INTERNATIONAL MARKET FOR PECORINO CHEESE

Although the Savoy were preoccupied with manufacturing industries, which they believed would bring Sardinia into the world economy, wheat cultivation and sheepherding ultimately connected the island to international markets. Historian Emilio Braga (1990, 367) calls the prominence of agriculture in Sardinian exports from 1890 to the 1950s "the victory of tradition," a reference to the export of traditional agricultural products (including wheat and cheese) during those years. The victory for wheat, however, was short-lived. Sardinian wheat soon was displaced from the market by Russian, and especially American, grain. As Kasaba and Tabak point out, after the conquest of the Americas "wheat cultivation gained a foothold on both hemispheres of the American continent, to expand spectacularly during the latter half of the twentieth century" (1995, 82). The decline in wheat prices was an important causal element in the restructuring of world agriculture at the time (Kasaba and Tabak 1995, 82–83).

With the crash of world cereal prices, wheat ceased to be a major crop in Sardinia, especially in the Central Highlands. Although in the 1920s the Italian government declared a *battaglia per il grano* (a fight for wheat), American grain continued to keep the price of local wheat depressed, and grain cultivation ceased to be a viable export activity. Pecorino cheese exports to the United States, after achieving an all-time record of 100,000 metric tons in 1928, fell to a steady 70,000–80,000 metric tons on average between 1932 and 1965 (Bussa 1978; Idda 1982). The new export market supported the expansion of flocks, which continued until the 1990s. From 555,902 head of sheep registered in 1875, herds swelled to 1,876,851 head in 1908; 2,054,138 in 1930; and to 3,000,000 in 1980 (Idda 1982). In 1990 there were, according to the national census, 3,600,000 sheep in Sardinia (Istituto Nazionale di Statistica 1994).

Before the demise of wheat cultivation, Telemula's economy was based on the complementarity of agriculture and pastoralism. From the Middle Ages until 1962, Telemula's farmers relied on the *biddazzone* system, whereby half the communal territory was used for pastures and the other half for wheat cultivation. The lands were rotated every two years. In this way the animals fertilized the agricultural lands and fed on stubble after the harvest. Families specialized in either agriculture or pastoralism, and they exchanged products among themselves through barter or through gifts. In addition to the lands they were given to till or to graze, each family was allotted a piece of land for a kitchen garden at the beginning of every year. The land around the village was terraced, and these terraces were the only parts of the communal territory that were actually inherited by customary right within families.

Villagers in other municipalities saw the advantages of the privatization of land before most of Telemula's people understood what it meant. Lowland villagers began to covet Telemula's lands in the Arbatax valley and bought the lands some families had received during the forced allotment. They did this before Telemulesi could establish a fair price for them. It is said that the first time a man from a different village approached a Telemula shepherd to offer him money for his land, the shepherd closed the deal right away, climbed back to Telemula, and went into the local bar. In disbelief, he happily told people at the bar that a man had given him money for his land: "Lui la vuole, ed io gliela vendo. Mica si la porta via!" ("He wants it, and I sell it to him; he can't pick it up and take it away!" author's translation). A few days later, he and other Telemulesi were astonished to find a fence around the land he had sold.[12]

The agricultural crisis and the opportunities for industrial employment in Europe and America drove many young people away from farming in Sardinia. Emigration made it possible for some Highland shepherds to buy idle lands in the valleys and to continue to expand the size of their flocks. Until the 1960s, most sheep breeding in Sardinia took the form of shepherds herding transhumant flocks. Highland shepherds took their animals to the lowlands during the coldest months of the year and then made the return trip to the Highlands in the spring. Although it is difficult to obtain exact figures on the regional distribution of sheep at the end of the nineteenth century, most of the growth in Pecorino cheese production in Sardinia was based on milk supplied to the dairy factories by transhumant shepherds from the Highlands.[13]

Italian emigration to the United States and Argentina at the end of the nineteenth century helped to create an international market for Pecorino Romano cheese. Soon Pecorino (cheese from sheep's milk), particularly Pecorino Romano, became popular among American Jews and other sectors of the American population. Pecorino Romano was then produced only in mainland Italy. (It is very salty, has a strong flavor, and is especially suited for Italian pasta.) As Pecorino cheese was imported into the United States and Argentina at a growing rate, the factories in mainland Italy, in the regions of Lazio and Tuscany, could not meet the new demand. Italian and foreign entrepreneurs soon saw the opportunities represented by production of Sardinian sheep's milk, which was then being hand-processed into cheese.

THE INDUSTRIALIZATION OF PECORINO CHEESE IN SARDINIA AND THE EXPANSION OF PASTORALISM

The first cheese factories in Sardinia were established in the 1890s in the Campidano area of Cagliari Province. These factories could count on a good seasonal supply of milk, since many shepherds from the Highlands rented lands there during the winter. Pecorino Romano factories were among the first dairy factories in Sardinia. Highland shepherds, who usually spoke only Sard and needed money mainly to pay rent to the local Campidanesi landowners, were easily enticed to provide milk to the dairy plants. Indeed it was these shepherds, who were and still are considered the most traditional and "backward" sector of the Sardinian population, who finally brought Sardinia into the international market. Pecorino cheese production made money increasingly important in the lives of villagers.

Older shepherds in the Ogliastra subregion who used to take their flocks to the Campidano di Cagliari area remember their first encounters with Italian and foreign entrepreneurs who were the owners or representatives of dairy factories. According to these shepherds, the entrepreneurs gave them a sum of money as a "credit advance" and they were obligated to supply the factories with their sheep's milk while they stayed in the Campidano region. The "credit advances" often required the shepherds to supply milk to the factories during the following year.[14]

In addition to buying milk from those shepherds who went down to the Campidano regions (when the Supramonte was covered with snow), Pecorino cheese manufacturers began to approach shepherds at their *ovili* (the shepherds' shelters) on the Supramonte plateau. Many shepherds began to sell milk at the trucks (usually parked down in a valley) owned by these manufacturers. The shepherds were responsible for transporting their milk containers to the trucks, either by mule or on foot.[15]

Sheepherding is a male occupation and women rarely if ever herd flocks. (The few women who had a herd are remembered with awe.) Women did tend one or two animals in order to provide fresh milk for their families. This practice survives today only in the most isolated parts of the Central Highlands (including Telemula). These animals—usually goats—are called *manalithas* in Sard (meaning "animals who are kept for fresh milk") and they are kept near the village.

TELEMULA'S GOLDEN AGE OF PASTORALISM

The expansion of the Pecorino Romano trade finally began to have important effects on Telemula in the late 1950s, and the *biddazzone* system was abandoned in 1962. The changes are captured in the comments of Naneddu, an old shepherd who recalls when he was a peasant and owned a *carro a buoi* (a yoke of oxen). He says that on the accustomed day for the yearly distribution of land plots "*nemus, nemus est torrau*" ("nobody, nobody came," author's translation). (He had gone to secure a plot of land for himself, but also to contract out to other peasants the use of his yoke of oxen.) Because his wheat and vegetable production were insufficient to provide for his family, he contracted out the use of his oxen for supplemental income. Seeing other peasants' lack of interest in growing wheat, Naneddu eventually did what many other men had done in recent years; he sold his oxen and used the money to purchase a flock of sheep.

The golden age of pastoralism in Telemula was from 1962 until the late 1960s. According to Effeddu, who is a nonregistered shepherd, most of the men in Telemula were shepherds in the 1960s. (There were 15,000 sheep.) It is difficult to imagine that Telemula's territory could have ever supported so many sheep since only 16 percent of its territory is flat enough to sustain such grazing and herding. Yet, Effeddu's recollection of the days of sheep pastoralism is probably accurate.

The expansion of pastoralism significantly affected the organization of household labor in the Central Highlands, including Telemula. Men took care of the animals, milked them, and made cheese manually when the product was not picked up by trucks from the cheese manufacturing plants. Shepherds' wives were responsible for tending vineyards and gardens in the valley and for managing the family's expenses. The children's labor was organized by both the husband and wife, although the oldest boy typically worked with his father at the *ovile* and with the flocks.[16] Both female and male teenagers were expected to find jobs working in other communities as *servi* (the girls in agriculture and the boys in sheepherding) to raise their own money and property to become *sistemati* (ready for marriage).[17]

The village acquired a pastoral image that continues to permeate most festivals and social activities. Although the shepherds and their families never participated fully in the *Festa di Sant'Efisio* (an annual festival that takes place in May), they did become important participants and hosts in the festivals of *Santa Marta* and *Santa Marta la Piccola,* both of which occur during the summer (Ayora-Diaz 1993a, 1993b). Unlike other villages and towns (Vargas-Cetina 1993a), in Telemula village festivals were never exclusively associated with the signing of contracts between land-owners and shepherds.

THE CRISIS OF THE PECORINO CHEESE MARKET

The Pecorino cheese market, and particularly the Pecorino Romano export market, has gone through several crises since its growth turned the Sardinian Highlands into "an island of shepherds."[18] Until the mid-1980s, however, it never faced a severe challenge because the market kept expanding, although at a slower rate than it had from the late 1800s to the 1950s.

Today the Pecorino cheese market is quite competitive. Argentinian *Pecorino sardo* (literally, "Sardinian Pecorino cheese") and French *fromages de chevre* (goat's milk cheeses) and *fromages de bebris* (sheep cheeses) compete in both the European and the American markets with Sardinia's Pecorino Romano. The volume of Sardinian Pecorino cheese exports to the United States during the 1970s fell to less than half the weight of Pecorino cheese exported to the United States in 1965, while the to-tal production in Sardinia continued to grow, reaching 15.4 million kilograms in 1980 (Idda 1982) and 37.2 million kilograms in 1984 (Comunità Europea 1988).

Sardinian cheese continued to be exported as Pecorino Romano until the 1990s. In 1990, several associations of shepherds began to demand that *Pecorino di Sardegna* be recognized as a *marchio d'origine* (trademark) in order to let the customer know that it was actually produced on the island. (The name *Pecorino sardo* had already been registered by Argentinian cheese makers and thus could not be used by Sardinian producers.) Shepherds and cheese manufacturers believe that this new trademark might help consumers recognize their product and arrest its price decline.[19]

European Community (EC) planners believe that the current troubles of Pecorino cheese are the result of inadequate marketing, rather than the characteristics of the product itself (Comunità Europea 1988). In 1985 the EC issued a bill to reduce the number of milk sheep. This law took several years to be approved, first by the Italian government and then by the Sardinian authorities, and it finally went into effect in Sardinia in 1992. Under this new program, Sardinian shepherds are encour-aged to reduce their flocks by 20 percent and to maintain them thus reduced for five years. If they do this, they will qualify for a European Union subsidy (Il Ministro dell'Agricoltùra e le Foreste 1990).

THE PROBLEMS OF PASTORAL UNDERDEVELOPMENT

The golden age of the Pecorino cheese market did not create general prosperity. Shepherds still milk their animals manually, practice transhumance, and endure difficult working conditions. While industrialists continue to tie the owners of flocks to their dairy plants through an unfavorable credit system, many affluent shepherds engage in what could be considered a form of child slavery—the employment of children and teenagers as *servopastori*, or boys who want to become shepherds. These boys receive a number of sheep and a quantity of cheese each year from the shepherd for whom they work, and after several years of work, they might have built their own flock and become self-employed. While the shepherds (including many who had themselves been *servopastori*) view this as legitimate work, others see it as a form of servitude that only confirms outsiders' perceptions of the pastoralists' "barbaric" customs.

Sardinian regional and national authorities also view livestock rustling as a problem, and indeed it is a crime according to Italian law. Livestock rustling in Sardinia, however, has the same social importance it has among pastoralists elsewhere (Flores Ochoa 1968; Herzfeld 1985), in that it helps shepherds build social networks beyond their own communities through the subsequent negotiation process centered on the return of stolen livestock. From this vantage point, it is considered an acceptable way to engage friends and make allies (Caltagirone 1989).

By the 1970s sociologists and bureaucrats believed that many of the social ills of pastoralism resulted from the poor standards of living of the shepherds and their families, their lack of formal education, their exploitation by industrialists, and the paucity of employment alternatives. A two-year senate inquiry into the causes of criminality in Sardinia led to legislation to reform the island's agro-pastoral sector.[20] Shepherds were given facilities to organize into cooperatives, so they could acquire high-quality pastures and Pecorino Romano cheese manufacturing plants.

The *riforma agropastorale* laws, initiated in 1976, are based on the social and economic circumstances of the 1970s, when the Pecorino Romano export trade was still relatively advantageous for cheese manufacturers, even though demand for the product had begun to decline. Pastoralism reform measures, however, are an obstacle to economic diversification in many Highland communities. Sheepherding now occupies 75 percent of all agricultural land on the island (Comunità Europea 1988). Although the EC absorbed the oversupply of Pecorino cheese when the export market declined in the 1980s (Regione Sardegna 1991, 54), the European Union now is downsizing its production and storage subsidies, which negatively affects the price of Sardinian cheese. According to a shepherd who is the president of a cheese manufacturing cooperative, the price of Sardinian Pecorino cheese sold to wholesale merchants had already fallen from L(lira)10,000 in 1991 to L6,000 per kg in 1992.[21] Nevertheless there are few buyers willing to make large purchases.

Sardinian authorities still view pastoralism as a problem, and they see shepherds as very traditional, violent people who resist social and economic change. Ironically, the Central Highlands area, once the locus of Sardinia's participation in the world market, has become a symbol of backwardness and underdevelopment.

THE LOCAL IMPACT OF STATE INTERVENTION

In the 1970s, when the export of Pecorino Romano cheese encountered a market bottleneck, the government recognized the need to help shepherds and the cheese trade. As a result several cheese manufacturing plants were converted to cooperative ownership under the control of shepherds. This happened throughout the Barbagia and Ogliastra subregions of Nuoro Province's Central Highlands. Private entrepreneurs, however, were already moving away from Pecorino cheese production and into more profitable ventures.

As early as the 1950s the government had supported shepherds' cooperatives in response to private manufacturers' apparent abuses. It was not until the 1970s, however, that the government seriously promoted the formation of these cooperatives. Several cooperative cheese factories were established in Barbagia, and milk supply cooperatives (associated with these factories) emerged in Ogliastra. In 1975 the Consorzio Regionale Sardegna, an umbrella marketing association for shepherds' cheese cooperatives, was established in Macomer. Through this association, cooperatives sought to present a united front vis-à-vis international buyers. Despite the regional government's support, the association could not arrest Pecorino cheese's price decline, and in the 1990s the cooperatives began to market their cheese on their own again. The association finally disbanded in 1992, and the regional government absorbed most of its debts.

The 1976 agro-pastoral reform targeted Telemula through a project to preserve communal lands and to create pastoral infrastructure. Telemula shepherds, however, did not receive sufficient political support for organizing a cooperative and so continued to supply most of their milk to private entrepreneurs. The village was considered a very traditional setting, so the authorities did not encourage pasture irrigation or other types of modern infrastructure. The Azienda Speciale project, drafted by government of Sardinia bureaucrats for Telemula (Regione Sardegna n.d.), was based on the premise that the locals would resist private land enclosures and would not cooperate to form collective associations. Signs of land erosion resulting from free-range pastoralism began to appear in Telemula in the 1970s. Today most of the communal territory has been degraded as sheep and goats have denuded most surface vegetation. The lands in the valleys of Nuoro Province are being used for vineyards, orchards, and kitchen gardens, and shepherds often have to travel to other parts of the island in search of winter pastures.

European Community regulations during the 1980s, particularly those controlling supply excess, sheltered shepherds from the full impact of the international market decline of Pecorino Romano. In the 1990s, part of Telemula's territory on the Supramonte had been targeted for a reforestation project that would expand the area of the Gennargentu park. Many shepherds have been displaced from their *ovili* and banned from the best shelters that had been built during the 1970s and 1980s. Sixty workers share thirty reforestation jobs in preparation for the opening of the national park. Former shepherds are looking for other occupations, such as reforestation or service work.

Pastoralism in Telemula is being eliminated through top-down policies. After monocrop agro-pastoralism had reached its growth limits, the village became part of an underdeveloped area. The regional government's strategy to eradicate "backwardness" is to eliminate pastoralism, the alleged cause of current social problems.

The Parco del Gennargentu, the national park soon opening to the public, will encompass most of the Supramonte plateau. This area covers the spring, summer, and fall pastures of many shepherds in Nuoro Province (Heatherington 1993; Kennedy 1993). The national park is expected to end Highland Sardinia's social and economic troubles by banishing pastoralism and pastoralists. From the planners' perspective, the shepherds must be pushed out of their current way of life; otherwise they will resist change in spite of the government's efforts. In the words of a Sardinian politician who described the plans for the national park:

> The shepherd is like the Panda bear; it is a species on its way to extinction. We are going to hire some shepherds so that they can provide an additional attraction for the tourists. Other than these few, salaried husbandmen, all the others will have to find another job.

The data from Telemula suggest that pastoralism in Sardinia is not the result of Highland villagers clinging stubbornly to tradition. Rather, pastoralism expanded in Sardinia because people saw the possibility of earning a better living. Many individuals made rational, entrepreneurial decisions and left other activities in order to dedicate themselves to tending flocks of sheep or goats.

CONCLUSION

Pastoralist problems in Sardinia today are officially blamed on the purported traditional character of shepherds, particularly those of the Central Highlands. This chapter argues, however, that the shepherds are not the traditionalists Italian politicians and the general public believe them to be. Many of these shepherds are new to their occupations and first became husbandmen because of the Pecorino Romano export boom, which reached the Central Highlands in the 1950s and early 1960s. Furthermore, I suggest that the unequal distribution of wealth among people engaged in Pecorino Romano production and export was not the result of the cultural incapacity of the shepherds or their families, but rather of processes often associated with monocrop export economies. Animals continue to be milked by hand; shepherds still must engage in transhumance; and their working conditions did not improve with the industrial production of cheese. All of these patterns show that monocrop-driven development does not necessarily extend to all parts of the production process or to all sectors of the population. After the collapse of Sardinian Pecorino cheese prices, there are more shepherds than before the export boom, but they do not seem to be much better off than their *contadini* (peasant) grandparents.

Sini (1982) has pointed out that Sardinia's exports are still predominantly cheap agricultural goods (mainly Pecorino cheese), while its imports are expensive goods. This imbalance creates a deficit in the island's balance of trade. Pecorino cheese production is in crisis, but the European (Comunità Europea 1988) and Sardinian (Regione Sardegna 1991) authorities continue to associate most of the economic troubles of pastoralism with seminomadic strategies of livestock breeding. These shepherds were generally less nomadic before the industrialization of Sardinian cheese, since the privatization of communal lands encouraged nomadism.

Had pastoralism not inserted Highland Sardinia into the international market, other products or services would have done so. It was the Highland shepherds, however, who accumulated the necessary surplus to modernize the island's economy, and their production strategies continued to be relatively viable even after the export market collapsed. Sardinia's Pecorino cheese is disadvantaged in international markets today because it competes with lower-priced inferior products that dominate supermarkets. The shepherds and their families, who cannot reduce their own production costs to suit the Pecorino cheese markets' low demand for Sardinian cheese, confront global processes they cannot control. The case of Telemula illustrates that many economic and social troubles today are not generated by supposedly tradition-bound local villages themselves. Rather, they are the result of the last stages of a handicraft to monocrop cycle that repeats itself worldwide.

NOTES

I dedicate this chapter to the memory of Herman W. Konrad. I thank Igor Ayora-Diaz and Tracey Heatherington for many discussions over the years, which helped me to sharpen my thoughts on this topic. Special thanks to Karen Fox for her editorial help and advice on economic theory, and to Angelique Haugerud, Peter Little, and Priscilla Stone for their detailed feedback on previous drafts of this manuscript. My twenty-two months of research in Sardinia, from 1990 to 1992, were made possible through the generous support of the McGill Faculty of Graduate Studies, the Canadian International Aid Agency, the Social Sciences and Humanities Research Council of Canada, the Wenner-Gren Foundation, the Canadian Association for Studies in Cooperation, and gifts from Mr. Gabrielle Giaccu and Ms. Gloria Vargas. I also received funds from a grant from the Social Sciences and Humanities Research Council of Canada awarded to Professor Philip C. Salzman, the head of a Sardinian research team at McGill University. I thank all the agencies and individuals who contributed to my doctoral work.

1. In Chiapas some indigenous communities are packaging "clean air stock bonds" or "carbon stock bonds"; industrial companies that purchase them acquire rights to emit specific quantities of polluting carbon into the air in other regions of the world.

2. Telemula and most proper names in this paper are pseudonyms.

3. Water creeks tend to dry after deforestation.

4. Here I am interested in monocrop economies that support the production of a prized local specialty. Henequen fibers in the Yucatán peninsula and Pecorino cheese in Sardinia are good examples. It is possible that this model could apply to the export cycles of products such as fruits and textiles.

5. It is possible to derive a similar model from the 1960s and 1970s writings of Andre Gunder Frank. Frank (1967, 1971) maintained that export economies engaged in a transfer of resources from peripheral economies to metropolis. This transfer was itself the cause of underdevelopment. He called the series of transfers that went from the countryside to the cities, and then to the world metropolis, "the development of underdevelopment" (Frank 1967). I find Frank's argument persuasive, but I do not have the data to endorse or challenge his model. In any case, I am not concerned with the details of the macroeconomic historical processes of monocrop commercialization, which would be better understood and explained by an economist. Rather, I wish to focus on the changes that people experience in their everyday lives under a monocrop economy.

6. It is likely that most local economies enter the market at some point and suffer from most of the problems associated with market dependency. Monocrop specialization, however, makes it more difficult to get out of extreme market dependency, because the land loses much of its productive potential. It is only through considerable investment that a region under monocrop specialization can make the switch to other forms of agriculture.

7. These figures are based on uncataloged animal holdings tables for the years 1985–1992, provided by the Telemula municipal archives.

8. There are also one truck driver, two bookkeepers, three men employed by an Italian government agency in road repair, and five people who are under a pension system known as *cassa integrazione guadagni*. (The latter are former employees of a paper factory that no longer needs their services. These laid-off workers receive 60 percent of their former salaries and are not expected to seek other employment.) Sixty men and women are employed part time by the Sardinian government in reforestation projects, sharing thirty jobs, and each summer five young men and women work as firefighters in the municipal territory. Some women find employment in sweatshops making clothes, but few remain in these positions long because of the low salaries and the harsh demands. (A woman who worked there for some time had to stitch collars to seventy shirts each hour, and she was not paid for her first three weeks at the factory because, according to the manager, she was on a trial period. These sweatshops are mostly illegal but they recruit from among the owners' or managers' relatives and friends, and thus neither their existence nor their owners' abuses are ever reported to the authorities.) There are several young men and women attending university in Cagliari or Rome, but employment prospects for university graduates are not very good in the Ogliastra region.

9. Although it is not possible to deny that Highland Sardinians engage in many violent acts, violence takes place under a specific code of honor. It is never random, as the authorities believe. Violence can be predicted and kept under relative control by regional mechanisms of conflict resolution, which are alien to those established by the Italian state or other Western nation-states.

10. These numbers probably underestimate the real extent to which men are engaged in sheep- and goat herding. Many young men prefer to declare themselves jobless rather than admit that they are full-time shepherds. This is because people who appear as unemployed in government records have priority when government-funded companies are hiring unskilled labor.

11. The House of Savoy, which headed the Kingdom of Piedmont, ruled over Sardinia between 1720 and 1861.

12. Author's field notes, December 1991.

13. The Sardinian lowlands have traditionally been considered mainly agricultural areas, in which livestock has little importance. The Highlands, in contrast, have been seen for centuries as "pastoral areas," although pastoralism has been practiced side by side with agriculture since the Middle Ages.

14. If they took their animals to the Campidano di Cagliari they would give their milk to the Italian entrepreneurs who made Pecorino Romano cheese; if they took their animals to the Campidano di Sassari, north of the Central Highlands, they would supply Greek entrepreneurs who owned feta cheese factories. Feta cheese was also exported to other parts of Europe and to the United States. Today feta cheese is no longer produced on the island, but Pecorino Romano continues to figure prominently in the Sardinian dairy industry.

According to Bussa (1978), feta cheese production took place in Sardinia between 1967 and 1972. My informants from Barbagia and Ogliastra, however, say that feta cheese was produced in Sassari before the 1960s, but is not produced there anymore. According to these same shepherds (or former shepherds, in some cases) the feta cheese that was produced in Sardinia competed with that of Greek origin, because the Greek entrepreneurs living in Sassari were quality-conscious.

15. For those families who still specialized in growing grains (wheat and barley), women and men generally worked together in the fields. A few men in the village had *carri a buoi* (yokes of oxen), and there were a limited number of grain mills in the area, which were all animal-powered. Young women and children usually supervised the grinding of wheat into flour. In Telemula, unlike other villages of Nuoro Province, women have always worked in the fields. Agricultural machinery was not operated by women until recent years, and men were always in charge of the most complex work tasks. Despite the wheat cultivation crisis on the island, people in Telemula continued to till the land to produce *grano duro* (durum wheat), which is indigenous to the island and was the villagers' main staple (Da Re 1990).

16. This was only one of many possible arrangements. In Bardia, a village of the Barbagia region, women were in charge of processing the milk when it was not collected by the trucks from the dairy plants. Women also took care of the sausages and hams the shepherds kept in their *ovili*. When their husbands undertook winter transhumance, women of Bardia were expected to accompany their husbands to the summer pastures.

17. Work as *servi* was rare for Central Highlands women. Work in the fields by Telemula women was an exception rather than the rule. Women from Bardia, for example, still refuse to engage in almost any form of agricultural work.

18. In Sardinia the Central Highlands are often called "an island within an island."

19. Argentina first produced its own Pecorino cheese to substitute for imported Pecorino cheese. Argentina now exports Pecorino cheese, which competes with the Italian variety in the international market.

20. Remo Dettori, personal communication, 1991.

21. Author's field notes, 1991, 1992.

REFERENCES

Allum, P. A. 1973. *Italy—Republic without Government?* New York: W. W. Norton.

Annis, Sheldon. 1987. *God and Production in a Guatemalan Town.* Austin: University of Texas Press.

Attwood, Donald W. 1988. Poverty, Inequality, and Economic Growth in Rural India. In Donald W. Attwood, Thomas C. Bruneau, and John G. Galaty, eds., *Power and Poverty: Development and Development Projects in the Third World.* Boulder, Colo.: Westview Press.

———. 1992. *Raising Cane: The Political Economy of Sugar in Western India.* Boulder, Colo.: Westview Press.

Ayora-Diaz, Steffan Igor. 1993a. Representations and Occupations: Shepherds' Choices in a Highland Village of Sardinia. Ph.D. diss., Department of Anthropology, McGill University.

———. 1993b. The Festa di Sant'Efisio in Telemula, Sardinia. Paper prepared for the American Anthropological Association Conference, Washington, D.C., 17–21 November.

Behal, Rana P., and Prabhu P. Mohapatra. 1992. Tea and Money versus Human Life: The Rise and Fall of the Indenture System in the Assam. *Journal of Peasant Studies* 19 (3–4): 142–172.

Birocchi, Italo. 1990. Il Regnum Sardiniae dalla Cessione dell'Isola ai Savoia alla Fusione Perfetta. In Massimo Guidetti, ed., *L'Eta' Contemporanea*, vol. 2 of *Storia dei Sardi e della Sardegna.* Milan: Jaca Book.

Bodeman, Yark Michal. 1979. Telemula: Aspects of the Micro-organization of Backwardness in Central Sardinia. Ph.D. diss., Department of Sociology, Brandeis University.

Braga, Emilio. 1990. La Forza della Tradizione e I Segni del Cambiamento: La Storia Economica (1820–1940). In Massimo Guidetti, ed., *L'Età Contemporanea: Dal Governo Piemontese Agli Anni Sessanta Del Nostro Secolo*, vol. 4 of *Storia dei Sardi e della Sardegna.* Milan: Jaca Book.

Brass, Tom, and Henry Bernstein. 1992. Introduction: Proletarianisation and Deproletarianisation on the Colonial Plantation. *Journal of Peasant Studies* 19 (3–4): 1–39.

Braudel, Fernand. 1973 [1967]. *Capitalism and Material Life 1400–1800.* Trans. Miriam Kochan. Glasgow: Fontana.

Bussa, Italo. 1978. L'Industria Casearia Sarda: Storia, Conseguenze e Prospettive. *Quaderni Bolotanesi* no. 1: 23–46.

Caltagirone, Benedetto. 1989. *Animali Perduti: Abigeato e Scambio Sociale in Barbagia.* Cagliari: Cagliari Editrice.

Casula, Francesco Cesare. 1982. L'Età dei Catalano-Aragonesi e degli Arborea. In Manlio Brigaglia, ed., *Sardegna: Enciclopedia,* vol. 1, section 3. Cagliari: Edizioni della Torre.

Comunità Europea (CE). 1988. *Programma Integrato Mediterraneo per la Regione Sardegna.* Computer printout.

Da Re, Maria Gabriella. 1990. *La Casa e I Campi': Divisione Sessuale del Lavoro nella Sardegna Tradizionale.* Cagliari: Cuec Editrice.

Del Piano, Lorenzo. 1991. I Problemi dell'Agricoltura e la Pastorizia dopo la Fusione con il Piemonte e nel Periodo Unitario. In Alberto Boscolo, Luigi Bulferetti, Lorenzo del Piano, and Giancarlo Sabattini, eds., *Profilo Storico-Economico della Sardegna dal Riformismo Settecentesco ai Piani di Rinascita.* Milan: Franco Angeli.

Flores Ochoa, Jorge A. 1968. *Pastoralists of the Andes: The Alpaca Herders of Parapatía.* Philadelphia: Institute for the Study of Human Issues.

Frank, Andre G. 1967. *Capitalism and Underdevelopment in Latin America: Historical Studies of Chile and Brazil.* New York: Monthly Review Press.

———. 1971. *Lumpenburguesía: Lumpendesarrollo.* Mexico City: Era.

Friedmann, Harriet. 1995. Food Politics: New Dangers, New Possibilities. In Philip McMichael, ed., *Food and Agrarian Orders in the World Economy.* Westport, Conn.: Praeger.

Hart, Keith. 1982. *The Political Economy of West African Agriculture.* Cambridge: Cambridge University Press.

Heatherington, Tracey. 1993. Environmental Politics in a Highland Sardinian Community. M.A. thesis, Department of Anthropology, McGill University.

Herzfeld, Michael. 1985. *The Poetics of Manhood: Contest and Identity in a Cretan Mountain Village.* Princeton, N.J.: Princeton University Press.

Idda, Lorenzo. 1982. La Pastorizia. In Manlio Brigaglia, ed., *Sardegna: Enciclopedia,* vol. 2, section 5. Cagliari: Edizioni della Torre.

Il Ministro dell'Agricoltùra e le Foreste. 1990. *Decreto Ministeriale Concernente: Regolamento Recante Disposizioni di Adattamento all Realtà Nazionale del Regime di Aiuto per l'Estensivizzazione della Produzione di cui al Regolamento CEE del Consiglio delle Comunità Europea.* N.797/85. 8 February.

Istituto Nazionale di Statistica (ISTAT). 1994. *Popolazione e Abitazioni. Fascicolo Provinciale Nuoro. 13° Censimento della Popolazione e delle Abitazioni.* Teramo: Istituto Nazionale di Statistica. 20 October.

Kasaba, Rasat, and Faruk Tabak. 1995. Fatal Conjuncture: The Decline and Fall of the Modern Agrarian Order during the Bretton Woods Era. In Philip McMichael, ed., *Food and Agrarian Orders in the World-Economy.* Westport, Conn.: Praeger.

Kennedy, Maya. 1993. Pastoral Identity in the Changing Cultural Landscape of Highland Sardinia. M.Sc. thesis, Department of Geography, University of Wisconsin-Madison.

Luxemburg, Rosa. 1967 [1912]. *La acumulación del capital.* México City: Juan Grijalbo.

MacWilliam, Scott. 1996. "Just Like Working for the Dole": Rural Households, Export Crops and State Subsidies in Papua New Guinea. *Journal of Peasant Studies* 23(4): 40–78.

Marongiu, Pietro. 1981. *Teoria del Banditismo in Sardegna.* Cagliari: Edizioni della Torre.

Marx, Karl. 1967 [1867]. *Capital.* Ed. Friederich Engels. Vol. 1, *A Critical Analysis of Capitalist Production.* New York: International Publishers.

McMichael, Philip. 1995. Introduction: Agrarian and Food Relations in the World-Economy. In Philip McMichael, ed., *Food and Agrarian Orders in the World-Economy.* Westport, Conn.: Praeger.

Meloni, Piero. 1982. L'Età dei Romani. In Manlio Brigaglia, ed., *Sardegna: Enciclopedia,* vol. 1, section 3. Cagliari: Edizioni della Torre.

Melville, Elinor G. K. 1994. *A Plague of Sheep: Environmental Consequences of the Conquest of Mexico.* Cambridge: Cambridge University Press.

Murray, Martin J. 1992. "White Gold" or "White Blood"?: The Rubber Plantation of Colonial Indochina, 1910–40. *Journal of Peasant Studies* 19(2–3): 41–67.

Nolasco, Margarita. 1985. *Café y sociedad en México.* Mexico City: Centro de Ecodesarrollo.

Page, Jeffery M. 1975. *Agrarian Revolution: Social Movements and Export Agriculture in the Underdeveloped World.* New York: Free Press.

Pigliaru, Antonio. 1975. *Il Banditismo in Sardegna: La Vendetta Barbaricina.* Milan: Giuffrè Editore.

Pilonca, Paolo. 1986. *Sardegna Segreta: Cronache del Villaggio*. Cagliari: Edizioni della Torre; Rome: Newton Compton Editori.

Regione Sardegna. n.d. *Comunità Montana 11—Ogliastra, Azienda Speciale Comunale [Telemula]*. 2 vols. Cagliari: Ente Regionale di Sviluppo e Assistenza Tecnica in Agricoltura (ERSAT).

———. 1991. *Quale Agricoltura per gli Anni '90? Proposta di un Programma di Ristruturazione dell'Assetto Agricolo Regionale*. Conferenza Regionale dell'Agricoltura. Cagliari, 6-8 Marzo. Relazzione introduttiva. Cagliari: Stampa Pisano.

Roseberry, William. 1995. Introduction. In William Roseberry, Lowell Gudmundson, and Mario Samper Kutschbach, eds., *Coffee, Society and Power in Latin America*. Baltimore, Md.: Johns Hopkins University Press.

Sini, Maria Luisa. 1982. La Riforma Agro-Pastorale. In Manlio Brigaglia, ed., *La Sardegna: Enciclopedia*, vol. 2, section 5. Cagliari: Edizioni della Torre.

Sotgiu, Girolamo. 1982. L'Età dei Savoia. In Manlio Brigaglia, ed., *La Sardegna: Enciclopedia*, vol. 1, section 3. Cagliari: Edizioni della Torre.

Thompson, Susan J., and J. Tadlock Cowan. 1995. Durable Food Production and Consumption in the World Economy. In Philip McMichael, ed., *Food and Agrarian Orders in the World Economy*. Westport, Conn.: Praeger.

Tore, Gianni. 1982. L'Età dei Punici. In Manlio Brigaglia, ed., *La Sardegna: Enciclopedia*, vol. 1, section 3. Cagliari: Edizioni della Torre.

Valdez, Alberto. 1991. The Role of Agricultural Exports in Development. In C. Peter Timmer, ed., *Agriculture and the State: Growth, Employment and Poverty in Developing Countries*. Ithaca, N.Y.: Cornell University Press.

Vargas-Cetina, Gabriela. 1986. Reproducción de la fuerza de trabajo en la Zona Henequenera de Yucatán. Estudio de caso: San Antonio Teuitz. Tesis de Licenciatura, Departmento de Antropología, Universidad de Yucatán.

———. 1993a. Celebrating Who We Are, Establishing that We Give: The Festa di San Giovanni in a Highland Sardinia Town. Paper presented at the American Anthropological Association Conference, Washington, D.C., 17–21 November.

———. 1993b. Our Patrons Are Our Clients: A Shepherds' Cooperative in Bardia, Sardinia. *Dialectical Anthropology* 18: 337–362.

———. 1994. Cooperation in Sardinia: Production, Exchange and Cooperatives among Highland Pastoralists. Ph.D. diss., Department of Anthropology, McGill University.

Vinci, Salvatore. 1992. Il Mezzogiorno negli Anni '90: Quale Nuova Politica di Sviluppo? In Beniamino Moro and Giancarlo Sabattini, eds., *Mezzogiorno: Ristagno o Sviluppo? Le Esperienze Regionali: Il Caso della Sardegna*. Milan: Franco Angeli.

Wells, Allen. 1985. *Yucatán's Guilded Age: Haciendas, Henequen and International Harvester 1860–1915*. Albuquerque: University of New Mexico Press.

Wolf, Eric R. 1982. *Europe and the People without History*. Berkeley: University of California Press.

Worsley, Peter. 1984. *The Three Worlds: Culture and World Development*. Chicago: University of Chicago Press.

Index

239

About the Contributors

Jane L. Collins is professor of rural sociology and women's studies at the University of Wisconsin (Madison). She is the author of *Unseasonal Migrations: The Effects of Rural Labor Scarcity in Peru* (Princeton University Press, 1988); co-editor (with Martha Gimenez) of *Work Without Wages* (Albany: SUNY Press, 1990); and co-author (with Catherine Lutz) of *Reading National Geographic* (University of Chicago Press, 1993). She has published additional articles on fruit and vegetable industry in Latin America in *World Development, Development and Change, Journal of Latin American Anthropology,* and *Comparative Studies in Society and History.*

Winifred Creamer is associate professor of anthropology at Northern Illinois University. She is author of *The Architecture of Arroyo Hondo* (School of American Research, 1993), and *Stress and Warfare Among the Kayenta Anasazi of the 13th Century A.D.* (Chicago Field Museum, 1993). Her research includes the study of ancient architecture, demography, and political organization in the southwestern United States and in Central and South America.

Catherine S. Dolan is a lecturer in development and gender studies at the School of Development Studies, University of East Anglia in England. She recently has published articles based on her field research on gender and contract farming in Kenya in the *Journal of Development Studies* and in *Gender and Development.*

Angelique Haugerud is associate professor of anthropology at Rutgers University and previously was editor of the scholarly journal *Africa Today.* Her publications include *The Culture of Politics in Modern Kenya* (Cambridge University Press, 1995); articles in *Africa, Experimental Agriculture,* and *Rural Africana;* and chapters in a number of edited collections. Her current research addresses wealth and culture in Kenya's central highlands, and the epistemological problems of studying change through long-term field research.

Peter D. Little is professor of anthropology at the University of Kentucky. He is author of *The Elusive Granary* (Cambridge University Press, 1992), and co-editor (with Michael Watts) of *Living Under Contract* (University of Wisconsin Press, 1994). His work has also appeared in *Current Anthropology, American Anthropologist, Africa, African Studies Review, Human Organization, American Ethnologist,* and a number of edited collections. His current research focuses on rural markets, conflict, and ethnicity in East Africa.

Stuart Plattner is program director for cultural anthropology at the National Science Foundation. He is the editor of *Economic Anthropology* (Stanford University Press, 1989) and author of *High Art Down Home* (University of Chicago, 1996) as well as other works.

Nicole Polier has taught anthropology and gender studies at Yale and Wesleyan Universities. She is preparing a book (Verso Press), and has published recent articles in *Journal of Historical Sociology, Ethnology, Identities,* and *Feminist Studies.*

Bruce D. Roberts is assistant professor of anthropology at Minnesota State University (Moorhead). Recent articles address livestock production, age, and gender among the Keiyo of Kenya, and the incorporation of maize into African agriculture.

Mitchell S. Rothman is associate professor and coordinator of anthropology at Widener University (Chester, Pennsylvania). His research focuses on the origin of complex societies, particularly in the Middle East. He is co-editor (with Gil Stein) of *Chiefdoms and Early States in the Near East* (Prehistory Press), and *Uruk Mesopotamia and Its Neighbors* (School of American Research Press), and author of chapters in several edited volumes.

Lois Stanford is associate professor of anthropology at New Mexico State University. Her current research includes a binational study of the role of entrepreneurs in the avocado industries of Michoacán and California, and a study of Hispano and Mexican-American farmer organizations in New Mexico. Her recent publications include a book co-authored with Robert Bolin, *The Northridge Earthquake: Vulnerability and Disaster on the Margins of Los Angeles* (Routledge, 1998), and a number of chapters in edited volumes.

M. Priscilla Stone is director of international studies at Washington University in St. Louis. Her publications include a co-edited volume (with L. Arizpe and D. Major) titled *Population and Environment: Rethinking the Debate* (Westview Press, 1994); articles in the *Journal of Anthropological Research, Human Ecology, American Ethnologist, American Anthropologist;* and chapters in a number of edited volumes. Her current research is a comparative study of crop genetic modification.

Gabriela Vargas-Cetina is professor of anthropology at the Universidad Autónoma de Yucatán, in Mexico. Recent works include the edited volume *Mirando . . . ¿Hacia Afuera? Experiencias de Investigación* (Centro de Investigaciones y Estudios Superiores en Antropologiá Social). Her current research interests are music and dance in the Mundo Maya tourist circuit in southern Mexico and Central America.

Bob White is assistant professor of anthropology at the University of California at Santa Cruz, and a research associate in the anthropology department at McGill University. His work on popular culture and politics in sub-Saharan Africa has appeared in journals such as *Research in African Literatures,* and he is preparing a book manuscript based on his recent research in Kinshasa.

Randy Ziegenhorn is visiting assistant professor of anthropology at the University of Iowa. He is author of *Networking the Farm: The Social Structure of Cooperation and Competition in Iowa Agriculture* (Ashgate Publishing Ltd., 1999).